CHANGING NEW YORK
THE ARCHITECTURAL SCENE
CHRISTOPHER GRAY

DOVER PUBLICATIONS, INC., *New York*

For Anna Margaret Riepma Gray, a newspaperwoman —

who brought me to New York and who gave me her love
for the daily intersection of writing and newsprint.

Published in Canada by General Publishing Company, Ltd., 30 Lesmill Road, Don Mills, Toronto, Ontario.
Published in the United Kingdom by Constable and Company, Ltd., 3 The Lanchesters, 162–164 Fulham Palace Road, London W6 9ER.

Changing New York: The Architectural Scene is a new work, first published by Dover Publications, Inc., in 1992.

Manufactured in the United States of America
Dover Publications, Inc., 31 East 2nd Street, Mineola, N.Y. 11501

Library of Congress Cataloging-in-Publication Data

Gray, Christopher, 1950–
    Changing New York : the architectural scene / by Christopher Gray.
        p.   cm.
    Includes index.
    ISBN 0-486-26936-1 (pbk.)
    1. Architecture—New York (N.Y.)   2. New York (N.Y.)—Buildings, structures, etc.   I. Title.
NA735.N5G73   1992
720′.9747′1—dc20   91-40254
                                                                         CIP

ACKNOWLEDGMENTS

ALTHOUGH IT IS MY own name that appears over the "Streetscapes" column, only in the narrowest sense is it solely from my hand. Michael Sterne conceived the idea and then let me alone with it. Gordie Thompson and Bill Hollander, successive copy chiefs at the real-estate section of the *New York Times*, have tactfully edited the columns. John Forbes, photo editor, Richard Rosen, section editor, and Rosalie Radomsky, Sarah Kass and Gene Rondinaro, successive news assistants, have done their best to keep me out of trouble.

In my own office, Jill Szarkowski has wrestled recalcitrant photo orders into line and still contends that I don't know how to spell "similar." For most of the period the indefatigable Raymond Fike was my principal outside researcher—that is, he carried out much of the research agenda at the Department of Buildings, Avery Library, New-York Historical Society, New York Public Library (and its feared Annex), Engineering Societies Library and on other dusty shelves. This is the real gruntwork (and fun) of architectural history—slogging through scratched rolls of fuzzy microfilm, interpreting the vagaries of various long-dead newspaper indexers, bird-dogging obscure cross-references. Since I have pegged my entire professional career on the importance of research and researchers, it is a source of enduring embarrassment to me that the *Times* will not credit those who serve as my principal investigators for the column. On fill-in research and updates for this publication Suzanne Braley, who succeeded Raymond Fike in late 1989, and Nina Kirschner, in charge of inside office research, have also been of great help. This small note does not do justice to their efforts.

Librarians and archivists who have been both regularly and exceptionally helpful, going well out of their way, include Kenneth Cobb, director of the Municipal Archives; Janet Parks, Irina Kouharets, Ted Gachot, Herbert Mitchell and Bill O'Malley at Avery Library; Laura Tosi and Gary Hermalyn at the Bronx County Historical Society; Claire Lamers at the Brooklyn Historical Society; Terry Ariano, Esther Brumberg and Gretchen Viehmann at the Museum of the City of New York; Jean Ashton, Mariam Touba, Dale Neighbors, Helena Zinkham, Pat Paladines and Wendy Shadwell at the New-York Historical Society; Mark Piel at the New York Society Library; Gerard Malanga and Ellen Wallenstein at the Department of Parks; Jeannette Eisenhart at Pennsylvania State University; Charles Young at the Queens Borough Public Library; Barnett Shepherd at the Staten Island Historical Society; and David Ment and Bette Weneck at Teachers College Library. Collectors Andrew Alpern, Barbara Cohen, Luther Harris and Frederick S. Lightfoot have also gotten me out of various photo jams.

David Dunlap, Margot Gayle, Carter Horsley, the late C. Ray Smith, Nicholas King and Suzanne Stephens, co-journalist/historians, have always been happy to share a tip with me. Others who have been exceptionally helpful include Skip Garrett at the Department of Parks, Bob Makla at the Friends of Central Park, Martha Ritter at the City Planning Commission, Tracie Rozhon at the Landmarks Preservation Commission, the late Halina Rosenthal at the Friends of the Upper East Side Historic Districts, Michael Sillerman at Rosenman & Colin, Arlene Simon at Landmark West!, Roger Starr at the *New York Times*, the faithful Vahe Tiryakian at the Department of Buildings, Paul H. Feinberg and my uncle, Siert F. Riepma.

Most important is the network of specialist and local historians whose toil is largely unrecognized. They tend to avoid writing books about New York since the available advances ($10,000 or less) make these into either charity or exercises in production writing (and fact pirating) rather than endeavors involving the search for knowledge. They are not on the fancy historic preservation boards or committees, for which the determining factor is access to money, not history. Rather they are generally working historians (or dedicated amateurs), the real custodians of the city's history, and those who have regularly contributed to my work deserve roll-call listing: William Alex, of the Olmsted Association; Andrew Alpern, a constant sounding board; Avis Berman; Deborah Bershad, of the Art Commission; Andrew Dolkart; Thomas Flagg; the late Dennis Francis; Gregory Gilmartin; Timothy Guilfoyle; Luther Harris; Sidney Horenstein, of the American Museum of Natural History; Regina Kellerman, of the Greenwich Village Historical Society; Joy Kestenbaum; Jeffrey Kroessler; Jonathan Kuhn, of the Department of Parks; the Honorable Sarah Landau; John Montague Massengale; Thomas Mellins; Michael R. Miller; Jane Preddy; Anthony Robins, of the Landmarks Preservation Commission; Peter Salwen; Charles Savage, of the Landmarks Preservation Commission; Vincent Seyfried; Robert A. M. Stern; John Tauranac; the late Elliot Willensky; Shirley Zavin, of the Landmarks Preservation Commission.

And to my family—Erin, Peter, Olivia and my late cat, Roman—I give my deep thanks for enduring and enjoying this weekly effort with me.

C.S.G.

INTRODUCTION

Whether it is a farmer arriving from Italy . . . or a young girl arriving from a small town in Mississippi . . . or a boy arriving from the corn belt . . . each embraces New York with the intense excitement of first love.—E. B. White, *Here is New York*, 1949

ON THE OTHER HAND, the first time I saw New York, I threw up. It was 1959 and my mother, a Midwestern preacher's daughter finally realizing her lifelong romance with the city, hoped to impress me by stretching her tiny budget around a black limousine from the airport to our new apartment, a type of dwelling I considered impossibly alien. She stopped the driver at the foot of the Empire State Building, shining and glistening that night. Sensing that I had set off my last cherry bomb, played doctor for the last time behind the Hebenstreits' garage and caught my last salamander, this nine-year-old's stomach lost the Kansas City lunch it had received only hours before.

We moved to a 1956 Doelger garden-apartment complex overlooking the Town Tennis Club, from which I eventually learned that, in dry weather, enough sparklers dropped from apartment 7G would ignite a perfect circle of expanding fire in the ground ivy. As I went to sleep to the sound of wop-wip-wop I mused over a disembodied Georgian-style skyscraper top to the south, with a gold ball on the top. For years I puzzled over that tower top: Where did it land? Was it an apartment or office building? New York was such a puzzle of seemingly unconnected parts—old brownstones over jazzy storefronts, buildings sliced in half for street extensions, giant conglomerations of structures like Bloomingdale's, buildings where you couldn't see the top and the bottom at the same time . . . like that odd tower (which I figured out only a decade later was River House).

It was different from the streetcar suburb where I grew up, carefully mega-planned by developer J. C. Nichols. There I had lived on a winding, three-block-long street, Greenway Terrace, that was insufferably comprehensible. The first block, next to Border Star School and the little shopping complex, had modest starter houses for beginning families. The middle block (mine) had slightly larger houses with larger yards. The last block was real Country Club District grandeur. (My "Mr. and Mrs. Bridge"–rich grandparents built their near-mansion there in 1927.) The economic stratification was mirrored architecturally, so obvious even a third-grader could see it—and I did.

New York, on the other hand, cried out for some decoding, some concordance. The typical north–south corridors, like Fifth or Third Avenues, had a certain crude homogeneity. But the crosstown slices—which is how I took my servings of New York on my daily east–west trips to school—were successive layers of Italianate tenement, Victorian brownstone, Edwardian town house, neoclassical storefront, Renaissance apartment, moderne taxpayer and 1950s white brick.

I monitored my school route with mathematical obsession to produce the maximum variety of exposure to this new scenery. Fixing—or at least observing—the building types, materials, styles and topography all became my way of making New York intelligible, my way of keeping my lunch down.

In my late adolescence I observed, with an outsider's acuity, the social nuances of housing for what Whit Stillman has called the Urban Haute Bourgeoisie; I still remember dinner-party wrestling over great questions like which was the better side of Park Avenue.

Later, in the fourth of an eventual seven years of undergraduate goofing off (sorry, Dad—but thanks), under Professor Elwood Parry I became interested in the history of photography and, under Professor George Collins, in the history of city planning. Period photography confirmed or revealed changes in the city I had only dimly imagined: a row of differing Edwardian town-house facades, for example, had started as one of identical Victorian brownstones. Professor Collins' course was really a shadow history of real-estate development, revealing that in many cases the "planning" was really just ad hoc development, and such an approach seemed to me to be a far more promising way to explain the history of New York's buildings than the airless art-historical approach that was the only one in my baccalaureate days. Adolf Placzek also provided me with extracurricular encouragement.

So in 1975, for lack of another occupation, I set out to find self-employment in unraveling the text of the physical city, becoming perforce a Court Street architectural historian. (The academy still considers the nuts and bolts of city-building inconvenient in its diffuse expansiveness.) By contrast, I certainly never had the attention span necessary to be eighty-eighth in line to study some major monument for months, years or even decades. Too much television in my youth, no doubt.

In 1986 Michael Sterne, the real-estate editor of the *New York Times*, had the idea that there could be room in his corner of the paper for such nuts and bolts, and paid me the unearned compliment of asking me to prepare what became the "Streetscapes" column, which first appeared on March 15, 1987.

My mission as Michael delivered it to me was to show how the city was changing by writing about interesting old buildings in the news. I have set for myself other criteria as well: to publish the best historical photographs, to investigate closely (not just take at face value) Landmarks Commission actions, to depict the custom and culture of the historic-preservation movement, to emphasize the "little" buildings that are, collectively, far more important to New York than its tour-bus monuments and to seek out and credit admirable research by other historians.

This last goal has been, in part, in aggravated opposition to the prevailing impression that the history of New York's buildings "must be written down somewhere" and is just waiting to be photocopied. The reality is that the brief articles I prepare often represent the only sustained attention a researcher has given the structure in question. Since each article has a modest research budget of twenty to twenty-five hours, this is no compliment to the present author but rather a municipal tragedy. To my unceasing amazement, even in bitterly contested Landmarks cases, with thousands or hundreds of thousands of dollars at stake, only rarely is more than cursory research done by either side. Preservation constituencies have as little use for historical fact as developers.

After four years of writing about "Changing New York" the amount of stasis in the city amazes me. For the hundred fifty-eight columns from 1987 through 1989 (not all of which are reprinted here), in only fourteen cases has demolition taken place—not a bad record for a column that is automatically drawn to endangered buildings. And what a change from the 1960s or 1970s, when Ada Louise Huxtable (in the *Times*) and Roberta Brandes Gratz (in the *Post*) had their pick of buildings falling before the onslaught!

It was from their writings that I first became aware of larger preservation issues, and their perceptive musings (and those of Nathan Silver in *Lost New York*) still form a study text for my own. But although the preservation politics of a particular issue is of interest, I am motivated, like them, by the grainy, gritty oldness of old buildings. Not the new-old, postrestoration, public-relationed old building, but one on

which it is possible to see the mark of decades or even centuries of humanity—the worn tread, the paint-encrusted storefront, the bowed cornice. The city is the most gargantuan art exhibit ever mounted, a blockbuster beyond even Tom Hoving, with miles and miles of different facade-canvases, some by masters and some by scoundrels, some bright and clean and some drowned in varnish, some antique and some freshly made.

The exciting thing is to make this tableau legible: designer, period, provenance, later changes. And the great thing is, no one can "collect" it (in the sense of acquisition), and yet it is free for all, the most democratic of arts. Just appreciate it, look at it, understand it, laugh at it and it will give you as much pleasure as Henry Frick got from a roomful of Fragonards.

The secret endeavor of this column has been to finally explain for myself some mysterious little structure, or odd siting or funny feature that has long puzzled me. That others have eavesdropped on my own curiosity, so much the better.

CHRISTOPHER GRAY

Note: Where pertinent, updates on the articles, written in November 1991, have been added. They appear at the end of an article in *italic* type.

A NOTE ON LANDMARKING IN NEW YORK CITY

This has been a column about historic buildings, not modern civics. But in the late twentieth century our history is more and more intertwined with our politics—from Columbus' "discovery" on down—and so in my articles the Landmarks Preservation Commission is frequently mentioned. This city agency was established in 1965 and has great control over the demolition and alteration of the landmarks it chooses to regulate. A professional staff advises 11 commissioners who decide what is and what is not a landmark, largely without formal criteria—but there is nothing wrong with an "I know it when I see it" approach. Landmarks can be exteriors, interiors (except houses of worship), parks and historic districts, where some crummy buildings are included with more attractive ones.

After designation begins a more problematic process of deciding how the building may be changed—for few human uses permit absolute stasis. Once designated, any change to a protected feature requires a (sliding scale of) review by the commission's staff. One owner's discreet rooftop addition may be a neighbor's garish eyesore; one preservation group's prescription for "correct" repairs may be financially ruinous to

an ultra-margined speculator. All of them have to deal with an incremental increase in paperwork and red tape, and even the holiest of property owners receives the "honor" of landmark designation with a certain amount of dread.

Left unremarked here is the fact that the raw, technical compliance with the law is quite small—it's pretty easy to make largely benign alterations to a landmark and get away with it. But the commission is generally successful with egregiously wicked mutilations, in large part because of a network of preservation groups who are ready to protest such things.

A reporter is naturally drawn to cases of controversy or to demonstrations of the commission's blind spots—of which there is no shortage—but in fact the screaming and yelling matches are the exception. Most Landmarks decisions are quite reasonable and unexceptional—but, of course, that's not really news. Also not news is that the Landmarks Commission has made an immense difference in the civility of New York City—but it's true.

CONTENTS

BOHEMIAN NATIONAL HALL

On East 73d Street, a Lingering Vestige of a Czech Heritage

1901 photograph of Bohemian National Hall rising above neighboring tenements on East 73d Street.

THE MUSEUM OF THE CITY OF NEW YORK

IT IS ONE of those midblock surprises on the far-to-the-east East Side of Manhattan well away from the well-traveled town-house and museum section.

Amid a block of anonymous 19th-century tenements and modern apartments between Second and First Avenues, a huge neo-Renaissance structure looms. At the top is the legend "Bohemian National all"—the "H" is missing from the last word. The building is vacant and the trustees have taken preliminary steps toward selling at least part of the property.

The Bohemians—the Czechs of the present Czechoslovakia—began emigration in earnest in the 1870's, with their population in New York rising to 27,000 in 1900. By the 1880's, the existing settlements around Tompkins Square began to shift to better, newer tenements in the far-to-the-East 60's and 70's, where the cigar factories, which employed many Czechs, were centered. In 1888, the Bohemian Brethren Presbyterian Church opened its first house of worship in the United States at 351 East 74th Street dedicated to the Czech martyr Jan Hus.

The Czechs had a score or more of clubs—athletic, intellectual, and social—scattered in various locations around Tompkins Square, but the uptown migration stimulated the movement for a single building to be shared by all. A subtext was the preservation of a nationalist spirit among the émigrés—Czechs had been restive under Austrian domination since the 17th century. Thus was born the Bohemian National Hall, an umbrella structure promoted by a consortium called the Bohemian Benevolent and Literary Association.

Gradually, money was raised from the clubs themselves, private donations, excursions, fairs and performances—one by Antonín Dvořák raised $200 in 1892. Part of the scheme was to support activities that combined charity and nationalism, like the Czech School, established in 1886.

By the mid-1890's, success was finally at hand. A site at 321–323 East 73d Street was purchased, a building fund was in place and the various clubs had been brought to order—except for the Sokol, an athletic society that withdrew at the last minute to build its own house at 424 East 71st Street. In October 1896, the Bohemian National Hall—Narodní Budová—opened, towering over its tenement neighbors.

The architect, William C. Frohne, had some experience with ethnic clubs, and had already designed the German-American Rifle Association at 12 St. Mark's Place. For the Czechs, he produced a broad palazzo of light brick and limestone.

The lower floors, with columned portico and quoined window surrounds, are similar to other New York architecture of the period, but the upper two floors—a great, two-story arcade separated by twin engaged columns resting on lion's-head bases—have an elaboration, a richness, that must have seemed distinctly European in its time. A great iron cornice topped the building, and carried a rather florid balustrade with 1896 in raised Roman numerals.

The building immediately was found too small, and in 1899 an addition to the east went up, identical in style and materials but with a simpler cornice treatment. The ground floor held a restaurant and bar, the upper floors individual club rooms, and the top floor a ballroom/theater.

The Department of Buildings did not like public assembly on the top floor for fire safety, but approved it after Frohne pointed out that other clubs—the Progress, New York Athletic and German-American Rifle Association—had similar arrangements. The basement held a bowling alley and shooting gallery.

After the turn of the century, movies became so popular that a special theater annex on 74th Street was put up in 1914. Always restive with their home country under Hapsburg rule, the Czechs used the hall as a focal point for liberation activities and $500,000 worth of Liberty Bonds were sold there in World War I. The peace settlement resulted in the creation of an independent Czechoslovakia.

The Czechs were less enthusiastic about the Prohibition years, 1919–1932, which cut deeply into their restaurant/bar income. In 1938 there was more political activity as Czechoslovakia was abandoned to the Nazis, but it lacked the vigor of the effort in World War I.

In *The Czechs in America* (1920), Thomas Čapek noted that American-born Czechs were less attached to the homeland: "Why do you weep?" he reports one teenager criticizing his tearful father during the Czech national anthem. The original spirit that created the Bohemian National Hall was faltering.

Gradually, there was less and less competition for the once-crowded club rooms, and they were let out as studios. The theater annex was leased out as a private operation in the 1940's (the Light Opera of Manhattan took over in 1975, and left only last year) and by the 1960's, the hall's letterhead openly promoted its availability to anyone for "Weddings, Dances, Social Affairs."

Last year, the hall's trustees began proceedings to separate the lot of the main building from that of the annex—a preliminary step to sale and redevelopment of either property, although they say that the demolition of the main building is not a possibility. If the Bohemian National Hall remains, it will be one of the last—and most impressive—vestiges of the once-strong Bohemian quarter in New York.

The annex was sold in 1987 and demolished.

GIMBEL'S

A "Big Store" Designed to Educate Bargain Hunters

Gimbel's department store on Sixth Avenue near Herald Square in 1915, five years after it opened; lower right, elevated rail station.

IN AN ERA of boutiques and mixed-use buildings, of luxury goods and marketing for the affluent, the basic, unadorned department store is something of a dinosaur—and the Gimbel's building, on Avenue of the Americas just south of Herald Square, is on the verge of being fossilized.

A partnership consisting of Larry Silverstein, Melvin Simon and William Zeckendorf Jr. has bought the vacant structure and now is examining various possibilities, none of which include returning one of the last of New York's "big stores" to its original use.

The "big store" concept began in earnest in New York with A. T. Stewart's full block at Broadway and 10th Street (1862) and picked up speed on Sixth Avenue between 18th and 23d Streets, where six full-blockfront department stores went up by 1901. Macy's pushed north to its present site on Herald Square in 1902, closely followed by Saks, on the blockfront to the south (site of the present Herald Center). At the same time, Pennsylvania Station was announced, and the Sixth Avenue spine around 34th was suddenly the new center for the large emporiums.

Gimbel's, established in Indiana in 1842, had expanded to Philadelphia in 1894 and began to search for a site in New York in 1905. In 1908, it secured an option on the blockfront just south of Saks, the west side of what is now the Avenue of the Americas from 32d to 33d, and hired Daniel Burnham & Company of Chicago to design its store.

Although the big department store of the 1890's had been exuberant, novel and full of luxurious extras to entice shoppers inside for an entire day, the new Gimbel's encouraged the briefest possible transaction—this was, after all, the store that claimed to introduce the "bargain basement" to New York. The result was the least interesting department store to be built in New York up through the 1950's. Monochrome, flat, regular, the new Gimbel's corresponded closely to Chicago architectural ideals of commercial architecture—that it should be direct, forceful, without humor or luxury—but in New York it read as boring.

The moralistic reserve of the building's design corresponds to a sort of missionary zeal about the store, reflected in a speech by one of the Gimbel brothers when the cornerstone was laid in 1909: "A great modern store helps to make the buying of goods absolutely safe to even the most inexperienced . . . . It is a great university for the training of character . . . and upright dealing."

The new store had 164 departments, 7,000 employees, 1 million square feet of floor space, two acres of window glass and 300,000 visitors on opening day, September 29, 1910. Lean and mean, Gimbel's was a thorn in the side of its rivals, especially Macy's, and Gimbel's apologized in its ads "for any inconvenience" that numerous spies from Macy's might cause legitimate patrons.

In 1922, Horace Saks, who had become friends with his neighbor-rival Bernard Gimbel, confided in him his dream of building a new Saks on Fifth Avenue catering to the affluent. He lacked the money, however. The result was a Gimbel's buyout of Saks—with Horace Saks remaining—and Gimbel's money building the present Saks Fifth Avenue. Gimbel's also acquired an annex at 116 West 32d in 1925, and constructed a magnificent three-story copper-clad bridge connecting the upper floors of the two buildings, designed by Shreve & Lamb, the firm soon to design the Empire State Building.

Even as the Gimbel's star was still rising, a fundamental change was occuring in New York's retail geography. Below 23d Street, the mass-market stores on Sixth Avenue had been barely a block away from the elite stores on Broadway, like Tiffany's and Brooks Brothers. But by 1910, the new generation of Sixth Avenue stores had developed tremendous plant investment, and their locations became fixed, while the elite stores—in smaller quarters—kept moving up Fifth Avenue. Sixth Avenue lost its position as an integral part of a broad retail market, and, once distant from the carriage-trade stores, became a middle-class shopping ghetto. Later, stores like Bloomingdale's, modest establishments that just happened to be in the path of the aristocratic migration, prospered. The old Saks was taken over by Korvette's in 1966, and only Macy's was able to make a successful turnaround, beginning within the last decade.

A store like Gimbel's—without the charm or personality of Macy's—had little to turn around. Last year the parent owner, Batus Ltd., decided it was worth more as real estate than as a business, and sold the site to the present owners. Last fall saw the final bargains at Gimbel's, basement or otherwise, and the new owners are considering mixed uses—residential, office and commercial, with some sort of addition on top of the existing building, but without changing its utilitarian facade. The fate of the 32d Street skywalk—one of the city's great works of metal—is not clear, but no one suggests that a single retail tenant will take Gimbel's place.

Now Gimbel's is quiet except for the drip of leaking pipes, the floors bare except for occasional hangers, the great mahogany-cased escalators—with wooden treads—motionless. Not beautiful, but reassuringly solid, it awaits the judgment of a real-estate market quite out of sympathy with the bargain philosophy of this big store.

The store was converted to a shopping mall with offices above in 1988, and features some major facade changes, including a terrific Buck Rogers/moderne neon lighting scheme.

THE NEW YORK ARCHITECTURAL TERRA-COTTA WORKS

A Jewel in the Shadow of the Queensboro Bridge

New York Architectural Terra-Cotta Works on Vernon Boulevard in Queens.

IT IS A surprise on the gritty water side of Vernon Boulevard, with the Queensboro Bridge looming overhead. Driving through a neighborhood where economic decay and vigor appear in equal parts—a fuel-oil company is well-kept across from a vacant one-story brick building—before you know it, you are upon this little masonry jewel, a burnt brown riot of pressed and shaped brick, chimneys with spiral designs, stepped gables and round-bottomed roof tiles.

It is so unlike its industrial environs that the two-story 20- by 60-foot building seems like the last vestige of a long-vanished residential settlement, a small-town library or civic building from the days when Queens was just a collection of villages.

But if you pass 42-10 Vernon Boulevard on the right day, when the plywood boxes and panels protecting the building from vandals are off for repair or renewal, you will see the elaborate terra-cotta plaques that clearly state the building's original purpose: "New York Architectural Terra-Cotta Works—1892."

Architectural terra-cotta as a building material—raw clay that is shaped into decorative forms, then fired—did not appear in quantity in the United States until the 1880's. In 1886, as a skyscraper boom swept the city, the New York Architectural Terra-Cotta Company was established. Situated in what was then rural Long Island City, Queens, the great complex had crucial river access to the skyscraper explosion going on across the way in Manhattan.

By 1891, the company had already supplied, or would soon supply, terra-cotta for Carnegie Hall, the elaborate Venetian-style Montauk Club in Brooklyn, the Ansonia Hotel on 73d Street and Broadway in Manhattan and scores of other buildings.

The Queens Terra-Cotta building, built in 1892 as the first structure solely for offices of the growing concern, was designed by Francis H. Kimball, the architect of the Montauk Club and, later, the Gertrude Rhinelander Waldo Mansion that rose at 72d Street and Madison Avenue and now is occupied by the Ralph Lauren store.

The long side of the Terra-Cotta building runs along Vernon Boulevard, interrupted by an offset, semicircular bay, and is terminated by stepped gables at either end. On the ground floor, the bay contains no door, but where a door might be expected there is a large classical enframement with a triangular pediment and the name of the company inset among intertwining vine and leaf work. Above that is the 1892 plaque and, at the right end on the main floor, is a doorway marked "OFFICE" in raised letters.

On the bay, the brick is pressed to a rounded profile, but on the balance of the building the brick is pressed flat. Just below the gutter

and the tiled roof runs a frieze of whimsically grotesque faces emerging from leafwork. Terra-cotta chimney tops remain above the main bay, two with spiral designs, one with checkerboard. The entire building is a rich symphony of hard-burnt brown, cream and umber.

Bankruptcy came to the company in 1928, in part due to changing architectural fashions, as cast-concrete replaced terra-cotta. A succession of declining uses ended in vacancy for the building in the 1960's, and it lay undiscovered until the 1970's, when some local residents mounted a campaign for landmark designation.

The campaign was not successful until 1982. Yet from hearing to designation took an unusually brief two-and-a-half months, so rapid that when the building was designated a landmark, the commission did not know the identity of the architect.

That fact was discovered later by Vincent Seyfried, a Queens historian who pored through local newspaper articles about the building from 1892.

After designation, Citibank, the owner since 1970, sealed the doorways, windows and terra-cotta plaques to protect them from vandalism. Susan Tunick, who led the successful landmark-designation battle, believes the owner is not protecting the building as well as it should—some of the brickwork has been crudely repointed and the plywood sealup is beginning to fail. But compared to most vacant buildings in marginal areas, this one receives luxurious care.

Long Island City is "hot" right now, abuzz with options and waterfront proposals. Because it is small and at a corner of the lot, the Terra-Cotta building is not an obstacle to redevelopment of this great site, with its brilliant views of the midtown skyscrapers, the Upper East Side enclaves, the Queensboro bridge and the red-and-white stacks of the Consolidated Edison plant to the north.

The Terra-Cotta building is a fair demonstration of what landmark designation can and cannot do. A building is not automatically saved upon designation, and buildings without economic uses are almost as vulnerable before as after designation. But designation can nominally preserve a building through the ups and downs of neighborhood renewal until all possible solutions for the building are exhausted.

The little brown jewel, the surprise on Vernon Boulevard, is patiently waiting for a solution.

The late Elliot Willensky remarked on the description of the building as "undiscovered until the 1970's," pointing out that it was in fact listed in the AIA Guide to New York City *beginning in 1967.*

THE METROPOLITAN CLUB

A Gilded Heritage Marred by Financial Troubles

Metropolitan Club, Fifth Avenue at 60th Street, in 1895, four years after founding.

THE RECENT PROPOSAL by the Metropolitan Club to sell the air rights over its landmarked clubhouse is but another chapter in the history of a club with perennial financial problems. The rights would be used by a developer to erect a 37-story apartment house over the the rear section of the club, originally built as a ladies' annex.

The Metropolitan was founded in 1891 to challenge the hegemony of the Union Club, then at West 21st Street and Fifth Avenue. J. Pierpont Morgan and other Union members were outraged by the blackballing of several of their friends. There also was a larger sentiment that 21st Street was too far south for both convenience and fashion.

The first meeting of the dissidents took place on February 20, 1891, and among the 25 conspirators were Goelets, Vanderbilts, Whitneys and Morgan himself, a legendary banker and first president of the new club.

For $420,000, the founders bought the northeast corner of East 60th Street and Fifth Avenue. At the time, most of the elite clubs were still below 42d Street.

If the Metropolitan was to challenge the Union, only the best architects would do, and this meant McKim, Mead & White, the designers of choice for the Gilded Age. Partner Stanford White "out-palazzoed" all previous efforts. "Merely a great box," said the *Real Estate Record and Guide* in 1894. Oh, but what a box! Vermont and Tuckahoe marble—now, sadly, overpainted—covered all the exposed facades in a chaste manner.

If the exterior was reserved, the interior was a catalogue of expensive decorative finishes. The foyer is entirely of marble and is one of the most intimidating entries in New York. Beyond is the lounging room running the length of the Fifth Avenue frontage, a swath of gilt, bronze and plaster relief designed by the French decorator Gilbert Cuel.

There are other significant rooms, among them the dining room on the third floor, also lavishly decorated by Cuel. These interiors were "the loudest work of art . . . ever presented to an astonished American public," according to the *Record and Guide*, and other journals were equally derisive. In retrospect, however, the Metropolitan represents the peak talents of a group of clients, architects and decorators guiding America to its station as a new international power.

Economy and wide appeal were not organizing principles for the founders, and decisions they made in 1890 have created issues that still challenge the club today. The few large rooms are set up for reading, cards and other sedentary activities. There is only a limited athletic program. And a club tradition of openness to women has diminished the "cigar-smoke" atmosphere that still seems to some to be the essence of an urban club.

Since the beginning, the Metropolitan has been plagued with deficits. In one period, the governors had to subsidize it with donations of $1,000 a year each, and twice mergers with the Union were considered.

The 1920's saw the replacement of the club's low-rise neighbors with skyscrapers. Once part of a parade of palaces along Fifth Avenue, it was suddenly a holdout in a canyon of tall hotels, apartments and office buildings. It was neither in the club district near Grand Central nor in a residential neighborhood, like the Union's new house at 69th and Park, completed in 1932.

Nevertheless, the club reached a healthy peak of 1,436 members in 1929, according to a history of the club by Paul Porzelt. But the Depression sent it down into the 700's by 1942, and in 1945 the clubhouse was nearly sold to satisfy loans. The club was clearly in trouble, which continued until membership fell to a low of 434 in 1970.

Since that time all clubs have enjoyed increased popularity, and the Metropolitan has cultivated reciprocal arrangements with other clubs, which has increased the use of the house. Nevertheless, its financial problems obliged the Metropolitan to make accommodations, especially to women, who were gradually let out of their annex and into the club itself. This gave the club a family air but also left it unlike others. It lacked the sports facilities of traditional clubs like the University, it was too far north for midtown businessmen, it was too grand to have a true family air like the River Club, and many women seemed to prefer the Colony and Cosmopolitan Clubs, where they could always be full members.

The Metropolitan was not successful in its goal of unseating the Union as top club. In its attempt, it created a lavish building that now needs repairs. The sale of the air rights would provide the money, but the approval of the apartment tower proposal by the Landmarks Preservation Commission is far from certain.

The tower proposal was rejected by the Landmarks Commission, but the club has removed the paint from the facade anyway, revealing some of the finest marble work in the city.

134 EAST 60th STREET

Holding Out in a Once-Gracious 1865 Brownstone

134 East 60th Street in 1912, third building, on left, from the corner of Lexington Avenue.

THE ROW HOUSE at 134 East 60th Street is a 122-year-old brownstone with a weathered facade that is indistinguishable from countless others in the city. Yet the building has received wide attention because a rent-controlled tenant, Jean Herman, has declined offers of up to $650,000 to leave from a developer, the Cohen Brothers Realty Corporation. Now the company has apparently given up, and its new office building on the Lexington Avenue blockfront opposite Bloomingdale's is under way, to rise 31 stories and overlook the little holdout brownstone it had hoped to demolish.

Beyond that test of wills, the house is of interest because its history is so typical of the brownstones that were developed by the thousands in Manhattan in the 19th century. It was built in 1865 by a Scotch-Irish family of builders, James and John Fettretch, when the close of the Civil War unleashed a wave of development above 42d Street. The Fettretch brownstones were the first on the block. Except for the corner house, which is wider and more elegant, the Fettretch buildings were identical: 20 feet wide, three windows across, with four stories reached by a stoop over the high basement. The basement held the kitchen; the main floor, a living room and dining room; and the upper floors held bedrooms and servants' rooms.

The facades of the houses were alike, Italianate-style brownstone except for the top floor—a slate mansard roof with dormers. The dark chocolate brownstone was ubiquitous in its day. To many, it seemed more luxurious than the brick facades of an earlier generation.

Henry S. Day, a barber living on what was then lower Sixth Avenue, now the Avenue of the Americas, bought 134 East 60th in 1866 for $26,000 and rented it out. His first tenant was Julius Birge, who was born in Germany in 1831 and came to the United States in 1851. Birge, a stockbroker with an office on Exchange Place, presumably commuted by horsecar on the Third Avenue Railroad.

Mr. Birge left in 1875, and then Mr. Day occupied the house with his wife, two children and assorted servants. The Days left in 1877, followed by a succession of families, including David Cohen, a broker, and Emily Whitaker, a widow, but Mr. Day retained ownership of the house until 1892.

The next occupants were Cecelie and Emil Potosky and their six children and two servants. Mr. Potosky ran a family cloak business. The Potoskys, who lived in the building from 1889 to 1895, seem to have been the last single family to occupy the whole house. Mr. Day sold the house in 1892 to Howland Pell, who was part of an old colonial family. The Pells lived in finer quarters off Fifth Avenue, and continued to rent the house, by 1900 to Henry and Frieda Urban. The Urbans brought with them a cook, a waitress and seven boarders.

Henry Urban, New York correspondent for the *Berlin Lokal Anzeiger*, and his boarders, who included Antonio Xavier, the Brazilian Consul, no doubt made a cosmopolitan dinner table. But the building was headed down a road that many older houses soon followed.

In 1928, the Pells leased the house to James F. Meehan, a Bronx builder and former Tenement House Commissioner. Mr. Meehan proceeded to convert the building to apartments. He removed the stoop and created stores in the lower two floors. At the same time, he was similarly altering 116, 117 and 153 East 60th Street.

By 1932, there were only five houses occupied by single families left on the block. Today, there are none. The brownstones that remain have been carved up into rentals with stores at street level, and the rest of the block is taken up with offices and large apartment buildings.

The Pells sold the house in 1937 to the first in a succession of corporations. The building continued a gradual but comfortable decline as brownstone apartments, without any foreseeable future except for demolition and replacement with a larger business building.

Today, the Fettretches would not recognize 134 East 60th Street. Its mansard roof has been sheared off and its rear unoccupied half removed. Only an occasional door frame or window shutter survives inside to recall its heyday as a house where children grew up, parents argued and made up, birthday presents were opened and family festivals were celebrated. Its brownstone skin has disintegrated to an ancient state, beautiful or shabby depending upon the observer.

Its ultimate fate still hangs in the balance, but in New York anything can happen, and it may just be that 134 East 60th Street will be around for later generations to point out, saying, "You know, that used to be an old row house, and what happened was . . ."

The tower at 750 Lexington was completed in 1988, a garish, overbearing shaft by Murphy/Jahn. Little 134 East 60th Street was first brutally mutilated and then ignorantly "restored" as a bank branch—but Jean Herman is still in residence upstairs.

THE CHURCH OF ST. PAUL AND ST. ANDREW

A Landmark with an Unwanted Status

Methodist Church of St. Paul and St. Andrew on West End Avenue at 86th Street in 1899.

D EPENDING ON YOUR point of view, it is either an architectural mishmash or a masterful example of scientific eclecticism. But the Methodist Church of St. Paul and St. Andrew on the Upper West Side, everyone agrees, has become one of New York's enduring real-estate controversies. After landmark designation in 1981 stalled a plan to demolish most of the church at West 86th Street and West End Avenue for redevelopment, its trustees began a legal battle to overturn the landmark status.

Although the State Supreme Court refused last November to hear the case, St. Paul and St. Andrew is likely to be a focal point for resistance to the landmarks law for years to come.

When it was built as the Methodist Episcopal Church of St. Paul in 1897, it was described in newspapers as having one of the most aristocratic and richest congregations in the city. The church was actually founded in 1834, and by 1890 its congregation was meeting at Park Avenue and East 22d Street. In the 1890's members began looking for an uptown site, finally purchasing the northeast corner of West 86th Street and West End Avenue in 1894.

The new location was in the heart of the newly developing West Side, "one of the choicest residential neighborhoods," according to a news-

paper story of the time. By the early 1890's, the West End Avenue blocks were largely covered with newly built brick and brownstone row houses. Churches soon followed, and construction continued up through the early 1900's until the church steeples dominated the skyline.

To design their new church, the Methodists hired Robert H. Robertson, an ecclesiastical specialist. Mr. Robertson had been the city's preeminent designer of Romanesque churches, but by 1895 the Renaissance tradition was sweeping the country. For the St. Paul congregation, Mr. Robertson produced a vast, tile-roofed shed in light colors of brick and terra-cotta, with two enormous towers on the West End Avenue front.

The church—which cost $200,000 to build—is in the basilica form of an early Christian church, with a simple, oblong shape and a row of windows just below the eave. But the monumental Corinthian pilasters on West End Avenue and the arched entrance on the West 86th Street side are distinctly Renaissance in character, while the six oversized angel figures above the West End Avenue entrance seem drawn directly from contemporary American art of the period.

The most striking feature of the church is its unequal pair of high, open towers on the West End Avenue front. Without bells, they have no apparent function and are haunting, evocative forms.

The interior is a more conventional Victorian preaching church of painted plaster and varnished oak. Two great angel figures—wings outspread—mark an arch over the chancel or altar area. The curved pews fan out in a circular design from the chancel, and on a typical Sunday even a small congregation scattered among the 1,200 seats can seem strong because of this sense of focus.

Architectural critics of the period gave the church mixed notices. The *Architectural Review* called the main entrance "full of poetic feeling," but described the towers as "ungainly and ill-balanced." Today, the church ranks among the most memorable.

By the 1920's, the steeples that had once dominated a low-rise skyline were being surpassed by high-rise apartment houses. But after 1930 development declined. The neighborhood was, in effect, frozen in time, with its great stock of 19th-century churches left intact. At the same time, the West Side's religious makeup was changing.

Although most of the Christian churches there were built before 1910, most synagogues went up after 1920, and in the 1930's the West Side became home to thousands of Jewish immigrants fleeing Nazi persecution. St. Paul suffered a loss in attendance, and in 1937 it took in and merged with the congregation of the Methodist Church of St. Andrew, which had been on West 76th Street between Columbus and Amsterdam Avenues.

In recent years, as the West Side has been rediscovered and revived, some churches have reported increased attendance. St. Paul and St. Andrew is not one of them. Sharp financial pressures forced the church in 1980 to plan to lease or sell most of the 17,500-square-foot property, but the city stepped in and designated it a landmark.

The Landmarks Preservation Commission, in designating the structure, called it an important example of scientific eclecticism. A group appointed by religious leaders in New York City to study landmark constraints on religious property called St. Paul and St. Andrew an architectural mishmash.

The church is now considering renewed legal challenges. In the meantime, the pair of towers continue to call attention to what has become not simply an architectural issue but a legal one as well.

No change.

THE COLISEUM

The "Hybrid Pseudo-Modern" on Columbus Circle

The Coliseum on Columbus Circle in 1956, shortly after it was completed.

THE 50'S MAY be back in style, but not soon enough to save the Coliseum at Columbus Circle. The exposition hall has been sold to Coliseum Associates for demolition to make way for a mixed-use project with two towers rising 68 and 58 stories. Construction is scheduled to begin late in the spring and by summer's end the blank, boxy Coliseum will be but a memory.

The Coliseum was begun in 1954 and completed in 1956 by the Triborough Bridge and Tunnel Authority under the direction of Robert Moses, who adopted a project that had been languishing for years. Mr. Moses developed a double strategy: Condemn the west side of Columbus Circle from West 58th to West 60th Streets—then a collection of old offices, tenements and minor retail uses—as a "slum" and then get the Federal Government, under the Title I slum-clearance program, to pay most of the acquisition cost.

To replace the "slum," he proposed a single exposition building facing Columbus Circle. Behind it would be middle-income apartments covering 53 percent of the two-block site—just enough to qualify for Title I assistance. His architects were Leon and Lionel Levy, who also were responsible for the design of the big pink United Parcel Service building at West 43d Street and 11th Avenue.

Esthetics were not Mr. Moses's highest priority, and even in the 1950's, the design of the Coliseum was not a popular one. "Utterly pedestrian," "hybrid pseudo-modern," editorialized *Art News*. Even worse, the editorial went on, was how the building had a "total lack of relation to its site," specifically the curve of Columbus Circle.

But the moral outrage rolled off Mr. Moses's back, and it is fair to say that what was built is significant as a low point for New York's public buildings. The Coliseum was simply a plain rectangle, with a single chamfered corner where Broadway cut into the block. An off-center, 20-story slab of offices had been added to the scheme to help subsidize other costs, and the relation between the two elements was awkward at best.

The windowless Coliseum building was sheathed in lifeless, uniform white brick, with vertical metal panels running from top to bottom. The office tower, a relentless grid, had the relative luxury of two colors of brick: white and gray.

Four large cast-aluminum panels, the seals of the Federal, state and city governments and the Authority, were executed by Paul Manship (who did the statue of Prometheus in Rockefeller Center) and bolted onto the main facade.

The Coliseum was functionally, if not esthetically, advanced. The three main entrances could serve a total of six shows independently, so that the philatelists and the photographers wouldn't collide with one another. The public-address systems could page the entire building, or a single corner.

The four exhibition floors, totalling 323,000 square feet, included an open, 150-foot-square, three-story well for sailboat masts, airplanes and other odd merchandise.

The opening program included the International Automobile Show, National Photographic Show and International Philatelic Exhibit—all at once—and in the next 30 years there were 1,246 shows in all.

Everything from King Farouk's jewels to Irish coffee was exhibited, touched, tasted, promoted and sold. The Coliseum was sort of a commercial circus, with at least one ring under the big top usually occupied. In 1959, it served as the American end of a American–Russian exhibition arrangement, the Moscow equivalent of which gave rise to the famous Nixon–Khrushchev kitchen debate in 1959.

But trade shows began to get larger and larger and the Coliseum's lack of space—just barely enough in 1956—began to be a liability. By the 1970's, New York was losing major shows to better-equipped cities. Plans for the Jacob K. Javits Convention Center, on the Hudson River north of West 34th Street, with 1.8 million square feet of space, were announced in 1979 and the Coliseum's days were numbered.

In 1985, the city and the authority requested proposals from developers for the site, and the winning scheme provided for a payment of $455 million to be used for mass-transit improvements. Demolition will begin this summer, with the office building to be submerged within the new project. The fate of the Manship sculptures is uncertain—the art world is not exactly lining up to save them—but the office lobby, unusually intact for its period, with attractive stainless steel/basketweave lighting fixtures, is scheduled for demolition.

The Coliseum itself has been empty since last year, impassively awaiting its fate, without hope of any last-minute reprieve by preservationists or block associations. The ever-changing, bright-red letters on the marquee have been fixed for months in a poignantly fractured farewell: "I OV NEW YORK."

Still standing, and still without architectural defenders.

THE SAMUEL R. SMITH INFIRMARY

"Pride of the Island" Facing an Uncertain Future

The Samuel R. Smith Infirmary in New Brighton, Staten Island, in 1895 photo.

DESPITE ITS SIZE and prominence, the Samuel R. Smith Infirmary—a great red-brick Victorian castle in New Brighton, Staten Island—is a building that has fallen through the cracks.

Apparently of landmark quality, it was considered by the Landmarks Preservation Commission in 1983 but never designated. The current owners say they intend to restore the building, but have made conflicting statements about their plans. One of the great institutional buildings of its borough, the Smith Infirmary could just as easily emerge from a current redevelopment project a renewed gem or a pile of rubble.

Staten Island—not part of New York City until 1898—had no private hospital until 1861, when the Richmond County Medical Society established the infirmary and named it after a local doctor "who devoted himself to the poor." It occupied a succession of buildings near the present Ferry Terminal, until in 1887 it acquired a hilly seven-acre site south and inland of the Terminal area on an irregular block bounded by Castleton, Webster and Brook Avenues and Pine Street.

Alfred E. Barlow, the architect, designed a rectangular red-brick château with four round corners topped by conical roofs. The castle imagery was reinforced by the high basement, mostly without windows, the small main entrance, and the projection of the upper floor out onto brick corbelling—as if the Infirmary's defenders were at the ready to pour boiling oil onto attacking Vikings.

The basic form of the Infirmary was apparently inspired by that of the New York Cancer Hospital (1885) in Manhattan, still standing at West 105th and Central Park West, where the "cornerless" rooms were thought to reduce the collection of germs.

Speeches at its opening in the summer of 1890 described the Infirmary as the "pride of the island," the county's "greatest charity," with a "splendid site and stately proportions."

Period photographs of the interior show an open, central stairway of decorative twisted ironwork, patterned tin ceilings and ceiling-high windows with diaphanous curtains. A newspaper account in 1891 described a typical room: "Beds are of iron, with woven wire springs, hair mattresses, snowy sheets and downy blankets."

The hospital was happy with its site, midway up a hill with dramatic views of New York Harbor, and soon added two surgical pavilions, a nurses' residence, a portable "fever pavilion," a boiler room and a crematorium. A low stone wall encircled the campus-like grounds,

which had ornamental shrubs, curving, graveled drives, and neat lawns. The name was changed in 1917 to Staten Island Hospital, and a new nurses' residence went up in the 1920's, along with a new, six-story hospital building.

When the Infirmary was established, the area was just beginning to develop, with modest residences below the hospital site and more substantial ones higher up. In the 1950's, low-income families began moving into the area below the hospital site, now largely black and Hispanic. Although the hospital was a convenient local resource, successive building programs had exhausted most of the available land, and parking began to be a serious problem. In 1979, the hospital abandoned its old site and moved to Dongan Hills, on the east side of the island.

A succession of developers tried in vain to renovate the old hospital without success, and it became derelict. The landmarks panel held hearings on the property in 1983, but failed to designate, apparently reluctant to regulate a vacant building considered by some to be a threat to the neighborhood. Last year, Forkash Construction, a partnership, bought the site and began renovating the 1920's hospital structure as a condominium, now sold out. The plan for the Castleton Castle complex calls for new town houses, athletic facilities, and renovated units in the remaining older buildings, including the original one.

The commission renewed its inquiries last year—a staff member contends that one of the owners has mentioned a plan to cover the red brick of the infirmary with modern stone facing—but Lillian Ayala, a spokesman for the commission, says that it cannot now act "since we didn't designate it originally."

Geofrey Alexander, one of the owners, states that the Infirmary building will not be changed. Scaffolding is now up around the Infirmary, the interior has been gutted—except for the iron stairway and some of the metal ceilings.

Although the exterior is still generally intact, there is nothing to prevent any owner—present or future—from covering over, or even demolishing, the "pride of the island," and its fate now hangs in the balance.

The building remains a vacant shell.

THE THIRD AVENUE "COTTAGES"

A Cool Low-Rise Oasis in a Hot Development Area

The "cottages" beneath the el at 77th Street and Third Avenue in 1937.

THE "COTTAGES," AS they are called locally, comprise a little low-rise oasis on Third Avenue between East 77th and East 78th Streets. Built in 1937, they occupy a prime potential development site, a full blockfront on the bustling avenue just outside the Upper East Side Historic District. Only two stories high, with a large garden, they are 50 years old this year. But it is hard to believe that they can long survive the superheated Manhattan real-estate market.

The Depression brought substantial changes to the Upper East Side. Older buildings were torn down and replaced with one- or two-story taxpayers erected to provide a better return on the property until times improved to permit more substantial development.

The Goelets, a New York merchant family dating back to the Federal era, had such a problem with a row of eight 70-year-old tenements on the west side of Third Avenue between 77th and 78th Streets. In 1936, new multiple-dwelling regulations required substantial upgrading, and according to the *Real Estate Record and Guide* in 1938, the cost was not worth the result.

The Goelets evicted their tenants and reimproved the property with a novel scheme, using a lot running almost 150 feet deep. They built a two-story apartment/store building with a tennis/badminton complex behind. Access to the apartments above the stores was not from Third Avenue, with its noisy, blighting el, but from 78th Street, where a walk leads to stairs to the eight apartments.

The cottages are of ingenious design, with glass-block windows on Third Avenue to seal out the rattle of the el, which was not demolished until 1956. Their front doors are at the second-floor level, where a setback creates a strip of tiny, 20-foot-deep, turfed front yards.

Designed by Edward H. Faile, an engineer who also designed the Goelet Building at 49th Street and Fifth Avenue, the cottage complex really has two fronts. The stores on Third Avenue are of plain brick with simple show windows, albeit with very soft purple art-glass transoms and big circular marquees at the cross-street corners. The garden side is basically Regency in theme, with white painted brick (now weathered bare), Chippendale-style ironwork and brick quoining. The apartments are all one-bedroom units, although the corner ones have tiny square sunrooms.

There is a protected feeling here, not as grand as the gardens of Sutton Place but just as serene and removed. This delightful amenity is not hidden from the passer-by behind brick walls—the usual model in New York—but only lightly screened by an iron fence. It is a gracious touch in a city where public and private rarely mix.

As originally designed, the project assumed further development at a later date, presumably including the demolition of the two-story building. The playing courts were the first to go, as the Goelets sold off a 100-foot-square plot on 77th Street to Sidney and Arthur Diamond.

In 1941, the Diamonds built the 11-story apartment house at 177 East 77th Street, which offers a second access to the cottages. They also took an overall lease from the Goelets to protect the light and air for their building, and in 1946 bought the entire site. The apartment-house construction eliminated the tennis and badminton courts and replaced them with a great garden, about 70 by 100 feet, of bedded ivy, dogwood, magnolias and larger trees.

The cottages overlook this secluded garden, with only the muffled sounds of traffic to remind tenants of the city's bustle outside. Despite the modest interiors, the private remove of the cottage complex and its unassuming air make it one of the great multiple dwellings of the city, comparable in gentility, if not in grandeur, to the best along Fifth Avenue.

In 1961, the Diamonds filed plans for a 20-story building to cover the site of the cottages and garden but never carried it out. As values on the East Side have risen, Arthur Diamond, now president of the 177 East 77th Street Corporation, says he gets regular telephone calls from parties seeking to buy and redevelop the site.

The present tenants believe that he has a sentimental attachment to the enclave, so they are not greatly concerned that he would sell. However, the stores are reportedly on month-to-month leases and only six of the eight cottages are occupied; two have been vacant for several years.

"For the moment," said Mr. Diamond, who has owned the complex most of its life, "it stays as it is. But nothing remains forever."

"Forever" has continued, but the Diamonds recently declined to meet with the New York Landmarks Conservancy, which wanted to discuss the possibility of a scenic easement over the gardens.

AUDUBON TERRACE

Attrition Taking Its Toll at a Cultural Complex

The Hispanic Society of America building in 1906 at Audubon Terrace between 155th and 156th Streets on Broadway.

IF IT WERE in, say, Toledo or Phoenix, it would be a major cultural attraction to which residents would make frequent visits. But Audubon Terrace—a magnificent assemblage at 155th Street and Broadway of a church and other structures that once housed five museums—is unknown to most New Yorkers, and now the second of its founding institutions is about to pull up stakes for another location.

Audubon Terrace was the effort of Archer Huntington, who used money inherited from his father, Collis P. Huntington, the railroad magnate, to found 12 museums. Early in his life, he decided he would establish a museum devoted to Spanish culture, and in 1904 he bought part of the old John James Audubon estate on the west side of Broadway between 155th and 156th Streets.

Huntington envisioned a complex of institutions for the 200- by 550-foot site: The Hispanic Society of America was the first building to go up (1904–1906), and was joined in short order by the American Numismatic Society (1906–1907), the American Geographical Society (1909–1911), the Church of Our Lady of Esperanza (1909–1912), the Museum of the American Indian (1916–1922) and the American Academy and National Institute of Arts and Letters (1921–1930).

Huntington's conception of Audubon Terrace, largely executed by his architect cousin, Charles Pratt Huntington, oriented the complex toward the north, where a subway stop and large intersection at 157th Street create a plaza. A grand landscaped terrace led up from 156th Street to the Hispanic Society on 155th Street.

But Charles Huntington died in 1919, and the later buildings of the 1920's blocked up the open space on 156th Street, making the new entrance on Broadway and producing a long, narrow courtyard. The buildings are instantly recognizable as museums. They are mostly Indiana limestone, in the Italian Renaissance style, with monumental Ionic colonnades and names carved in the friezes—Da Gama and Columbus, for instance, on the Geographic Society.

The Hispanic, Numismatic and Indian institutions are visited most often and each has its special character. The Hispanic Society has an imposing interior—a Spanish-style court in plum-colored terra-cotta, filled with Spanish artifacts from Goyas to medieval pottery to marble sarcophagi.

The Numismatic Society has a pristine 1950's exhibit room, all smooth blond birch cases with displays that will surprise the visitor who considers coins boring. The first two floors of the Indian Museum have charming and unpretentious installations with 1920's oak cases filled—but not crammed—with some of the greatest works of native American art.

This totally understated approach is long out of fashion in the

museum world, but it is refreshing to a visitor accustomed to over-dramatic spotlights and elaborate displays of artworks that can presumably stand on their own merits.

Audubon Terrace has an innocent charm about it—no lines for blockbuster exhibitions snaking down the long, red-brick courtyard, no big banners, no huge bookstores, just the museums and their artwork. Grand in aspiration and its collections, it is small and friendly in scale.

Although the area had bourgeois expectations in 1904, it is now just another remote Manhattan neighborhood, far from the cultural concentration along Museum Mile on Fifth Avenue. The Geographical Society left in 1971 and the building that once housed one of the premier collections of maps in the Western Hemisphere is now Boricua College, a four-year, private institution created in 1974 to meet the needs of Puerto Ricans and other Spanish-speaking people.

The Museum of the American Indian has made no secret of its dissatisfaction with its location, and has long stated its desire to move to a new, more prominent location. In February, the museum director, Roland Force, promised with apparent reluctance to maintain some presence at Audubon Terrace if the museum receives the old Custom House at Bowling Green as a gift from the Federal Government. But just last week, the Smithsonian Institution authorized negotiations that could lead to the museum's relocation to the Mall in Washington.

The other institutions seem satisfied, if not overjoyed, with their location, but last year's attendance at the entire complex was about 50,000, against 3.8 million for the Metropolitan Museum of Art. The relationship between attendance and location is obvious, and another few defections would seriously dilute the character of Audubon Terrace.

The question of new quarters for the Museum of the American Indian will probably be resolved this year, and how it handles its "commitment" to Audubon Terrace may offer a strong clue to its ultimate fate. Although the complex was designated a city landmark in 1979, nothing prevents the institutions from relocating, since only the buildings themselves are protected by the designation's shield.

Archer Huntington collected smaller institutions on Audubon Terrace to make it something special. The years may have eroded that image, but its faded glory remains.

Congress subsequently arranged for a new museum to be built in Washington, with satellite exhibits in the Custom House in New York— and 2,000 square feet of general Smithsonian exhibits in the original Indian Museum building. That deal is still on—if years away—but now the Hispanic Society and Boricua College are in court wrangling over possession of the building when the Indian Museum actually moves out.

THE DAKOTA STABLES

A "Soft-Site" Garage
on the Booming West Side

The Dakota Garage, Amsterdam Avenue and 77th Street, in 1944.

THINGS LOOK PEACEFUL on "stable row," a collection of a dozen public and private garages, most of them former stables, on Amsterdam Avenue from 75th to 77th Streets. But to a developer it is really a collection of sites crying out for development: old, low buildings, with no residential tenants, that are not landmarks—and are right in the middle of the fashionable West Side.

The biggest and, perhaps, best building is the old Dakota Garage, on a 12,000-square-foot plot at the southwest corner of Amsterdam Avenue and 77th Street.

The garage—actually built as a stable—went up in two sections from 1891 to 1894. Originally containing 158 stalls and space for over 300 carriages, it was erected by Edmund Coffin, a banker, as a real-estate investment. (Mr. Coffin was father and grandfather, respectively, to the Revs. Henry Sloane and William Sloane Coffin.) He hired as his architect Bradford Lee Gilbert, then prominent for introducing steel-skeleton construction to New York City with his Tower Building at 50 Broadway in 1889.

Though a stylistic gem, the Dakota Garage does not appear to have been structurally unique. It was typical of stable construction of the time—stalls for horses on the basement and second floors—with ramps, and heavier floors to accommodate drainage systems—and elevators to take carriages to the third, fourth and fifth floors. Stables were sited on Amsterdam because they were convenient to the new row houses nearer the Hudson River, but not so close as to bother their residents with stable smells and noises.

Mr. Gilbert produced a Romanesque Revival structure almost entirely of brick, with little applied decoration. The warm orange walls are set off by rich, salmon-colored trim at the windows and the cornice. Arches above the windows and at the cornice are of specially manufactured brick, with ends tapering to only two inches in width.

Two stepped, Flemish-style entry portals with serpentine decorative carvings mark street-level areas—there were originally four. But the building is a work of color and line rather than applied ornament, in contrast to most buildings of the period, which were often overloaded with decoration. This simplicity gives it a fresh, even modern, character despite its age.

The architect also directly quoted several major elements from his Tower Building, demolished in 1914 but considered one of the most important skyscrapers in the city's history. On both structures he used small areas of serpentine ornament, round arches at the top of multistory arcades, and similar two-tone color schemes in brick.

Originally known as the Mason Stable, in 1912 the building became the Dakota Stables, after the demolition of a namesake building nearby (there is no clear connection between either stable and the Dakota apartment building). It appears to have been built as a "livery" rather than a "boarding" stable, since residents of the new brownstones and apartments in the neighborhood preferred to rent entire outfits whenever necessary—horses, carriage, tack and driver—rather than keep their own on the premises.

In 1915, after a few years of storing both cars and carriages, the Dakota was altered into a legitimate garage, with new steel reinforcing concrete floors, gasoline pumps and even automobile turntables on the ground floor. In the 1950's it was renamed the Pyramid, apparently after the pyramidlike, stepped entry portals.

Today the Dakota Garage is considered one of the "soft sites" of the Upper West Side, where land values have soared in the last decade. Much of the area is occupied either by residential buildings—where tenant-protection laws make demolition unlikely—or landmark buildings, making structures like individual supermarkets and garages practically the only sites for new construction.

The Landmarks Preservation Commission has not been keen on the Dakota Garage, saying the ground floor has been "severely compromised"—although a designated landmark a block away, the Belleclaire Hotel, has no original ground floor left.

David Berley, a partner in Sylan Associates, which owns the property, said the building "will remain as a garage for the next 10 or 15 years." "We're owners, not developers," he said. "We like the income." But at the same time, he said, there is a demolition clause in the garage operator's lease.

There are no signs of impending demolition, but garage operations can fold quickly. There are no adjacent co-ops that want to preserve the view, no activist block association, no one likely to stir up controversy. If the end comes for the Dakota Stables, it will probably be swift—and certain.

Correspondent Stephen Langenthal later wrote that the Pyramid name was in fact brought in (by a later operator) from a prior garage by the same name on West 69th Street.

GRAND CENTRAL POST OFFICE

A New Tower Belatedly "Completes" Terminal City

Grand Central Station and Post Office at Lexington Avenue and 45th Street in 1910.

THE SEVEN-STORY Grand Central Post Office, at 45th and Lexington, is one of those older, grimy midtown buildings lost among taller structures. But it is also among the last remaining buildings of the original "terminal city" complex around Grand Central Terminal. Although the details are not yet definite, a development group expects to begin work this year on a 25- to 30-story addition on top of the postal building. The developers plan to use the old building as the base, keeping its facade and remodeling its interior.

Designed in 1906, the post office was part of the New York Central Railroad's "great air rights plan." Covering over its huge marshaling yards—roughly 12 square blocks—the railroad erected a steel platform with raised streets, sidewalks and foundations for a sprawling complex of offices, hotels and apartments. This terminal city included such buildings as the old Commodore and Biltmore Hotels, apartments on Park Avenue above 47th, and office structures at 52 Vanderbilt Avenue and 250 Park Avenue.

The post-office building is now the oldest survivor of this group, older even than Grand Central Terminal, which was completed in 1912. Both were jointly designed by Warren & Wetmore and Reed & Stem.

The post office was originally conceived as a double blockfront on the west side of Lexington Avenue from 43d to 45th Streets, but only the northern half was built. The height was to be 20 stories, but only seven floors were built at first—other buildings had followed such construction in stages. Opened in 1909, practically the entire structure was given over to postal operations, including a long, open truck bay along Depew Place, across from the present Pan Am Building.

The post office is a Roman Doric mass of red granite on the first floor and Indiana limestone above. The middle four stories have large vertical bays of steel windows alternating with piers of limestone.

Like much Federal architecture, it is massive—made up of great limestone blocks, with first-floor walls almost five feet thick. The decoration, although limited, is rich and inventive. A limestone band at the second floor has a rectangular, interlocking meander pattern, intertwined with what appears to be leafwork and berries. Up close, the berries turn out to be acorns, and some are "missing," leaving only empty caps.

This decoration also appears on the bases of the two Roman Doric columns on the Lexington Avenue side—unusual places for ornaments.

The riveted steel window bays carry an intricate, criss-cross fretwork—sort of industrial Gothic. The attic floor slopes backward, an unusual touch, perhaps meant to suggest the future addition.

In 1938 and 1939 the interior was completely remodeled. The present windows for stamps and other services—with their mild, moderne styling—are from that period.

The upper floors also appear to date from the same alteration, and have a definite Federal feel. Some offices have intact metal and glass partitions, wooden floors, Venetian blinds, and gray metal desks and furniture. They could be movie sets for the 1940's. Most of the doors have labels, such as "Postal Police" or "Medical Supervisor," but many are dark inside. The wide halls—some 200 feet long—are often empty, and footsteps echo in a way that suggests a massive Government building in Washington.

In recent years terminal city has become attractive real estate. The Biltmore and Commodore have been given new facades, and 466 Lexington Avenue was stripped to the steel and rebuilt. In 1982, Carol Clark, who was then a staff member of the New York Landmarks Conservancy, nominated the post office to the National Register of Historic Places since local landmark statutes do not apply to Federal properties.

The Postal Service, considering redevelopment, blocked the nomination, but later consented. In 1984 it signed an accord with the state parks agency—which oversees government work on historic buildings. The Postal Service agreed to encourage—but not require—any developer to retain the original exterior "to the greatest extent possible," and to permit the city landmarks agency to strip the interior of decorative elements before any interior demolition.

This year the Postal Service designated as developer a group made up of Sterling Equities, Gerald D. Hines Interests and the Prudential Insurance Company. David Childs, a partner with Skidmore, Owings & Merrill, the architectural firm hired by the developers, said work will begin later this year on the tower over the old building.

Though not in the way the original builders imagined, one of the last elements in terminal city is falling into place.

A 40-story tower is now under construction.

BROOKLYN BOROUGH HALL

A Greek Revival Temple Fronts an 1848 City Hall

Fulton Street el, left, and Court Street flanking Brooklyn Borough Hall in 1908.

Brooklyn Borough Hall has aroused debate from the start, so the recent controversy over its prolonged restoration is perhaps in context. But if all goes well, it will be in service by early 1988 as borough offices, and as a reminder of Brooklyn's glory days before it became part of New York City in 1898.

The term "Borough Hall" is something that a real Brooklyn booster may bridle at, or correct. For it was built as City Hall when Brooklyn was still its own master. Brooklyn was incorporated as a city in April 1834, and its new Council began discussions of a fitting seat of government three months later.

In 1835, a triangular plot bounded by Fulton, Joralemon and Court Streets was acquired, and an architectural competition followed. But construction did not begin until 1845, after a decade of false starts, switching architects, lawsuits and near bankruptcy for the fledging city.

Finally, Gamaliel King, a local architect and builder, came up with an acceptable design for a severe Greek Revival, four-story building with a temple front. Wisely, he used the light-gray Tuckahoe marble cut for an earlier design; the contractor had been suing for years for payment.

The main facade faced north onto the triangle, with a giant stairway leading up to an Ionic-style portico with six free-standing columns. Exterior decoration was reduced to a minimum—even the modest egg and dart detailing at the second floor was restricted to the area under the portico. The entire structure was taut, attenuated.

Except for the projecting temple front, the completed City Hall was rectangular in plan, although two wings projected slightly from the back. Instead of a dome—a standard feature in government buildings of the period—King had a wooden cupola, with a clock, that doubled as a fire lookout and a bell tower. A figure of Justice was placed on the top.

Although it was first occupied in late 1848, some rooms in the City Hall were not finished until the 1860's. It had a relatively straightforward plan—an east–west corridor running down the middle of a series of unexceptional rooms except for a double-height courtroom and a columned, double-height central gallery.

Unlike other government buildings, which were either built for the ages or operated by agencies too cheap to alter them, the new City Hall saw regular and successive changes. The completion of the interior took

20 years. And then there were water problems, for the basement floors were set on sand fill. Apparently, there also were problems with King's interior stairs, and they were replaced. Long before the present restoration effort, all of the original stone flooring had been removed—an unusual change for such a durable material—and only one original door survived intact. The "restored" stairs are largely conjectural, since only traces of the originals survived.

In 1895, two years after a fire watch had ended, a midday fire destroyed the cupola, sending the bell and the statue of Justice crashing through the roof. A new cast-iron cupola went up in 1898, the same year the city became a borough.

Gradually, the area around Borough Hall became a civic center, attracting courts and municipal buildings, but Borough Hall remained the focus, perched on a small, green rise. The construction of an elevated rail line in the 1880's and later street widenings undercut its presence, however. In the 50's, the building of a civic center complex led to the demolition of all the buildings on one side of the triangle across from Borough Hall. With the demolition, the park lost its sense of enclosure, and Fulton Street was cut off short of it, compromising the centrality of Borough Hall.

The aim of the master plan was to leave Borough Hall at the end of a long swath of park running all the way to the Brooklyn Bridge, a conceit that would have worked only with a building the size of the Capitol.

The idea of restoring Borough Hall came in the early 70's, but it was not until 1982 that the Department of General Services let a contract for the project to the architectural firm of Conklin & Rossant. Since 1983 the building has been closed as work proceeded—overbudget and overdue. In 1983, completion was scheduled for 1985.

On schedule or not, the project is now in the home stretch. The exterior is a spotty, light-and-dark gray from test patches made before a final cleaning. The interior is almost entirely new, since there was nearly nothing original left to restore. Thus the building is a peculiar amalgam—an antique facade seemingly applied to a modern interior. All in all, there is something a little unsettling, a restlessness, to Borough Hall, as if the city inside the borough is still trying to break out.

Completed in 1988.

THE NEW YORK BUTCHERS' DRESSED MEAT COMPANY

A Building Long Past Its Prime on a Choice Site for Offices

© 1906, *THE AMERICAN ARCHITECT*

A SLAUGHTERHOUSE DOES NOT exactly fit in with the contemporary image of New York as a center of finance and communication. Thus it is no surprise that the vacant New York Butchers' Dressed Meat Company building, on the west side of 11th Avenue, from 39th to 40th Street, is scheduled for demolition by the city, eager to capitalize on the growing building boom in midtown west.

Although such a move has been long opposed by Community Board 4, the city's Department of General Services will soon propose that an office building be constructed on the site.

The block-long building was built in two sections–the 39th Street corner in 1903–1905, and the 40th Street corner in 1917–1919. The New York Butchers' Dressed Meat Company itself was a joint effort by local butchers and provisioners who sought to break the hold of the Midwestern "beef trust," which they contended had been able to arrange prices to suit themselves.

The location of the complex reflected the importance of the West Side as an industrial center. Water transport and especially freight rail yards (those of the New York Central, Pennsylvania and the West Shore lines were all in the West 30's) had combined to create favorable conditions for suppliers of food and other commodities.

Designed by Horgan & Slattery, the original building was built six stories high with the lower two floors faced with limestone and the upper floors with dark orange brick and white terra-cotta. The incised, shadowed rustication of the lower floors is set off against raised, white banding on the upper section.

Neo-Renaissance in style, the building has an unmistakably civic or semi-public character. A powerhouse is the first guess by most people until they see the six giant sculptures of rams and steers at the sixth floor.

Now surrounded by barbed wire and cyclone fencing, the one-time slaughterhouse is a derelict, its windows either bricked up or open to the weather, its green copper cornice partly detached.

In its heyday, the building had a "roof garden" for livestock. Herded up a seven-story ramp—still visible from the west—the animals were released into tile-lined pens on the top floor, where, a 1905 newspaper article said, "their last hours will be among comparatively peaceful and harmonious surroundings."

The roof garden, however, was probably more functional than humane, since the killing floor was the next level down.

This slaughterhouse served, among others, Orthodox Jews, whose religion requires animals to be freshly killed under rabbinical supervision. The plans for the building thus provided for a "rabbi's dressing room" on the killing floor below the roof garden.

Notwithstanding the hostility of its Eastern customers, the Midwestern beef trust still knew a good thing, and by the 1930's Armour had acquired the New York Butchers' Dressed Meat Company and its building.

Slaughtering continued until the late 1950's, when railhead slaughterhouses lost their advantage to truck-related operations, such as the United Parcel Services facilities and the Greyhound bus station that were built in the vicinity.

The Jacob K. Javits Convention Center, opened in 1986, has spawned a variety of proposals that portend a resurgence of large-scale development interest in this former industrial area. The convention center extends to the south side of 39th Street, across the street from the building. The area—once a haunt of prostitutes—has been distinctly cleaned up.

The city took title to the building in 1975, and, according to William Ryan, the district manager for Community Board 4, it is now planning to present a proposal for a 99-year lease on the site to the Board of Estimate for approval.

The Department of General Services confirms that the proposal involves construction of an office building erected by a private developer. Borough President David N. Dinkins of Manhattan delayed a vote on the proposal, but has not yet taken a position on the project itself.

The Community Board has also been asking the Landmarks Preservation Commission to designate the property, but there is a loophole since the city is exempt from the Landmark regulations.

The convention center establishes a different calling for the West 30's—smoked glass, pristine grass plots and impeccably clean streets.

In the meantime, like the animals awaiting slaughter that preceded it, the old New York Butchers' Dressed Meat Company building is apparently spending its last hours in "comparatively peaceful surroundings," waiting for the end.

Demolished in 1991.

THALIA THEATER

A Closed Revival House That May Itself Be Revived

The Astor Market, which opened in 1915, at the southwest corner of 95th Street and Broadway.

WHEN THE THALIA Theater closed in May many people thought the two-story building at West 95th Street and Broadway, which housed the famed revival house and a performing-arts center, would be demolished. It would have been a fairly typical tale of new development on the Upper West Side.

Instead, the proposed redevelopment of the property is mired in unusual litigation. A group that holds a master lease on part of the building claims the right to buy and develop the site. But the current owner, Symphony Space, proposes a building that not only would preserve its functioning performing-arts center and the old movie house, but also the exterior of the building.

The building, which also houses several shops and offices, was built in 1915 as an innovative public market. The Astor estate owned a lot of Upper West Side property at the turn of the century and one of the heirs, Vincent Astor, was a member of the city's Commission on Markets. He decided to build a model market on his 165- by 125-foot plot at the southwest corner of West 95th Street and Broadway.

The Astor Market had 201,000 square feet of selling space on the main floor, with stalls for lease to butchers, greengrocers and other merchants. A fish market was on the lower floor, now the Thalia space. The concept of the Astor Market was to decrease the cost of living for the middle and lower classes, a special concern of Vincent Astor.

A 1915 newspaper article said the building was modeled on the style of a Florentine market, with high, arched show windows and a great sgraffito frieze with the theme of food. "Cattle, sheep, pigs, chickens, ducks and fish . . . are held in composition by garlands of vegetables and fruits," the article said, going on to call the structure "the most-attractive market building in the country."

But the Astor subsidy could not sustain the market and in 1917 the property was purchased by Thomas Healy, who later built the landmark Pomander Walk mews next door. Mr. Healy converted the market into retail and office space and installed the Symphony Theater on the first floor—the present Symphony Space auditorium.

In 1931, a second theater, the Thalia, was installed in the basement space around the corner on West 95th Street. Generations of Thalia patrons have assumed that its oddly sloping floor—with a depression in the middle—was the result of poor planning or unusual site conditions. But the Thalia's parabolic reverse floor—apparently the first of its kind in the country—was just what its designer, Ben Schlanger, intended.

In Mr. Schlanger's view, most movie theaters were poor adaptations of theater designs. The Thalia incorporated not only Mr. Schlanger's patented floor system—designed to give everyone in the audience the same view of the screen—but also lighting, seating and projection provisions intended specifically for movie presentations.

Mr. Schlanger left a mark on theater design, and the upward slant of the first few rows of modern theaters apparently derives from his work. The Thalia's Art Moderne interior could be a candidate for landmark designation.

It is not clear if the Thalia was originally a revival house, but Richard Schwarz, who operated the Thalia from 1977 until its closing, believes that it began showing old films when World War II interrupted the normal flow of first-run films.

The Thalia closed after Mr. Schwarz was able to get only a month-to-month lease because of conflicting claims to the property. The theater, he said, needed improvements that he could not make with only a short-term lease. The present owner of the building, Symphony Space, is a nonprofit corporation. Its president, Isaiah Sheffer, says the organization wants to seek redevelopment of the property, preserving both theaters and perhaps even the original Astor Market facade and frieze, now covered with paint.

But another group whose principal partners are Pergola Properties and Bradford Swett has a master lease on the stores and offices in the building and the Thalia and claims an option to buy the building well below market value.

The group is interested in a straight redevelopment, demolishing the entire blockfront. Symphony Space contests the validity of the option, and hopes the Thalia can show another revival by going back into business.

Regardless of who wins, the high rents being charged stores in the area, combined with an oversupply of new apartment buildings, may preserve the building for longer than anyone expects. Symphony Space is booked into next summer.

GRAHAM COURT

Grande Dame Tries to Regain Her Respectability in Harlem

A section of the courtyard in 1901 at Graham Court, building on Adam Clayton Powell Jr. Boulevard between 116th and 117th Streets.

IF HARLEM HAS an equivalent to the Dakota, the famed apartment building on Central Park West, it is Graham Court, a full blockfront on Adam Clayton Powell Jr. Boulevard, from 116th to 117th Streets.

Built in 1901 by the Astor family, the building has recently seen hard times—decay, drug problems and a near foreclosure by the city. But it has been purchased by a new owner, who promises a better future.

William Waldorf Astor became head of the family estate in 1890, and in the same year moved to England in an attempt to avoid the constant press attention to his family and his $100 million fortune. Although he lived abroad, Astor regularly returned to the United States to supervise his building projects. In addition to Graham Court, they included the Hotel Netherland in 1893, the Hotel Astor in 1904 and the Apthorp Apartments in 1908.

For Graham Court, Astor retained as architects Clinton & Russell, who would also design the Hotel Astor and the Apthorp. They produced a great, eight-story boxy mass in the mode of an Italian palazzo. The first two floors are of rusticated limestone, with tan or gray brick above and a crowning story of foliate terra-cotta capped by a copper cornice.

While the basic facade is unremarkable, the courtyard plan of the building makes it unusual. A full blockfront on the avenue and 175 feet deep on the side street, the completed building had great height and presence for Harlem, where a five-story corner flat was still considered a big building in the early 1900's.

The courtyard, reached by an open arcaded entry from Seventh Avenue, is 79 feet by 108 feet square and was originally planted with grass and ornamental shrubbery. Its gate is now locked against intruders.

One of the great issues in apartment design at the turn of the century was the disposition of the courts—often reduced to mere air shafts. But because of its size, Graham Court could have a courtyard shared with no other building.

The court itself creates a genteel but cozy feeling, grand but also comfortably secure from the outside—an unusual amenity in a city where there are few private unroofed spaces. It also gives cross ventilation to every apartment.

The planning of the apartments was a bit crude. Andrew Alpern, in his book *Apartments for the Affluent* (reprinted by Dover Publications as *New York's Fabulous Luxury Apartments*; 25318-X), says the building has an "awkward circulation pattern" and the bedrooms tend to be small

and narrow. But each apartment combines features—oak kitchen cabinets, mosaic foyer floors, mahogany and oak flooring, paneled dining rooms and multiple fireplaces—that later, simpler buildings could only sample.

Early tenants—the building was initially restricted to whites—were such professionals as Dr. Joseph Lumbard, an anesthetist at Harlem Hospital, and Henry Redfield, a Columbia law professor. Overbuilding in Harlem destroyed the rental market early in the century, and gradually the whites-only restrictions were dropped. In 1928, the first black tenant moved into Graham Court.

By the 1960's, the building had become a typical story of marginal maintenance and some troublesome tenants making life difficult for everyone else.

In 1979, Mohammed Siddiqui, a pharmacist whose license was suspended for three months last year for "negligence" in handling prescription drugs, bought the building for $55,000 and a promise to pay $150,000 in back taxes.

But he fell behind on his tax bill and, according to the tenants association, let the building slide further into disrepair. In the meantime, some residents said drugs were being sold illegally from apartments in the building.

Last September, the city moved to foreclose for $600,000 in back taxes. But Mr. Siddiqui finally paid the taxes last February and in April, he sold the building for $2 million to Leon Scharf, a West Side building owner.

Mr. Scharf said he is spending $1 million on improvements this year, and is optimistic about the future of the building. "Eventually, maybe we would go to a co-op plan," he said.

"I just got my apartment painted for the first time in 10 years," said Margaret Porter, who is the secretary of the tenants' association. "And a new intercom system is going in. It's encouraging."

As Mr. Scharf begins his work, the cast-iron lampposts in the courtyard lie broken or missing. The plantings are scruffy. The cornices have been stripped off and the front doors have the bars and locks typical of many neighborhoods.

But there is, even now, an underlying elegance and a few Graham Court tenants have begun to restore their apartments—stripping paint and prying up linoleum from the mosaic floors.

THE RIALTO THEATER

A Times Square Cinema Nurtured by the "Merchant of Menace"

The Rialto Theater building on Seventh Avenue at 42d Street in 1954. Facade had been changed slightly from the original 1935 style.

I T IS APPARENTLY the largest glass-block facade in New York City, an unusual Art Moderne theater of blue and white glass with streamlined aluminum fins.

But the building that once housed the old Rialto Theater is scheduled to make way next year for the joint city-state 42d Street Development Project, unless the building's long-term lessees can prevent condemnation, or the project falls through. In fact, a new theater, the Cineplex Odeon Warner, has recently opened in the old Rialto space.

The 1935 Rialto, at the northwest corner of 42d and Seventh Avenue, was designed with a 750-seat theater with stores on the ground and subway levels, a special subway entrance and offices and a restaurant above with a circular dance floor.

The architects of the Rialto were Thomas Lamb and Rosario Candela. Lamb was a prolific theater architect; he also designed the Empire Theater at 236 West 42d Street, among others. Candela had designed many luxury apartments on Fifth and Park Avenues in the 1920's.

But the Rialto had little precedent. Above a first floor of unexceptional storefronts, the second floor was composed of alternating deep blue glass with white marbling and strips of metal. Above these were protruding aluminum fins similar to those found on engines and other mechanical equipment. The third floor was composed entirely of cream-colored glass blocks in alternating curved and faceted bays.

A parapet wall and an 80-foot-high corner tower, also in the same glass, crowned the building. The upper section had an illuminated strip sign carrying local and entertainment news.

Lewis Mumford, the urban historian and architectural critic, writing in the *New Yorker* in 1936, described the colors as "unspeakable" and said the overall design was a "wisecrack." But a 1935 newspaper article called the building "the most ambitious glass structure thus far," and the same system was used in building the Queens-Midtown Tunnel in 1940.

The Rialto opened for Christmas of 1935 with Frank Buck's *Fang and Claw*. The theater's manager, Arthur Mayer, saw the Rialto as distinctly masculine in tone. Most theaters, he said in a newspaper interview after the opening, were "rococo, luxurious palaces for the uxorious," both in styling and choice of films. His theater, both in styling and presentations, sought to satisfy the "ancient and unquenchable male thirst for

mystery, menace and manslaughter." He was soon called the "merchant of menace."

The restaurant was apparently removed around 1950, and its space taken over for a succession of studio uses, including the Joe Franklin television show. As West 42d Street declined, so did the theater, and by the 1960's it was satisfying another seemingly "ancient and unquenchable thirst"—for pornographic movies. In the early 1980's, it had a short run as a theater for stage plays.

The Times Square area has been the focus of various redevelopment plans. The most recent involves the renovation of most of the theaters, and the replacement of the Rialto building with an office building. The decision on what buildings to preserve was based, in part, on a 1981 report by two historians, Adolf Placzek and Dennis McFadden, who said the Rialto had "no outstanding merit." Their report also found the Candler Building, at 220 West 42d Street, was not eligible for landmark regulation.

But in 1980, the Candler Building had already been independently recommended by New York State for listing on the National Register of Historic Places. And the Landmarks Commission recently held hearings on the designation of another Art Moderne theater, the Metro, on Broadway near 99th.

The Rialto building is owned by the Kohlberg family trust. An officer at the Chemical Bank, which administers the trust, said the bank will not oppose the condemnation proceedings. But the Brandt Organization, which holds a 100-year lease on the building from the trust that dates to 1953, is opposing the project. It would terminate Brandt's lease, now well below market value. The Brandts have recently subleased the Rialto Theater to the Cineplex Odeon Corporation, which has spent $1.5 million to reopen the theater.

A spokesman for Cineplex Odeon said the Times Square project, which would mean the demolition of the building, was considered "only a possibility, not a certainty."

Correspondent Nick King later wrote in with his recollections of the "merchant of menace" period, when screams and groans were broadcast out onto the sidewalk and the theater dramatically advertised that there was a "nurse on duty" at every performance.

THE 18th PRECINCT STATION HOUSE

A Sunset Park "Fortress" Rescued From Destruction

Old police station on Fourth Avenue in Sunset Park section of Brooklyn. Photo made in 1886 was taken from a double-page bookplate.

THE CASTLELIKE STATION house of the old 18th Police Precinct has long been a landmark on Fourth Avenue in the Sunset Park section of Brooklyn. When it was vacated in 1970, deterioration of the 1892 building accelerated, and a fire in 1980 seemed to have sealed its fate. But the Sunset Park School of Music purchased it at auction in 1984, after landmark designation, and it is now painstakingly collecting the $2.5 million it needs to restore the building.

The Sunset Park area, southwest of Greenwood Cemetery, developed as industry took over the lower Brooklyn waterfront between Red Hook and Bay Ridge. As piers and factories began to line the shore in the 1860's, row houses began to line the sidestreets.

In March 1892, the City of Brooklyn opened a new police station for its 18th Precinct—the Sunset Park area—at the southwest corner of Fourth Avenue and 43d Street. It was designed by Emile Gruwe, who produced an unusual castlelike building, fundamentally Romanesque in styling, but also drawing from other styles.

The building's round corner tower is flanked by two projecting bays, on the avenue and the side street. The avenue side has a great round-arched entrance portico and, at the top, a Venetian-style arcade with terra-cotta diaper work. The side-street elevation has a tall bay of stairway windows and a tiny inset balcony that is of little conceivable use but has great visual appeal.

On Fourth Avenue, barely set off from the main building, is a two-story stable with more modest detailing. It was used for horses of the mounted patrols that were often used in newly developed areas with marginal transit facilities. Although now painted red, all the original brick is a warm orange, contrasting with varying material: terra-cotta, nearly white limestone, dark brownstone and polished granite.

The symmetry of the station house is in counterpoint to a chaotic variety of decorative forms: a corbeled parapet of rounded brick, rope moldings of terra-cotta, zigzag and Romanesque carving, rock-faced brownstone and decorative ironwork.

The use of a castle form was not necessarily incidental in Gruwe's design. Nineteenth-century police stations often served near-military purposes, as officers were often asked to control political and labor violence. Thus the station's fortresslike appearance to some extent mirrored real police duties of the time.

The *Brooklyn Daily Eagle* recorded the opening day ceremonies on March 8, 1892. Henry I. Hayden, the Brooklyn Police Commissioner, said in a speech that "a man about to commit a crime would stand appalled at the sight of a station house such as this."

The *Eagle* called the building a "stately mansion" and described the station house as "the finest in Brooklyn or Manhattan." Gruwe also designed a near-twin to it in the same year, at 486 Liberty Avenue in East New York. That building is no longer an active police station.

In 1970, a new station house was built several blocks away, and the old building was left vacant. It was auctioned by the city in the 1970's, but was later taken back after the owners failed to pay property taxes.

A fire in 1980 destroyed much of the roof, and rain, snow and pigeons began to destroy the interior. In 1984, the Landmarks Preservation Commission designated the building a landmark, and the city—at the request of local officials—put the property up for auction once again. This time the building was restricted to a nonprofit use devoted to "musical enrichment and education."

The Sunset Park School of Music, founded in 1980, was the only such school in the area and the only bidder, acquiring the building for $15,000. Under the terms of the sale, the school was given until July 1986 to repair the roof, raise a minimum of $750,000, and begin a major rehabilitation.

So far the school has raised only $220,000, has repaired the roof and has engaged an architect to prepare drawings for a bare-bones renovation of the stable only. Work on the main building—neither safe nor legal for occupancy—seems a long way off.

But political and community support for the school is strong, and according to Barbara Perkins, director of communications for the Department of General Services, the city has not threatened to take back the building.

Work on the stable will begin this fall and be completed by 1988, said Anthony Masiello, director of the school. He said he is daunted but not discouraged by the larger task of renovating the station house.

"It's been an eyesore for many years, and it's still an eyesore," said Mr. Masiello. "But we're working on it."

Work has not yet begun.

THE 81st STREET THEATER

The Curtain Falls, but Preservation Is in the Wings

Theater on Broadway at 81st Street in a photograph made in 1938.

OLD THEATER BUILDINGS in development areas are usually either demolished or given landmark designation—often over the owner's protests. But on 81st and Broadway, a hybrid solution is nearing completion, and part of a 1914 theater building is being preserved as part of an apartment development.

The completion of the subway in 1904 made Broadway north of Columbus Circle a Champs-Elysées—a solid burgher quarter of brownstones and apartment houses. Several big building projects—like the Ansonia (1904), the Apthorp (1908) and the Belnord (1910)—gave a cosmopolitan electricity to the street, Manhattan's only real boulevard.

Perhaps because of the historic presence of theaters on Broadway further south, theater construction was an important factor on upper Broadway as well. Ten theaters were built on Broadway between 59th and 110th Streets in 1911 and 1912. In 1914, Arthur L. Shakman, a real-estate developer who lived at 90th and Broadway, built the 2,000-seat 81st Street Theater on the southwest corner of Broadway.

A contemporary newspaper article described it as a building for "high-class vaudeville and moving pictures," but it was really two structures—a three-story business building on Broadway and an auditorium behind with sidestreet frontage.

Shakman's architect, Thomas Lamb, specialized in theaters, designing nearly 300 in his 40-year career. At the 81st Street Theater, the auditorium section, executed in plain brick, was separated from the commercial section by a small light court, and the commercial building was built of cream-colored terra-cotta. The upper floors carry arched openings with recessed windows, giving the feeling of a colossal arcade. Original newspaper reports described the building as Italian Renaissance in style, but there are also elements of the English Renaissance, a style to which Lamb was partial.

By 1920, most of the vacant land on Broadway had disappeared, and the street acquired its characteristic counterpoint of tall apartment buildings and low commercial ones.

By 1925, the Keith vaudeville chain had taken over the theater. But vaudeville itself was in transition, as movies began to get top—and, finally, sole—billing in theaters originally built for vaudeville. In 1954, CBS began using the building as an early color television facility. In 1967, the building was leased by the Teletape Corporation, and *Sesame Street* was taped there from 1970 to 1982.

Landmark Restorations acquired the 81st Street Theater in 1984. Louis Greco Jr., the company's president, said he planned from the beginning to demolish only the nondescript auditorium structure at the rear—a 17,500-square foot plot—and retain Lamb's white terra-cotta commercial building on Broadway.

At the same time, the New York Landmarks Conservancy, a private group, heard that a deal was in the works. Believing that demolition of the entire building would follow, it asked the Landmarks Preservation Commission to designate the structure.

However, at the request of Mr. Greco, the Conservancy did not push the request. He promised a private, written agreement with the Conservancy guaranteeing that the commercial part of the building would not be changed.

The landmarks panel did not act, and now a condominium-apartment tower on the old auditorium plot is nearly completed. Conran's, the British home furnishings company, will occupy the old section this fall. Mr. Greco has not yet delivered his preservation guarantee to the Landmarks Conservancy, but the old section is not now a buildable site, and is thus likely to be preserved.

The entire enterprise has been a novel one, conducted in a sort of twilight area between official landmark regulation and none at all. The architects of the new building, Beyer Blinder Belle, are unhappy with the developer's choice of bright red brick for the apartment tower—it clashes with the white commercial building. The developer is going to paint, not actually restore, the terra-cotta itself, a move that is considered tacky and cheap in preservation circles. And the Conservancy doesn't think the show windows Mr. Greco is installing are historically appropriate.

But nonetheless the private agreement to preserve the old 81st Street Theater building demonstrates an unusual alternative in a field usually characterized by life-or-death preservation battles. Despite problems with the design, the project preserves an attractive amenity and even a trace of the vanishing variety of Broadway.

Mr. Greco has still not delivered his preservation agreement, and the residential building is completely vacant.

PUBLIC SCHOOL 35

A Window on the Blackboard World of the 1890's

Public School 35 on the northwest corner of 51st Street and First Avenue, circa 1930.

THE END OF a seven-year preservation battle in the Beekman Place area of Manhattan may be at hand. Public School 35, out of service for 20 years, is scheduled for auction next Wednesday. Although not a designated landmark, the 94-year-old school will be sold by the city with preservation restrictions, putting to rest community fears that a new building might rise on the site.

The late 19th century saw both a physical and intellectual expansion of the city's school system, with changes not just in instructing the students, but in caring for them as well. Doctors and nurses were brought into the system, personal cleanliness and physical exercise were encouraged, and the school environment itself was considered.

A building program was begun in the late 1880's under George Debevoise, the Board of Education architect, who designed at least a dozen schools in three years. Debevoise emphasized light and air in his designs; tuberculosis was still a scourge of working-class and poor families.

In 1890, the *Real Estate Record and Guide* examined one of his buildings (at 77th and Amsterdam Avenue) and announced with astonishment, "For the first time in the history of school building it has been possible to photograph an interior." That year, Debevoise filed plans for P.S. 35 at the northwest corner of 51st and First Avenue, to serve the growing working-class district between Third Avenue and the East River. Completed in 1893, it was Romanesque in style, with transitional elements of the emerging neoclassical sensibility of the 1890's.

The overall design is basically symmetrical, but the ornament and roof treatments are picturesque. The facade is of yellow brick with brownstone trim. The individual components are reasonably attractive, but the monotonous regularity of the windows gives the building a leaden, industrial quality. Although the exterior is not very successful, it is unusual to find a public school building—or any large institutional building—surviving from this period with such integrity.

If the exterior does not make this building memorable, the interior does. The ceiling heights seem tremendous, just right for high-flying spitballs and displays of student artwork tacked up above blackboards. The rooms themselves are large and square, with a roominess that is expected only in grand clubs and public buildings.

Most of the finishes are intact: tin ceilings, elaborate cast-iron radiators, oak trim (under coats of paint) and the distinctive public school "scissor stairs," with dividers of ironwork and wire glass and landings between floors.

Many other buildings have a patina of age, or are largely unchanged, but the interior of P.S. 35 offers a direct link to public-school education of the 1890's, in the way a simple one-room schoolhouse can give an idea of prairie life.

In 1891, after construction was under way, Debevoise left the Board of Education. Later, the board accused him of "connivance" with subcontractors in the installation of cheaper plumbing fixtures than the city paid for in many school buildings. But criminal charges were never filed.

As early as the 1910's, schools like P.S. 35 were considered outdated. Debevoise's successor, C.B.J. Snyder, introduced fireproof construction, mechanical ventilation and better toilet facilities. But P.S. 35 remained in use as a public school until the 1960's, and then saw a succession of occupants, including the United Nations School and a shelter for homeless women.

In 1980, the city moved to sell the building at auction, at first contemplating simple demolition by the successful bidder. But community groups began a push to have the building designated a landmark. Their effort was unsuccessful, and would have been largely symbolic anyway, since the city is exempt from its own landmark regulations. But community pressure did bring about preservation restrictions on the auction, which took place in 1983.

Under the terms of that sale, the exterior had to be preserved, although a rooftop addition of several floors was allowed. There was a winning bidder, but the required rehabilitation never started, and P.S. 35 is up for city auction again Wednesday, with preservation restrictions similar to those of 1983. The opening bid is set at $9.3 million.

The irony is that the interior is not covered by the preservation restrictions, and the building will probably be gutted if only to permit a new structural system to support the additional floors.

The auction will indeed preserve the exterior of this late-Victorian building, but will probably insure the demolition of what makes it special.

Three successive sales have not been consummated and John Beckman, a spokesman for the Department of General Services, says that the building will remain a shelter for women "for the time being."

THE MOUNT MORRIS BANK

A Derelict Is Freshened Up, but Its Fate Is Still Uncertain

The Mount Morris Bank at Park Avenue and 125th Street, circa 1895.

F OR OVER A decade, one of Harlem's greatest buildings has been derelict, a few dingy curtains blowing in its broken Queen Anne windows. This July it looked as if the old Mount Morris Bank at the northwest corner of 125th Street and Park Avenue was finally about to undergo restoration.

But the work was only protective, designed to slow further deterioration, and the fate of the unusual seven-story bank-apartment complex is still uncertain.

The Mount Morris Bank, which was chartered in 1880 to serve the growing community of Harlem, originally was situated at 125th Street between Park and Lexington Avenues. Still a suburb at that time, Harlem had had its own railroad stop at 125th Street and Park Avenue since 1837.

The bank prospered and in 1883 built a building that combined bank offices (on the lower three floors) and apartments (the top four floors) across from the station at 125th and Park.

Designed by Lamb & Rich, it is one of Manhattan's most picturesque buildings, a great Queen Anne–Romanesque architectural stew of red brick, rock-faced brownstone, stepped gables, window bays and chimneys projecting above a peaked roof.

The building had three arched entrances on 125th Street: one for the apartments, one with steps leading down to the vault area and one at the corner—a grand, projecting brownstone porch that served as the main entrance to the bank.

There were some exquisite details on the upper floors: brick with rivet-heads molded in, terra-cotta panels with radiant forms, a date stone with the year 1883 in script set against a basket-weave pattern. In 1889, the building was extended in the rear following the same style.

The interior, still intact in the 1950's, was embellished with mahogany, Numidian marble and bronze. Like other banks of the period, the Mount Morris had special windows for ladies to save them "the inconvenience of waiting in line," according to *King's Handbook of New York City* published in 1893. The handbook described Mount Morris as successful, with nearly $3 million in deposits.

In 1890, the *Real Estate Record and Guide* called the building "hardly surpassed by the great bank buildings erected in Wall Street during recent years."

But today the galvanized iron cornices are rusted out to the thinness of paper. Inside, the plaster ceilings have collapsed and the old doors and windows are strewn about.

By 1900, Harlem was no longer a separate village, with a need for separate institutions. In 1913, the Corn Exchange Bank—with 22 branches—took over the single-office Mount Morris Bank. About that time the porch—which extended beyond the building line—was cut back.

By the late 1920's Harlem was emerging as a black community. New housing in New York was historically restricted to whites; blacks were restricted to older neighborhoods with deteriorating housing. But because of overbuilding in residential housing a couple of decades earlier, owners of many new buildings in Harlem were opening their doors to blacks.

By the 1950's, however, 125th Street—and Harlem in general—was in trouble. Residential buildings that were new in the 1910's and 1920's were deteriorating. Chemical Bank had taken over the Corn Exchange Bank in 1954, and closed out its operations in the old Mount Morris Bank building.

The city acquired the property in 1972, and by 1975 a delicatessen and the Samuel Temple Church of God in Christ were the only occupants of the building. Complete vacancy followed several years later.

The Landmarks Preservation Commission considered the building for designation in 1984, but never acted. This summer, it looked as if restoration was finally beginning. In June workmen began to paint all the ironwork, patch the roof and install new windows.

Although the work was crudely done, and the interior was not being touched, it seemed as if the building would finally see new life. The paint and new windows rejuvenated the building's appearance, but late in July it became clear what was really going on.

The workmen began using cinderblocks to seal up the lower two floors; at the request of the Community Board, the Department of General Services was simply sealing up the building. Because no one at the city has a particular plan for the building and there is no outside time limit beyond which the city must sell property it has acquired, the fate of the bank is uncertain.

THE NEW YORK HOUSE AND SCHOOL
OF INDUSTRY

Where the Poor Learned "Plain and Fine Sewing"

New York House and School of Industry at 120 West 16th Street, 1892.

THIS SUMMER THE New York House and School of Industry at 120 West 16th Street promised to shape up as a major preservation battle for the fall. Built in 1878, the two-story building was marked for replacement by an apartment house, and the Landmarks Preservation Commission has scheduled a hearing on it for September 15.

But in late July, the owner discovered that the State of New York had taken the property by eminent domain. Now, it will remain as a residence for the mentally retarded, no longer immediately threatened.

Charity was a growth industry in mid-19th-century New York. Cities were indifferent to the health and housing needs of the poor and the working class, leading concerned private citizens to form several new charities a year. Many were unusually specific. For example, one asylum took only Protestant half-orphans.

Most had a moral purpose, encouraging those in difficulty to improve their lot by "industry," rather than by vice, crime or insurrection.

The New York House and School of Industry was founded in 1851 to teach poor women "plain and fine sewing." For some time, it was quartered in an old wooden farmhouse on its present site, but in 1878 the organization built an asymmetrical brick building designed by Sidney V. Stratton.

The building is still largely unchanged, with a projecting two-story oriel window on the left, a central entrance and top and bottom triple windows on the right. Above the main door, a tablet bears the organization's name and the date of construction in elaborate script, still legible, although slathered with paint. The overall form of the building is picturesque, and windows make up the greatest element of decoration: the oriel has panes of bottle ends and some of the windows have 44 panes in the top sash over four panes in the bottom.

Mosette Broderick, an architectural historian who has linked Stratton to the firm of McKim, Mead & White, says the building "appears to be the first instance of the Queen Anne style in New York City." The style emphasized the use of red brick, unusual forms and craft elements— like the bottle glass and plaques over the doorway. The lack of a projecting cornice is also a Queen Anne feature.

The 1878 report of the House of Industry states that, in the preceding year, 148 women had been employed, 9,927 garments were sold and day care and the sewing school for children had been established.

By the late 30's the charity was taking contract work from hospitals and asylums, noting that "changes in fashions and customs, and frequent addition to labor and local laws need constant watchfulness." In 1951, the House of Industry was absorbed by Greenwich House, a social-services agency established at the turn of the century. Sewing work was replaced by typewriters, as Greenwich House began a program of "brush ups" to help older women enter or re-enter the work force. But in 1955 Greenwich House sold the building to the Friends of Hebrew Culture, a civic and social organization that occupied the building for the next 20 years.

By 1980, the Young Adult Institute, a nonprofit organization under contract to the state's Office of Mental Retardation, was using the building as a residence for 25 young adults, but only under leasehold. A spokesman for the agency said that the state had been in litigation over the terms of the lease since 1983.

In 1985, the building was purchased by Jack Rosenthal, a developer who notified the Young Adult Institute last year that it would have to leave at the expiration of its lease last July 31 to make way for a 12- or 13-story condominium tower on the site. But on July 21, the city landmarks panel notified him that it would hold a hearing on landmark designation on September 15. A week later, the state told him it was taking his building by eminent domain.

"I feel like I am in Russia," said Mr. Rosenthal. "They could have told me six months ago, before I had made all the arrangements, but they took it away two days before their lease expired. That both things happened at once"—the Landmarks hearing and the state condemnation—"it's very curious."

Both the state and the Landmarks Commission say that they were unaware of the other's actions; the landmarks agency is also holding hearings on other Chelsea properties this month.

Although the state is exempt from the city's landmark regulations, a spokesman says that it will not oppose designation and seeks only to preserve the building as a residence for the retarded.

THE NEW YORK SAVINGS BANK

Landmark Hearing Set for 14th Street Building

New York Savings Bank, 14th Street and Eighth Avenue, circa 1910.

O<small>N</small> T<small>UESDAY THE</small> Landmarks Preservation Commission will hold a public hearing on the old New York Savings Bank, at the northwest corner of Eighth Avenue and 14th Street. The building has been the subject of controversy, with mysterious demolition, a stop-work order and an architect's plan for a tower addition that the owner's attorney says does not exist.

The bank was founded in 1854, and four years later moved to its present location, on the border between Greenwich Village and Chelsea. By 1876 it was of middling size, with $3.2 million in assets. By that time 14th Street was a major east–west thoroughfare, linking the principal shopping district surrounding Union Square with the growing colony of industry and shipping along the Hudson River. Indeed, the New York National Bank thought the intersection was desirable too, and located on the southwest corner in the early 1870's.

In 1896 the New York Savings Bank began work on a new building at the site. Completed in 1898, it was Greek in style, according to the *New York Tribune*, of "pure white" South Dover marble with a giant temple front on Eighth Avenue and a lofty dome at the center of the long side on 14th Street. The interior was decorated in Siena marble, with bank counters of marble and bronze, a coffered, vaulted ceiling, and stained glass illuminating the lantern of the dome. Aside from minor changes to windows and the front entrance, that description still largely applies.

"The building stands out with especial prominence in its neighborhood, which is not remarkable for beauty of architecture," according to the *Tribune* story. However, Montgomery Schuyler, an architecture critic of the period, writing in the *Architectural Record* while the building was under construction, considered it unbalanced, perhaps because the dome and temple front are too grand for such a constricted site. In 1973 a six-story apartment house at 85 Eighth Avenue covered the balance of the blockfront adjacent to the bank up to 15th Street.

In 1963 the New York Savings Bank merged with the Bank for Savings, producing the New York Bank for Savings. This summer Goldome, the successor to the merged bank, moved out of the building, leaving it empty. In early July, the owner of the building, Landmark Realty, which bought it in 1982 and kept the bank as a tenant, said there were "no plans" to do anything with the building after the bank vacated.

Over the same period, the Landmarks Preservation Commission was moving to schedule several Chelsea properties, including the New York Savings Bank, for its September 15 hearing. The items were officially scheduled on June 23, and word began to circulate that they were up for consideration for landmarking. Official notification was mailed to the owner on July 14.

But on July 17 a demolition crew began to remove metalwork and decorative elements from the bank, including portions of the copper roof, without a building permit. A stop-work order was issued by the Department of Buildings. The owner of the building, Joel Wiener, president of Landmark Realty, declined to be interviewed, but his attorney, Kenneth Block, could not explain the demolition. "The owner did not authorize the work," said Mr. Block. "I don't know how it came about." However, he said there were no plans to sue the contractor, Mitron Associates of Brooklyn, for trespass. The contractor, who did not return several phone calls, is the same one that illegally demolished four buildings on West 44th Street, two of them S.R.O. hotels, in January 1985.

Asked if there is a building contemplated for the site, Mr. Block said: "We don't have any plans for a building on top of or adjacent to the bank. We have no plans, period." But the adjacent apartment house, 85 Eighth Avenue, is owned by Manhattan Realty, of which Mr. Wiener is also the president, and is undergoing a cooperative conversion.

An amendment to the offering plan dated May 13, 1987, reserves unused development rights from the apartment house, which is six stories high, to the sponsor, and refers to "the building contemplated" for the bank parcel, saying that it could rise to 32 stories. And Richard Blinder, architect for Landmark Realty, said in early September, "In July we prepared a zoning diagram for Mr. Wiener to develop a mixed-use building which would preserve most of the exterior of the bank—including the dome and most of the tower."

The question now seems to be whether the commission will decide if the building is really landmark eligible and, if so, whether it will permit a tower addition over the bank. The commission does not rule out tower additions to landmark buildings, and has received a dozen or so requests in the last few years for such additions over the New-York Historical Society, St. Bartholomew's Church and other major buildings.

None of the applications has been granted, but the New York Savings Bank is distinctly a lesser structure, and pressure is mounting for the commission to either demonstrate that a tower over a landmark is indeed feasible or rule them out altogether.

Project on hold—building vacant.

ST. ANN'S CHURCH

A Son's Homage, Hallowed by Time

MOST OLDER INNER-CITY churches struggle for survival, largely unrecognized by the outside world. But St. Ann's Church, at St. Ann's Avenue at 140st Street in the South Bronx, has always had a claim to regional and even national attention.

Now two groups, independent of the parish, have been set up to promote their own interpretations of the significance of St. Ann's while also helping the parish itself.

St. Ann's was built in 1841 by Gouverneur Morris Jr. as a public memorial to his mother, Ann Randolph Morris, and as the centerpiece of a family burial ground at the family's estate in Morrisania, as the section came to be called. Morris retained perpetual burial rights for his family and veto power over any new minister.

The church faces south from a small rise, and in its first years looked out over a landscape of isolated manor houses and farms.

The exterior of the church is of local rock-faced stone with window and door openings trimmed in red brick, with pointed Gothic-style arches. The steeple and the interiors are more like those of Colonial-period churches, such as St. Paul's Chapel (1766) in Manhattan. The church still sits on an open plot, about 400 by 500 feet, with one side open to St. Ann's Avenue, but later tenement construction has boxed in the rolling land.

Over time, more than a score of Morrises prominent in American affairs have been buried in the churchyard, including Gouverneur Morris (1752–1816), who had a key role in drafting the Constitution, Gen. Lewis Morris (1726–1798), a signer of the Declaration of Independence, and Gouverneur Morris Jr. (1813–1888).

With its historic associations, St. Ann's accquired a patriotic character, and a 1918 pamphlet published by the vestry said financing by outside sources was a "sacred duty."

Its goal of an endowment fund of $200,000 was repeated in a similar 1940 brochure. According to the 1918 work, the "original American families have left" and "newcomers have swarmed into the district." A 1925 pamphlet described the parish's "Americanization program" for these newcomers.

The original tenement settlers were apparently German and Irish, but by the 1940's a few blacks began to appear in photos of parish activities. As the blacks began to leave the neighborhood, a new wave, predominantly Puerto Rican, moved in. The church now has Spanish and English services.

The last of the white parishioners disappeared in the 1970's, and at the same time the neighborhood hit a low spot, with drugs and arson making the area a near-wasteland. Today, almost half the lots are vacant—to some extent restoring the original, sweeping view from the church.

Some new housing has been built and the area is now in better shape. St. Ann's is a focus of activity for the area, with day care, children's activities, classes, and a theater group, Pregones, in residence. There is also the traditional Bible study as well as other parish activities.

Until 1986, it was not much different from other struggling urban churches. But last year a group including Morris descendents, the Historic Preservation Committee of St. Ann's, was set up.

This group, now including Gouverneur Morris Helfenstein, a Manhattan real-estate broker, and Governor Kean of New Jersey, seeks to restore the church and its grounds and create an endowment for this "national shrine," with activities organized around the bicentennial of the Constitution. The group's figure for an endowment is, coincidentally, $200,000.

Then this year the Episcopal Diocese of New York set up a Bicentennial Committee to raise funds for the ministry of the church. As yet, only one formal fund-raising activity has been planned. The

St. Ann's Church at St. Ann's Avenue at 140th Street, circa 1950.

one-day program, "The South Bronx Today: A Challenge to the Constitution," is scheduled for April 30, 1988.

There is an unstated contrast between the two groups—the Historic Preservation Committee concerned with the restoration of the site and with its patriotic associations, the Bicentennial Committee concerned with raising money for day-to-day services in what is still a desperately needy community.

The two groups are remaining separate, although the Bicentennial Committee would like to absorb the Preservation Committee, and place more focus on the needs of the people in the parish.

Day-to-day life in the parish is generally unaffected by such lofty issues. As one parishioner said, the Morris connection has been useful, but largely irrelevant to such daily issues as paying the electricity bill, staffing the soup kitchen or converting the basketball court to a theater while satisfying fire laws.

"We are not as concerned with rebuilding the building as we are with rebuilding the community," said the Rev. Roberto Morales, the priest in charge of the parish.

THE HOTEL MARTINIQUE

Grimy Grande Dame Housing the Homeless Off Herald Square

THE HOTEL MARTINIQUE, at the northeast corner of 32d and Broadway, could be any once-elegant midtown hotel now fallen on hard times. Its French Renaissance facade is dabbed with colors as if by a giant paint brush—the colors of drying clothes on the window guards.

The clothes belong to the hotel's current residents, 436 of New York City's 5,200 homeless families.

The Martinique has reflected the history of its location. By the 1890's, the center of hotel and theater life had penetrated up Broadway past Herald Square north of 34th Street. The Metropolitan Opera had been built at 39th Street in 1883 and a string of hotels extended up to Times Square.

In 1890, these were joined by the original Martinique, a 16-story hotel at 56 West 33d. In 1901, an annex was built on the east side of Broadway, north of 32d Street.

In 1903, plans to build Pennsylvania Station to the west were announced. Macy's opened on Herald Square in 1904 and in 1907 what is known as the PATH system reached its present Manhattan terminus at 33d Street. In that year, William R.H. Martin, owner of the Martinique, filed plans to more than double the size of the hotel by erecting an addition on the northeast corner of 32d and Broadway.

Martin, who had been head of the Rogers, Pect clothing company since 1877, hired as architect Henry Hardenbergh, also the designer of the earlier sections. Mr. Hardenbergh had designed the Dakota apartment house in 1880 but by the early 1900's was a hotel specialist, with the old Waldorf-Astoria (1893) and Plaza (1907) to his credit.

For the Martinique, Hardenbergh used his signature elements: a skin of heavily detailed but light-colored masonry, a chamfered corner and a tiled mansard roof.

The enlarged Martinique, with a total of 600 rooms, opened on Dec. 21, 1910. The French Renaissance style of the exterior was carried into the major rooms, "copied after the Apollo Gallery in the Louvre," according to a period newspaper article.

Like other transient hotels, the Martinique also attracted a coterie of permanent guests. A few years after opening, these included Cornelia A. Walker, a physician, and Job E. Hedges, former Deputy Attorney General for the State of New York.

For a decade, the Martinique's location remained prime. But the theaters finally settled in Times Square, and the best stores left Sixth for Fifth Avenue.

Loft and industrial buildings went up, and the Martinique became just another fading hotel in a gritty area. In the 50's, it was one of the few in the city to still offer rooms without baths, and most of the grand rooms were gradually converted to stores.

In 1973, the city began using the Martinique for "short-term" shelter of homeless families, and now the hotel is used exclusively by the city.

Most families spend about a year at the Martinique—with its dimly lit, squalid hallways and a history of problems with asbestos removal— before finding an apartment. The midtown location offers little for children, whose only space for play is an office plaza across the street.

The city, using its own funds plus state and Federal aid, spends about $1,500 a month to keep a family of four in the Martinique; the normal housing allowance for welfare families is set by the state at $270 a month.

Officials of the company that owns the hotel, Martinique Hotel Affiliates Inc., declined to be interviewed. But they did not come in for severe criticism in random interviews with eight residents, who were far more critical of what they consider to be an unrealistically meager housing allowance, which makes it difficult for them to move.

The Hotel Martinique at 32d Street and Broadway, circa 1910.

The hotel is covered by a city moratorium on the demolition or conversion of single-room occupancy hotels.

The grand character of the place is now fragmentary—the original room doors have been replaced with steel ones with spray-painted numbers. But the main foyer is still largely intact, a great high space with rich red Italian marble and gilt coffered ceiling. It is the kind of building that receives preservation awards when restored.

While the hotel's role in housing the homeless far outweighs issues of historic preservation, many fine architectural features of the Martinique remain—features that may one day lead to its restoration.

*A new owner is converting the building to a transient hotel. Although the promise was that "most" of the largely intact interior would **be** preserved, the ornate lobby has been destroyed.*

THE CENTRAL PARK TENNIS HOUSE

A Neoclassical Structure in an Unstructured Setting

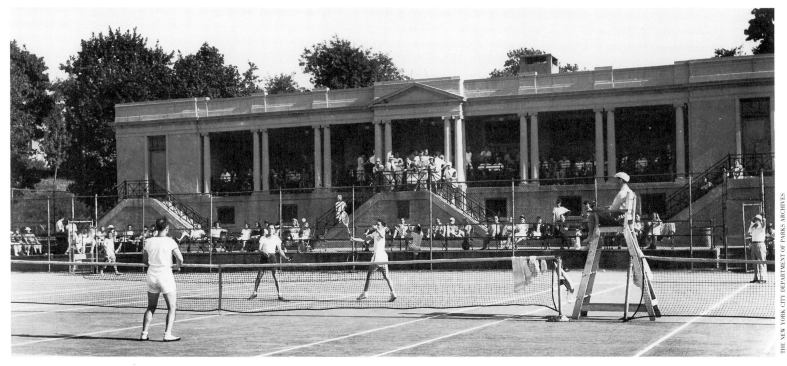

Contestants playing tennis at the Central Park Tennis House in 1943.

THE CENTRAL PARK Tennis House controversy—whether to build new or renovate—has been joined since last spring. Parks Commissioner Henry J. Stern had scheduled his decision for October 5, but now says it may be delayed until later this year.

The original design of Central Park by Frederick Law Olmsted and Calvert Vaux was characterized by romance and flexibility. Set in a gridiron city, the park had almost no straight lines, no formal elements, only picturesque informality. Most areas were adaptable, with a few places set aside for specific uses, and structures were kept to a minimum.

Olmsted and Vaux did make concessions to the interest of New York citizens in sports in Central Park—but generally they just provided wide open areas on which to play.

One example was the provision for tennis, which was introduced in America in the 1870's. In 1892, *Sun's Guide to New York* said there were more than 250 courts scattered over the park. But they were grass courts, with temporary nets and chalk markings on sweeps of lawn that could be used for other purposes.

Sometime after 1910, permanent courts were built in the South Meadow—just east of Central Park West, north of the reservoir and south of the 96th Street transverse—and they gradually acquired backstops and fencing.

By 1927, there were 30 courts (the present number) and there were calls for a fieldhouse with lockers and showers. In 1930, the Tennis House was completed and more than 5,000 season permits for the courts, costing $2, were issued.

The building was designed by Gustavo Steinacher, a Cornell graduate who was chief engineer for Central Park. The courts are oriented north–south in three rows running east and west, and Steinacher sited the Tennis House along the southern line of the courts, backing up to the bottom of the hill stretching up to the reservoir.

The building has a short central hallway with concessionaires and offices, and men's and women's locker rooms in the wings on either side. A long open loggia faces north, high over the courts, giving protection from the sun and a good view. The loggia is screened by a row of columns, and the building has modest neoclassical detailing.

Except for later coats of paint, currently white and yellow, and the usual deferred maintenance, the Tennis House is unchanged since its construction. It is remarkably familial for New York City. There is a definite "tennis crowd" with many regulars schmoozing and watching the play.

But if the Tennis House did not change, other things did. In the 1970's, the landscape work of Olmsted and Vaux was reexamined, and the park came to be viewed as an artistic document of the romantic landscape, where a large neoclassical structure such as the tennis house was an intrusion, like a modern storefront on a beautiful old brownstone.

In 1985, a private donor contacted the nonprofit Central Park Conservancy and expressed an interest in contributing money to improve the tennis facilities in Central Park. The Conservancy, in consultation with the Department of Parks, recommended a new tennis house, in a grove north of the courts. They cited drainage problems with the present house and its incompatibility with the original Central Park design.

The city's Landmarks Preservation Commission gave permission to demolish the existing tennis house in April 1986 and there were no protests at that time. But earlier this year, a group of tennis players began complaining that the new house would be too far away from the courts, too small, too expensive—and that the present house was just fine. Thus began a bitter battle over what many consider a perfectly pleasant piece of civic design.

Those favoring demolition have called the present building "unsightly," a "stylistic malaprop" and "an eyesore and a pillbox." But critics of the proposed new tennis house say it will be a rather labored, unconvincing neo-Victorian structure, although better sited in terms of the original park scheme.

Even those favoring preservation, sensing the temper of the times, have proposed "Victorianizing" the existing building.

Gradually, the history of Central Park is being rewritten, and later additions not deemed proper are being edited out.

Whether the new site or the existing site is decided upon, it seems that the existing house, the wrong style in the wrong place, is doomed.

All plans are shelved.

BROOKLYN MUSEUM

A Touch of Imperial Rome Gracing Eastern Parkway

The Brooklyn Museum, circa 1915, with main stairway, now removed.

THE BROOKLYN MUSEUM has never even approached completion of its original master plan, designed in 1893 by McKim, Mead & White. But last year it held a competition for a completion on more modest lines. The museum's decision on how to treat its 1930's lobby will indicate how far the pendulum is swinging away from orthodox modernism.

The museum was established in 1823 as the Apprentices' Library, designed to provide educational opportunities for workingmen. In 1890, it was reorganized as the Brooklyn Institute of Arts and Sciences and the City of Brooklyn—then with a population of 838,000—promised to build a new building, to be designed by competition, on a site on Eastern Parkway that was adjacent to Prospect Park.

The *Brooklyn Daily Eagle* described the competition, calling for a building of about 1.5 million square feet, as "one of the most important in the history of architecture." It was to be more than a museum, with departments for engineering, mathematics, chemistry, geology, zoology, art, archeology and sculpture, and an attached observatory.

McKim, Mead & White won the competition with a neoclassic design, grand and imposing in the manner of imperial Rome—a great square, with four interior courts divided by criss-cross halls. The main hall was to run north to south, from the present Eastern Parkway entrance to a corresponding entrance facing south.

The cornerstone was laid in 1895 and the first section opened in 1897. By the mid-1920's, when building stopped, not much more than the north facade had been completed, with its 28 giant statues and Ionic temple front over a grand stairway.

The full north–south hall had not been completed, but the entry hall—at the present third-floor level—was still quite grand, a forest of huge Doric columns interspersed with classical statuary.

Although conceived as the cultural center of a great independent city, the Brooklyn Institute of Arts and Sciences was soon placed in competition with other major institutions.

The consolidation of 1898 produced the present city, in which Brooklyn was simply another borough, and the infant institution had to compete for city and other funds with the Metropolitan Museum of Art, the American Museum of Natural History and other organizations.

In the 1930's the Brooklyn Institute of Arts and Sciences began a slow evolution to the Brooklyn Museum, as it began to concentrate on art and sculpture.

At the time, the building was described as "quite outmoded" in the *W.P.A. Guide to New York City*, and a new director, Philip Youtz, brought a set of Modernist ideas and a friendship with William Lescaze, the avant-garde designer.

Joan Darragh, a staff member who is editing a history of the museum building for publication next year, said Youtz wanted a more "democratic" museum, which to him meant a street-level entrance and simpler interiors.

The grand stairs and the sculpture hall were soon removed, beginning a program of erasing the neoclassic character of the museum that continued into the 1960's. Although Youtz, an architect, signed the drawings for the new lobby, Ms. Darragh believes that Lescaze strongly influenced it.

The *Guide* praised the new, ground-floor lobby as "an example of the best in modern architecture . . . devoid of the elaborate decoration which so often clutters up the entrances of public building." It was all flat surfaces, slim handrails, indirect lighting and sleek black glass panels.

In 1955, a rear stairway was added by the Brown, Lawford & Forbes architectural concern in the same general style, a dreamy essay of nickel-plated tube hand rails, black stone and white walls. Except for an addition in 1980, all building stopped.

By the time of the 1986 competition the museum had built only 300,000 of the 1.5 million square feet of the original plan, and could not realistically use the original space allotment.

The winning-scheme, submitted as a joint venture by Arata Isosaki & Associates and James Stewart Polshek & Partners, provides 680,000 square feet of space extending back over about half of the original museum plot in a Postmodernist scheme.

A condition of the competition was the restoration of the steps, an expensive gesture for a feature that does not increase interior space.

The future of the lobby—the sleek centerpiece of the revisionist plan of the 1930's—is still undecided as the museum and its architects hammer out the fine points of the new plan through 1988, when the final design is to be announced.

Plans for the lobby are still in "a thoughtful stage," according to Joan Darragh.

THE SPEYER SCHOOL

"Essentials of Wholesome Living" in a "Settlement House" Setting

The Speyer School, at 514 West 126th Street, in 1906.

THE SPEYER SCHOOL, at 514 West 126th Street, is an empty derelict, its windows broken or blocked up, its elaborate ornament gradually decaying.

A focus for three major episodes of social and educational activity since its construction in 1902, the picturesque structure will now be sold as offices for community organizations.

The school was an outgrowth of a "free kindergarten" established by St. Mary's Episcopal Church, at 521 West 126th Street. In 1899, the church joined with Columbia's Teachers College to expand the school to include grade-school pupils of what then was a lower middle-class neighborhood.

In 1901, James Speyer, German-born heir to a family banking firm and a member of the city's Board of Education in the 1890's, gave

$100,000 for a new seven-story building, including a roof deck. Its architect, Edgar Josselyn, produced a German Renaissance–style structure—rare in New York City even today—with a three-story-high stepped gable, apparently a specific response to Speyer's German background. Within the building were a gym, showers, classrooms, a community library, a roof garden and apartments for the Teachers College staff.

There was a strong "settlement house" component to the school. It sought to do "what can be done under the conditions of crowded city life, to provide some of the first essentials of wholesome living," according to a 1903 article by Jesse D. Burks, the first principal. Since the mid-19th century, settlement houses had tried to establish social programs in poor communities. Speyer himself had been a founder of the University Settlement House in 1885.

In many ways, the school lived up to the rhetoric. The library served a community that had none, and various "community clubs" were established to bring residents together. The children in the school were taught health and sanitation—the showers in the basement were not found in public schools.

There was also an emphasis on outdoor activities on the roof, which included a garden, at a time when the playgrounds of most city schools were still in rear courtyards.

The structure, which served about 260 pupils through the eighth grade, was open Monday through Saturday from 8 A.M. to 10 P.M. to accommodate community programs.

By 1915, Teachers College changed its emphasis from elementary to secondary school education and it permitted the city to use the building as an annex of Public School 43 on 129th Street and Amsterdam Avenue. In 1919, the college leased the building to the city.

The building continued to be used as a public school, but in 1936 a new experiment was announced: The building became P.S. 500, with a mix of 225 pupils, both the gifted and the backward.

The experimental school was established to see if separating students with special needs from the average students would improve their performance over the existing system, which called for generally homogeneous classes.

At the end of a five-year experimental period the school was closed for lack of funds, but its report was widely published. It suggested that separating "dull–normal" students from the average students actually slowed them down, but that it benefited the gifted.

The school building was apparently abandoned during World War II—photographs taken in 1945 show broken skylights and water damage down to the second floor. The Episcopal Diocese of New York owned the building from 1964 to 1977 when it housed many civil-rights programs.

The Rev. Neale Secor was pastor at St. Mary's over part of that period.

"The welfare rights movement started there," he recalled. "It had one of the earliest Head Start programs and Martin Luther King was in the building only a week before he was assassinated. Isaiah Robinson, the first black president of the city's Board of Education, was often there. It was a center of social concern."

But then "the money dried up" and the diocese gave the building to the Paul Robeson Community Center, an umbrella group, in 1977. The center occupied it for a few years, but moved out when heating oil became too expensive, and it has been inactive for several years.

Now the center's director, Babette Edwards, says she hopes to sell cooperative shares in the building to other community organizations, although how community organizations could afford to buy into a building and pay the carrying costs is not yet clear.

It is now scheduled by a new owner for conversion into a 40-bed shelter for homeless persons with AIDS.

THE CORN EXCHANGE BANK

A "Noble Monument to Thrift" with an Unusually Modern Air

MOST LANDMARK CONTROVERSIES close with a bang not a whimper, the end of a crescendo of angry public hearings and threatened lawsuits. But the old Corn Exchange Bank's unusual skyscraper complex at 11–15 William Street, in an area with more businesses than block associations, is scheduled for demolition without a determination by the Landmarks Preservation Commission on whether it is a land-mark.

The Corn Exchange Bank, founded in 1853, is typical of the commodity-related financial institutions of the 19th century, such as the Chemical Bank and Shoe and Leather Bank. In 1855, the bank moved into an existing building at the northwest corner of William and Beaver Streets in the heart of the growing financial district.

By 1893, the bank, serving primarily grain, provision, cotton and coffee trades, had $10 million in deposits.

In 1894, after relocating temporarily during construction, the bank completed a new headquarters on its existing corner. The 11-story building designed by R.H. Robertson was described by the *New York Times* as "a noble monument to the thrift and industry of the bank."

Except for the copper cornice, the facade is of stone, a rich mixture of red granite on the first three floors, limestone above and polished red granite columns at the top and bottom. The arch-topped window bays mimic the Romanesque forms of the Corn Exchange Bank's earlier building on the site.

There is some stone carving, such as a winged female statue at the corner holding a sash with the date 1894. But the distinctive character of the building is its sleek, solid verticality, with plain, broad vertical piers rising more or less continuously to the top. Most skyscrapers of the period were still heavily decorated or used rougher materials, such as brick or terra-cotta. This is an unusually modern-looking work.

The building was not the tallest of its day in New York City; the Manhattan Life Building at 66 Broadway took the honor in 1894 with 18 stories. But in a city where three- and five-story buildings still predominated, it was "immense and elegant," in the words of a period guidebook.

An adjoining 20-story annex on William Street was added in 1903, in a matching style. The annex has some exceptionally fine foliate ornament at the upper floors, but again the annex is even more significant as an experiment in skyscraper design. Together the 1894 and 1903 buildings form an impressive pair, as appropriate for bankers as conservative suits of the best wool.

Gradually the bank's skyscraper became lost in a canyon of ever-taller buildings, like the 57-story City Bank Farmers Trust Building on the northeast corner of William and Beaver Streets built in 1931.

The Corn Exchange Bank merged with the Chemical Bank in 1954 and sold its buildings in 1956.

The property went through a succession of owners including the Goldman DiLorenzo real estate company from whom the city took the buildings in 1978 for nonpayment of taxes.

When the buildings were sold at auction in 1983 for $13.1 million, the price was the highest ever paid at a public auction for a single property.

The city sold the buildings without preservation restrictions and for several years the New York Landmarks Conservancy, a private, non-profit group, has been urging the Landmarks Commission at least to consider the buildings for designation. And on October 23, Community Board 1 formally asked the commission for a hearing on the buildings.

But Park Tower Realty, the current owner, has had valid demolition permits for over a year, and Marjorie Pearson, director of research for the Landmarks Commission, said that it is now unable to act. The Conservancy also urged Park Tower to incorporate the facades of the bank buildings in any new development.

Corn Exchange Bank building and annex at 11–15 William Street, 1956.

But Cathy Straus, a spokesman for Park Tower, said only that their architects, Kohn Pederson Fox, will incorporate "some of the architectural elements" of the old buildings into the new, 450,000-square-foot office building they are planning for the site.

Scaffolding now surrounds the buildings, architectural elements have been removed and some demolition on the rear of the lot has begun.

Demolished.

FISS, DOERR, & CARROLL AUCTION MART

Who Holds the Reins on Fate of a 1907 Horse-Auction Mart?

Fiss, Doerr, & Carroll auction mart, left, and stable on East 24th St., 1907.

A PRESERVATION BATTLE MAY be on the horizon over the Fiss, Doerr, & Carroll Auction Mart on East 24th Street that could cast light on state-city sovereignty in landmarks matters.

The firm of Fiss & Doerr, established on East 24th Street in the 1870's, was "the largest dealer of horses in the world," according to an 1895 advertisement, and had additional branches in Albany, Buffalo, Lancaster, Pa., and Jersey City. At its "rain or shine" Monday and Thursday auctions, it promised "extensive variety—square dealing."

By the turn of the century, the firm had become Fiss, Doerr, & Carroll. In short order, the architectural firm of Horgan & Slattery designed a seven-story stable at 155 East 24th Street and a one-story auction mart at 147 East 24th, both completed by 1907 on the block between Lexington and Third Avenues.

Both buildings, which extended all the way to 25th Street, were linked by ramps and passages at several levels. The stable, faced with orange brick, is indistinguishable from other industrial buildings of its period. The adjacent auction mart, with a limestone, Beaux-Arts facade and high, arched attic windows, is far more interesting.

This building, an exuberant mixture of Roman classicism and Beaux-Arts grandeur, enclosed a huge interior ring 65 feet by 197 feet, where animals for sale were exercised for crowds of up to 1,000 people in a suspended gallery. The roof was supported by a steel arch, with a suspended, coffered ceiling.

It was perhaps the most unusual horse-related building ever built in Manhattan, and it certainly is the most unusual to survive. *Architects' and Builders' Magazine* said that Horgan & Slattery had decided "to abandon all former conventions" in its design.

In 1913, Fiss, Doerr, & Carroll erected 139 East 24th Street, a much-reduced and simplified version of the original auction mart at 147 East 24th. And at some point, the firm took over an existing 1887 stable at 145 East 24th Street, built by an earlier owner.

But the Fiss, Doerr, & Carroll complex of four buildings was to be the last gasp of equine architecture to appear in New York, as mass production brought automobile prices down to new lows, displacing horses.

In 1928, the auction mart was sold to the R & T Garage Company, which installed two intermediate floors for parking and removed the

balcony and ornate ceiling. But the exterior, although deteriorated, remains largely unchanged.

In 1969, Baruch College acquired the seven-story stable building at 155 East 24th for classes and offices. The college itself was taken over by the state after the city's fiscal crisis in the 1970's.

Earlier this year, Baruch announced an expansion program that would mean demolishing most of the 24th–25th Street block, including its own existing building, for a new structure. Using condemnation procedures if necessary, it will apparently move to gain the part of the site it does not own, including the auction mart.

The venerable Kauffman Riding Equipment Store is a tenant in the building at No. 139 and opposes the Baruch expansion. But the owner of Nos. 139, 145 and 147 (the auction mart) is the L.B. Oil Company. To its principal, John Tuckler, the possible condemnation is "just a business proposition," significant only in terms of what the company receives as compensation.

The auction-mart building is the only one with significant architectural character, and it is probably eligible for the landmark designation Community Board 6 recently requested. But it sits inconveniently in the middle of the projected building site, and it is not even clear if local landmark regulation would apply to the state.

Dorothy Miner, counsel to the New York City Landmarks Preservation Commission, calls it a "cloudy" issue, resolved on a case-by-case basis.

Theodore A. Holmes, counsel to the New York State Dormitory Authority—which would actually build the new Baruch buildings—said projects proposed by his agency are subject to environmental reviews.

But if the state decides that the Baruch plans cannot accommodate the old auction mart, Mr. Holmes said, a decision to demolish it may be beyond the control of the landmark agency and the building's inherent character would be irrelevant.

The Landmarks Commission declined to designate the buildings as landmarks and the state says that plans for new dormitories on the site are moving ahead.

THE CONEY ISLAND PARACHUTE JUMP

For the Boardwalk's "Eiffel Tower," Restoration or Regulating a Ruin?

The Parachute Jump at the World's Fair in 1940.

AMONG THE MANY advances in military aviation in the 1930's was a tower to train paratroopers patented by Comdr. James H. Strong in 1936. He licensed one such six-chute tower for a Chicago amusement park. But for the 1939–1940 World's Fair in New York, Commander Strong developed a 250-foot-high version with 12 parachutes.

After the fair ended, the 170-ton jump was disassembled and taken to Coney Island, where it was reerected just off the Boardwalk, at 16th Street, and towered majestically over its neighbors for a quarter of a century.

The Parachute Jump, appropriately sponsored at the World's Fair by Lifesavers, was built for $750,000 and rides went for 40 cents apiece. The drop, abrupt at first, slowed as the parachute quickly filled. The float to earth was held on course by guy wires and cushioned by shock absorbers on landing. Patrons of the 15-second ride sat two abreast and were belted in.

It was billed as the tallest, largest amusement ride in the world and so gained extra notoriety when it occasionally jammed, as it did in 1939 when J. Cornelius Rathbone, a Social Register polo star, and his wife, Nancy, were stranded aloft for four hours.

The jump hit a different kind of snag when Commander Strong sued to block its reopening for the 1940 season of the World's Fair. He held patent rights and would not let the ride return to operation until the licensing dispute was settled.

The Tilyou family bought the Parachute Jump for $150,000, according to Janet Adams, an architectural historian formerly with the city's Landmarks Preservation Commission. In 1941, it was back in business at Steeplechase Park, one of the many amusement complexes in Coney Island. The jump was rivaled in scale only by the 150-foot high Wonder Wheel, situated nearby.

Several hundred thousand people rode the Parachute Jump each year. In 1943, an article in the *New York Times* called it a "must" for visiting paratroopers.

But Coney Island had already seen its heyday. A few years earlier, in 1939, a report by the master builder, Robert Moses, said that it had become "a mecca for people of the smallest means." Older resorts like Coney Island, which were reachable by subway, were beginning to lose their cachet as the automobile brought even distant beaches within reach.

In 1965, the Tilyou family closed Steeplechase Park, including the Parachute Jump. After a proposal to redevelop the site for housing failed, New York City purchased the land in 1969 for park purposes. At a public auction in 1971, the Parachute Jump failed to attract any bidders.

Now, despite repeated proposals to demolish the rusting Parachute Jump, its owner, the New York City Parks Department, is supporting landmark designation and even restoration of the structure. But whether it will ever operate again as a ride, even if restored, is in question.

In 1977, the Landmarks Preservation Commission designated the structure a city landmark. The chairwoman, Beverly Moss Spatt, called it the "Eiffel Tower" of Brooklyn, but the Board of Estimate overturned the designation in the same year and the Parks Department announced the impending demolition of the Parachute Jump.

The steel structure managed to survive, however, and last July the Landmarks Commission held another hearing on designation, this time with the support of the Parks Department. In his endorsement of landmark designation, Parks Commissioner Henry J. Stern cited a 1983 report estimating that the cost of actually restoring the Parachute Jump was "not much more than" the $455,000 necessary to halt the deterioration of the structure.

It is not clear whether, even if rebuilt, the Parachute Jump could be operated profitably. Milton Berger, who handled public relations for the Tilyou family, said that the ride required a staff of 30. It had to be shut down even in moderate winds, he said, and even though there were no serious accidents during its operation, "the liability insurance would be astronomical."

The landmarks panel now faces a difficult decision. Normally the theory is that designation does not "freeze" a building or structure and that almost any structure can be altered to renew its economic viability. But the Parachute Jump cannot really be converted into anything else. If reviving the ride is impossible, the commission may have to permanently regulate a ruin. Restoration is not contingent on landmark status.

It is as a ruin that the Parachute Jump is most magnificent. Seen from a distance, it is rivaled in height by a dozen or so towers of public housing that have gone up in Coney Island. But looking up from directly underneath, viewers can see clouds scudding overhead, seemingly through the spidery steelwork.

The surf drowns out the sounds of the city, the old guy wires dangle loosely in the breeze and the Parachute Jump takes on the aura of majestic antiquity, a haunting artifact from some lost civilization.

Designated a landmark in 1989, but still rusty.

THE AUDUBON THEATER

On Upper Broadway, the Genesis of the Fox Empire

A 1952 view of the Audubon Theater, built in 1912, at the corner of 166th Street and Broadway.

After the completion of the city's first subway in 1904, Upper Broadway saw accelerated building of apartment houses, theaters and stores as the street became a sort of regional rialto. The West Side's new housing and river views attracted more and more people from older neighborhoods who could still commute to the business districts on the clean, safe IRT subway extending down to City Hall.

William Fox, an arcade and nickelodeon operator, also saw opportunity there and his Audubon Theater, built in 1912 on Upper Broadway, is scheduled for demolition, to be replaced by a medical research center.

Fox, a Hungarian immigrant who operated the City Theater at 114 East 14th Street for another owner, purchased the block bounded by 165th and 166th Streets, Broadway and St. Nicholas Avenue—roughly 200 feet on a side—and filed plans for a two-story building combining a theater, stores, offices and a second-floor ballroom.

As architect, he hired Thomas Lamb, who had designed the City Theater in 1909 and eventually was to design more than 300 others. For the full-block site, Lamb put a plain brick section enclosing the theater auditorium on the St. Nicholas Avenue side, but wrapped the rest of the structure with a polychrome terra-cotta facade topped by a projecting cornice.

The entrance to the theater was on Broadway, flanked by paired, engaged columns. Above the marquee is a polychrome terra-cotta relief of a woman standing in a ship's prow.

Between each window at the second-floor projects is the head of a light brown animal, a fox. The theater, one of several Fox built all over the country, was originally to be called the Washington Heights Hippodrome, perhaps because animal acts were planned.

Contemporary accounts say that the 6,800 people attending the opening of the theater on November 27, 1912, created so great a crush that police reinforcements were called out.

The theater presented both vaudeville and films, with both bills changing twice a week. According to Michael R. Miller, a theater historian who visited the Audubon's auditorium in the 70's, it was decorated in English Renaissance style. Old photographs show a large painting of a Revolutionary War scene, "Washington on the Heights," over the proscenium arch. A roof garden seating 2,800 people was planned, but apparently was not built.

By the 1920's, Fox controlled a $300 million organization covering production, distribution and exhibition of films. But after the market crash of 1929, he lost control of his empire and was later sentenced to jail for fraud in bankruptcy proceedings. In 1935, the Fox Film Corporation was merged with 20th Century Pictures and became 20th Century-Fox. In the 1940's, the theater was renamed the Beverly Hills, and soon after, the San Juan.

In 1965, Malcolm X, the Black Muslim leader, was assassinated at a rally in the large ballroom above the theater.

The city took the building over in 1967 for back taxes. The city had planned to convert it to a mental-health center, but the plan was never realized. The San Juan Theater operated until the late 1970's. Now, the building is vacant except for a city housing office.

In 1981, the city proposed the sale of the site for the construction of a hotel, another plan that was not realized. In 1983, the Columbia-Presbyterian Medical Center, across Broadway, announced that it would erect a biotechnology research laboratory on the site in partnership with the city.

H. Bernhard Haeckel, director of project development for the medical center, says that the proposal will come to public review sometime next year. The medical center originally had hoped to save at least part of the building, but a 1984 report called the structure too deteriorated to preserve. "The cornice poses an immediate danger," Mr. Haeckel said.

The medical center declined to release a copy of the report, saying a new one was under way, and there is no protective shed around the building, which appears to be intact.

The Landmarks Preservation Commission has asked only that architectural elements be salvaged from the building. Landmark designation would have only modest effect, since the commission cannot prevent the demolition of city-owned buildings.

A battle royal has developed over this building and its fate is still unresolved. For the record, the Landmarks Commission—in responding to my information request—concealed its own internal evaluation that the building was of "outstanding significance," a fact I discovered only much later.

THE COLONIAL CLUB

A "West End" Exception to the "Men Only" Barrier

The Colonial Club on southwest corner of Broadway and 72d Street, circa 1895.

THE "WEST END," as Manhattan's West Side was originally called, was an entirely new neighborhood when it was built on largely virgin territory beginning in the 1880's. Poor crosstown and downtown transit increased the area's identity as a separate, self-sufficient quarter.

Now the much-altered building at the southwest corner of 72d Street and Broadway—the West Side's first social club—has just been excluded from the proposed Central Park West Historic District. Leases in the building are set to expire in the summer of 1988 and it could become a development site.

Founded in 1889 as the Occident Club, it changed its name to the Colonial within a year, the new name deriving from a stated endeavor "to perpetuate the memory of Revolutionary days," including the retreat of Washington's army from Long Island along the line of Broadway to Harlem Heights in 1776.

Members first met in an old rowhouse at 127 West 72d Street, but their number grew to 400 in one year and this encouraged the club to erect its own building at the junction of the West Side's two major arteries in 1892.

Designed by Henry Kilburn, the clubhouse was a sort of colonial palazzo, mixing rich renaissance forms with light Adam-style detailing. With Bedford limestone on the ground floor and pale yellow Roman brick and gray terra-cotta above, the building was "delicate and clear," said an article in the *Real Estate Record and Guide* the year it opened.

Inside, the new clubhouse had a ballroom that was 82 feet long with 25-foot ceilings, a cafe, apartments for members and smoking, dining, writing and billiard rooms.

The Colonial Club was unusual in that it permitted women as guests of its male members. The separate ladies' entrance and ladies' rooms in the building were actually quite liberal innovations since men's clubs in midtown excluded women altogether.

There was also a ladies' bowling alley, with a half partition that screened the women—but not their pins—from the men, who used the adjacent lanes. Given that the Colonial was in the heart of a district of homes rather than businesses, admitting women was perhaps a necessity, but it did serve to further distinguish the Colonial from the bulk of other clubs. The *New York Tribune* said in 1892: "A bond which tied men who live west of Central Park to the so-called club region has been broken."

Membership rose to 700 in 1893, and the *Tribune* called it "a young giant in the club world," its building "an ornament to the neighbor-

hood." The club's rapid growth was financed largely by members' $1,000 bonds, secured by the land and building, and their example inspired other construction on Broadway.

At 73d Street the Ansonia was planned in 1899, and between 71st and 72d the Dorilton and the IRT kiosk were planned in 1900. Other West Side clubs followed the Colonial, among them the West Side Republican (1898) and the Progress (1904).

But the rapid rise of the Colonial Club was halted by sudden difficulties. In July 1903, the treasurer reported financial trouble and in November the club lost its house in foreclosure. Conversion to offices came in 1906, and the billiard and smoking rooms were torn out and replaced by stores. Over time, the grand ballroom was divided, cartouches were destroyed by added windows and existing round windows were enlarged and squared off.

Still the clubhouse maintained most of its delicate terra-cotta-and-iron detail, and, more importantly, remained an important visual anchor at the West Side's most important intersection. In the intervening years, most of the other major buildings in the area—like the Dorilton and Ansonia—have been designated landmarks, but the Colonial Club has not. Rarely are buildings so heavily altered protected by the Landmarks Preservation Commission.

Over the last few years the owner of the building, Broadway 72 Associates, has arranged for most or all of the leases to expire in the summer of 1988, and some commercial and office tenants say that demolition may be in the offing. But Maurice Fischoff, who handles renting for the owner, says that "no decision has been made" on what will happen.

In August, the landmarks agency announced hearings in January on the Central Park West Historic District, which reaches to the east side of Broadway, just barely excluding the Colonial Club building. Often, the panel also calendars significant buildings just outside the boundaries of proposed districts, recognizing that designation of a district may push development pressure to its outer boundaries. No such action has been taken.

But if the preservation issue is ever joined, the question will be whether a highly visible but much altered historic building meets the test for landmark protection.

The offices are again being rented—on short-term leases.

HOLBEIN STUDIO

Art Came Alive Over a Stable

Holbein Studio building at 154 West 55th Street, circa 1939.

THE OUTCOME OF a tenant–landlord battle may decide the fate of an unusual Romanesque-style structure on West 55th Street that was built in 1888 with a ground-floor stable and studios for artists above.

One of the two remaining tenants has requested landmark status for the structure, the Holbein Studio building. The possibility of such status could bring an increase in the owner's offers to the tenants to vacate, so demolition could proceed before action by the Landmarks Preservation Commission, or could cause the offers to be withdrawn failing permission for demolition.

In the 19th century the prosperous families living near Fifth Avenue usually built their carriage houses on streets informally set aside for stables, such as the West 50's near Seventh Avenue. In the 1870's, the banker Charles T. Barney built a group of stables on the north side of 55th Street, between Sixth and Seventh Avenues.

According to a 1920 newspaper account unearthed by Gary Reynolds, an art historian, the painter Jonathan Scott Hartley suggested that the space above the stables be converted into studios and rented to artists. Barney reportedly said: "It wouldn't pay. There's nothing in American art; nobody wants it." But he was persuaded and his Holbein Studio attracted such artists as Childe Hassam, John Singer Sargent, Cecilia Beaux and George Inness.

Barney, who collected Gothic and Renaissance art, noted the success of the venture and in 1888 built another studio across the street, designed by E. Bassett Jones, that came to be considered part of the Holbein complex.

This three-story building at 154 West 55th Street, the only one of the complex to survive, was unusual in that it was designed from the outset for artists' studios and a stable. Except for the removal of the carriage doors, the exterior of the building is intact.

Romanesque in style, the Holbein Studio has two great arch-topped carriage entrances and a smaller doorway leading to a coachman's apartment on the second floor. On the third floor are four skylit studios. A terra-cotta plaque with the word "Studio" is set into the brickwork above the stairway door and dragons decorate various parts of the brick-and-stone facade. The four studio spaces are almost entirely intact, with massive carved stone fireplaces, oak doors and oak wainscoting.

The carriage space was reportedly used by William C. Whitney, a financier who was Secretary of the Navy from 1885 to 1889. Whitney, a brother-in-law of Barney, had a house on the southwest corner of 57th Street and Fifth Avenue. His daughter-in-law, Gertrude Vanderbilt Whitney, later founded the Whitney Museum.

Census records indicate a succession of coachmen on the second floor, among them the 30-year-old Laurence Fitzpatrick in 1900, with his wife, eight children, a sister and four stablemen. But the third-floor studios were occupied by artists like Jonas Lie, later president of the National Academy of Design. Lie, who lived in his studio, heated his morning bathwater overnight "in a wash boiler, which he set on a two-burner gas stove each night before going to bed," according to an account in the *New York Times* in 1948.

Apartment houses began to take over the street in the early 1900's, and the ground floor of 154 West 55th Street was converted to a movie theater in 1928. The theater space now accommodates construction offices, but the upper floors remain residential.

In 1979, the Landmarks Preservation Commission included the Holbein Studio building in a list of more than 200 West Midtown structures that were or might be eligible for landmark status. But it has designated fewer than 25 of that group.

This year, a partnership that included William Zeckendorf and the late Sol Goldman began construction of a 58-story hotel on West 54th Street, backing up to the Holbein Studio, and indicated that the site of the building would serve as a truck entrance for the hotel. Papers filed with the New York State Division of Housing and Community Renewal in August indicate that the building will be demolished after "voluntary agreements" with the two remaining tenants. The third tenant left in June after a settlement reportedly in excess of $500,000.

One of the remaining tenants, Gerald Intrator, said the owner has told him that if the tenants do not agree to move, the hotel could simply put a truck entrance through the ground floor, which would certainly destroy the original front wall.

Mr. Intrator has now asked the landmarks panel to designate the building, which would probably prevent both demolition and alteration. The owner cannot obtain a demolition permit until the building is vacant, but could alter the facade to remove its historic character and thus reduce its chances of designation.

The Landmarks Commission ducked this one, and the owner installed a truck entrance.

TIFFANY STUDIOS

In Queens, a Remembrance of a Luminous Legend

The Tiffany Studios on the northwest corner of 44th Avenue and 97th Place in Corona, Queens, circa 1901.

THE OLD TWO-STORY brick building in Corona, Queens, at the southwest corner of 43d Avenue and 97th Place looks no different from many other industrial structures: It is functional, but worn, and surrounded by cars. But the flaking letters of a huge old painted sign just barely coalesce into a magic name: "Tiffany Studios."

The building, a survivor of Tiffany's legendary metal and glass operations, is now under contract of sale and both seller and buyer hope to put together a consortium of artists and manufacturers that will approach the glory of the original Tiffany operation.

Louis Comfort Tiffany, who established the studios, did not follow his father into the jewelry trade, but began a career as an artist in the 1860's. On a painting trip to Europe he was impressed with Italian and French stained glass and began to experiment with different types of glass manufacturing in the late 1870's.

In 1893, Tiffany established his own glass house, the Stourbridge Glass Company, at the northwest corner of 43d Avenue and 97th Place in Corona, a block north of the Long Island Rail Road tracks.

Tiffany imported a foreman and workers from the English town of Stourbridge, famous for glassmaking since the 16th century, and introduced his famous favrile glass from this factory. In 1901, the firm acquired most of the block across the street, between 43d Avenue and the railroad, from 97th Place to Junction Boulevard.

Staff architects designed a long, low brick building, undecorated except for a delicately corbeled brick cornice. The building was later destroyed, and the 1901 building is the one that survives today, along with a large work shed added in 1914.

The length of the building screens a courtyard space reached by a vehicular tunnel. A large boilerhouse at the center originally provided power and heat for the surrounding buildings, which were added to accommodate metalwork facilities.

Within his complex, Tiffany carried out experiments in glass colors and pottery glazing, perfected techniques of assembling stained-glass windows, and generally kept up his competitive position against other artists like John La Farge.

"We are going after the money there is in art," Tiffany said at the beginning of his career, according to the 1918 memoirs of an early partner, Candace Wheeler.

By 1901, Tiffany was at the peak of his profession, with a position in decoration comparable to that of McKim, Mead & White in architecture. But Tiffany's high Victorian sensibility and dense decoration fell out of favor beginning in the 1910's, when the onset of new forms of art reflected a disdain for the past.

By the 1920's a foundry had been installed for a separate bronze company, and in 1932 Tiffany Studios filed for bankruptcy. Ownership of the complex passed to the Roman Bronze Works, which had served as a subcontractor to Tiffany in prior years.

Roman Bronze, established in 1897, had popularized the lost-wax method of casting in the United States, according to Philip Schiavo, its president. This method permitted large works to be cast in one piece, and much of the sculpture at Rockefeller Center, like the statues of Prometheus and Atlas, were cast at the Corona building.

In World War II, the foundry was given over to defense work, disrupting the organization of the artisans, and in the 1950's new subtenants were taken into the complex. Now, electronics and garment operations occupy the high, open second floor of the building where stained-glass panels were once painstakingly assembled.

Mr. Schiavo, whose father and grandfather also worked for Roman Bronze, has now contracted to sell the complex to John B. Maltz, a real-estate broker specializing in industrial properties, and Howard Bodner, a real-estate attorney. Together they hope to attract another major sculpture-related tenant, and then lease or sell space to lesser art firms, reserving a central gallery and studio areas for artists coming to supervise castings.

They have replaced the old wooden windows—that, according to one tenant, incorporated bits of Tiffany glass—with aluminum ones, and plan other renovations, like removing the huge central boiler that lies unused in the courtyard.

Mr. Schiavo said that the Archives of American Art has agreed to take the firm's records and a vast collection of casts and molds dating back to the early 1900's that lie covered in dust in the basement. He and Mr. Maltz hope that the new Tiffany complex will be operating by 1989.

Roman Bronze is still in occupancy, but the Archives of American Art says that the firm wanted to sell its archives and the organization only takes donations.

THE WEST SIDE IMPROVEMENT

On the Lower West Side, Fate of Old Rail Line Is Undecided

View north along Washington Street from Bank Street in 1936 showing passenger train running through Bell Telephone Laboratories building.

IT WAS HAILED in its time, but now the West Side Improvement is to some an awful blight and to others a magnificent opportunity. The elevated railroad, completed in 1934, snakes around and even through industrial buildings on the Lower West Side of Manhattan. It will either be demolished or returned to service, depending on the outcome of litigation that began in 1985.

The Hudson River Railroad was first established in the 1840's, with tracks leading down the Hudson shoreline—11th Avenue, 10th Avenue

and West and Hudson Streets—to a terminal at Chambers and Hudson Streets. By the 1860's, the Lower West Side was a bustling center of shipping, and loft and factory development extended up to the West 50's, following the railroad.

However, the grade-level railroad route became known as Death Avenue as fatal accidents became common. In essence, the West Side Improvement was first proposed in 1925: a shorefront, three-level elevated structure, with local traffic at grade, railroad lines in the middle and express auto traffic above.

By 1929, the project was revised with an elevated roadway—the West Side Highway—along the shorefront and an elevated rail viaduct a few hundred feet inland. The automobile part took on a separate character and the name for both sections—The West Side Improvement—came to describe the rail part alone, depressed in an open cut or underground north of 30th Street, but elevated below that point.

The viaduct runs at the second-floor level, snaking through the West Side and occasionally down the middle of avenues, but generally between, on top of, and even through buildings. The railroad acquired some properties outright and easements over others.

At some points buildings were demolished, but at most others—such as the National Biscuit Company and Merchants Refrigeration buildings at West 16th Street and 10th Avenue—special spur lines were inserted at second-floor levels. The result was an overhead rail network partly hidden—because of its midblock routing—from major traffic arteries. It did create an "El" effect, casting shadows where there was once light. But it also removed the grade-level trains.

The first rail freight trip on the new line took place in August 1933, and full operation started in 1934. The New York Central Railroad president, F. E. Williamson, was quoted as saying, "This simple event today may well mark a transformation of the West Side."

But the Depression had already reduced rail freight shipments by 50 percent, and after World War II truck shipping rose in popularity. The elevated structure did not become the hive of shipping activity it was intended to be.

By 1978, traffic on the line was down to two carloads a week. But construction of the Jacob K. Javits Convention Center, which crossed the route, required a one-year interruption in service in 1980 and two major freight customers relocated to New Jersey. Although the connection was restored in 1981, service did not resume.

Conrail, the line's owner by 1984, announced plans to abandon it but had to offer it for sale to any group that might still operate a freight line. The city supported abandonment and demolition of the line. A transportation consultant, Peter Obletz, offered $10 to acquire the line for a minimal freight operation and Conrail accepted—it could then avoid demolition costs of perhaps $5 million.

Mr. Obletz's bid has been under continuous challenge from local real-estate developers and property owners, but to Mr. Obletz's satisfaction, the city has now apparently had a change of heart—there are now studies under way for light rail service along the route connecting the convention center and Battery Park City. The Metropolitan Transportation Authority, without any specific plan, is negotiating with Conrail to acquire the line, but the property owners claim the route has already been effectively abandoned and the easements over their properties lapsed. The matter will be resolved either by the Interstate Commerce Commission or a special rail court.

Meanwhile, the majestic West Side Improvement still threads its way through the Lower West Side, rusting and waiting for either a new use, or demolition.

Mr. Obletz has given up, but the MTA is still pursuing a project to haul garbage over the line.

WEST-PARK PRESBYTERIAN

An 1890 West Side Church Fighting
Landmark Status

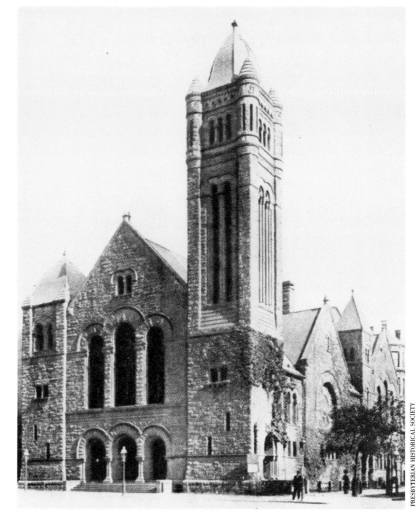

West-Park Presbyterian, 86th Street and Amsterdam Avenue, in 1910.

PRESBYTERIAN HISTORICAL SOCIETY

DESIGNATING RELIGIOUS PROPERTIES as landmarks is a sensitive subject. Churches have opposed such designation, fearing a loss of not only religious freedom but the flexibility to deal with property that often is difficult to maintain.

Recent practice has been to let architecturally significant churches remain unprotected as long as they are not in danger of demolition. Now the West-Park Presbyterian Church at 86th Street and Amsterdam Avenue is about to lobby vigorously for exclusion from a proposed historic district, but it may still be subject to designation as an individual landmark.

West-Park was founded in the 1850's as the Park Presbyterian Church on the rural West Side. The congregation built a frame building at 84th Street and West End Avenue in 1854, calling on a resident of the area, Leopold Eidlitz, as architect.

The church struggled until 1879, when it hired Anson Phelps Atterbury as its pastor. He was related to the Phelps-Dodge mining family and used his connections to improve the church's condition. The Columbus Avenue elevated railway had just opened and Mr. Atterbury correctly foresaw a huge increase in population for the West Side.

In 1883 he secured the northeast corner of 86th Street and Amsterdam Avenue for a new building. Leopold Eidlitz was again retained and he designed the large brownstone chapel still facing 86th Street, leaving the corner vacant. In 1889, Henry Kilburn designed the main sanctuary on the corner in a style matching the older section.

The entire complex, completed in 1890, is in the French Romanesque style, with rock-faced "Longmeadow brownstone trimmed with Lake Superior red stone," according to the *New York Times* of 1889.

Although it may be considered stiff and awkward compared to the best Romanesque revival work, the church is still above average in quality for New York City, and its lush, reddish-brown stone is a rare work of rich color.

The West Side boom of the 1880's and 1890's attracted congregations from downtown, and soon churches were competing for members. Park Presbyterian joined forces with the West-Park Church in 1911.

In the late 1970's real-estate development in the area picked up again and the demolition of buildings, like All Angels Church at 81st Street and West End Avenue for an apartment house, encouraged the Landmarks Preservation Commission to review West Side churches more closely.

In 1979 the commission staff described the West-Park church as "superb" but the building has never been designated a landmark. In 1981 the commission did designate the nearby Methodist Church of St. Paul and St. Andrew, over the strenuous objections of the congregation, which was seeking to redevelop the site.

The landmarks panel has always treated church designations with great care. For example, church interiors are exempted from regulation. As long as an architecturally significant church is not threatened the commission tends to leave it alone.

But two years ago, a local preservation group, Landmark West!, began a campaign for a historic district between Central Park West and Amsterdam Avenue. It did not include 86th Street west of Columbus, but the landmarks commission's proposed district extends all the way to Amsterdam and includes the West-Park church.

The church has just installed a $100,000 elevator and has no plans for demolition, but the pastor, the Rev. Bob Davidson, says it will vigorously oppose landmark designation. Mr. Davidson said citizens groups should seek zoning changes to protect their neighborhoods, not landmark designation, which requires the costly upkeep of church buildings and prevents the construction of modern, more easily maintained structures.

"The zealots for landmarking end up penalizing the religious institutions and providing a bonus for the developers with scenic views" over the low-rise churches, he said.

There may be a case to be made for eliminating 86th Street—which is occupied mostly by apartment houses—from the proposed historic district. Indeed, the *AIA Guide to New York City* says of the church, "Were it not overwhelmed by the grim apartment building to the north, it would be one of the West Side's loveliest landmarks."

The final district eliminated this section of West 86th Street.

1451 LEXINGTON AVENUE

A Sad Brownstone Monument to
an Aborted Plan for a Sliver

Brownstone, center, 1451 Lexington Avenue near 94th Street, in 1911.

IT WAS TO BE the narrowest—and perhaps most notorious—of the sliver buildings, 33 stories on an 18-foot-wide lot at 1451 Lexington Avenue, between East 94th and 95th Streets.

The structure was not built and the brownstone it would have replaced has remained a vacant shell, a thorn in the side of the Carnegie Hill community, which fought the proposed sliver building. Now the 110-year-old brownstone may soon be sold and the neighborhood is not sure whether to expect renovation or demolition.

The six houses at 1449–1459 Lexington Avenue are typical of the brownstones that covered sections of midtown and the Upper East Side. Built in 1878 and 1879 for $8,000 each, they were erected by a builder, Michael Duffy, who, alone or in partnership, built more than 40 row houses on the block.

Thom & Wilson were Duffy's architects for most of these projects and they produced the typical high-stoop brownstone, three windows wide, with machine-incised detailing in the neo-Grec style.

A former city alderman, Duffy was arrested in 1896 on a charge of bribing another alderman to vote in favor of a particular streetcar franchise for 34th Street. When he declared bankruptcy in 1888, a newspaper account said, "The ex-boodler was rude, belligerent and boastful from the stand," being particularly aroused when an $81 debt to Bloomingdale's was brought up.

First to occupy the house at 1451 Lexington Avenue—it was initially held for rental and not sold—was the family of Orren Hutchinson, an agent for Poland Spring Water. The family remained at 1451 Lexington only two years, until 1881.

The second family to occupy the house was that of Raphael Ettinger, who moved in in 1881. Ettinger, born in Germany in 1838, came to America in 1856 and worked in the worsted-goods business. Ettinger's household included his American-born wife Jenny, two daughters, Flora and Tessie, two sons, Sidney and Leonides, and Hedwig Tipper, an 18-year-old Austrian servant.

Ettinger died in 1904 and his family moved into an apartment building on East 97th Street. By 1922, the Lexington Avenue house had been converted to apartments.

One reason the Ettingers moved may have been the declining desirability of houses on the major avenues. As the north–south streets became more crowded and commercial, families that wanted private houses tended to relocate to side streets. Subway construction and sidewalk narrowing on upper Lexington Avenue had the same effect.

Gradually, the other buildings in the Duffy row were altered to apartments or other uses. The building at 1451 Lexington had six units. Its stoop was removed, windows changed and the facade painted over, but the original house remains identifiable.

For most of this century, the block did not change much. But in the early 1980's, as conventional development sites on the East Side became scarce, builders put up tall buildings on narrow sites. Buildings of 20 stories and more went up on frontages of 34 feet, 22 feet and even 20 feet. Then, in the fall of 1981, Spages Construction Company Inc. filed plans for a 320-foot-high, 33-story apartment house, named the Empyrean (which means "the highest heaven"), to go up on the 18-foot-wide site of 1451 Lexington.

Such a high, narrow building at a prominent location—other slivers had been on side streets next to other tall buildings—alarmed the neighborhood and galvanized opposition to the practice, resulting in a law passed in 1983 that restricts sliver buildings. The law says that on lots that are 45 feet in width or less, the height of a building cannot exceed the width of the street it faces. Michael Parley, a zoning consultant, said the law effectively limits construction on such sites to about eight stories.

The Empyrean had other problems, however, and was denied approval by the Department of Buildings in 1982. Spages retained ownership of the property, and in recent months a "for sale" sign has hung on the facade.

The president of Spages Construction, Philip Spages, said previously that he had entered into a contract to sell the building, but would not say for what purpose or to whom, and the neighbors await with interest the latest chapter in the history of 1451 Lexington Avenue.

A later owner has rebuilt the house and restored the exterior, sparking similar work by neighboring owners.

1020 MADISON AVENUE

A Lonely Row House Ignored by Two Historic Districts

1020 Madison Avenue, center, just south of 79th Street, in 1939.

THE FIVE-STORY HOUSE at 1020 Madison Avenue, built in 1913, looks no different from the other row houses in its Upper East Side neighborhood. But it is a sort of orphan, inexplicably marooned just outside the invisible boundaries of the two historic districts that cover most of the area.

Beginning in the 1870's, Madison Avenue developed as a polite, definitely second-fiddle alternative to mansion-lined Fifth Avenue above 59th Street. Although some important families, like the Cuttings and Herters, built major houses on Madison after 1880, it was still primarily a street of comfortable row houses interspersed with churches.

After the turn of the century, private-house construction slowed all over Manhattan and apartment houses gained in popularity. On Madison, the primacy of the private house was also eroded by increasing traffic and commercialization as shopfronts sprouted in once-private brownstones.

In 1911, a large town house, 870 Madison, went up at 71st Street and in 1913, 1020 Madison Avenue was completed just south of 79th Street—the last private house to be built on a changing avenue.

It was actually part of a three-house complex developed by Charles Buek at the southwest corner of 79th and Madison. He acquired the last vacant corner of the block running from 78th to 79th Streets between Fifth to Madison Avenues. It was called the Cook block and all its lots permitted only single-family dwellings.

According to a 1912 article in the *New York Times*, Buek first attempted to build an apartment house on the corner, but the block's homeowners prevented it, citing the deed restrictions. Thus thwarted, Buek built three houses in 1912 and 1913: 20 East 79th, a French neoclassical limestone house; 22 East 79th, at the corner; and 1020 Madison, just to the south.

The corner house and 1020 Madison were designed "in the Spanish style" according to a 1912 article in the *Real Estate Record and Guide*. The high-relief ornamentation on 1020, designed by F. E. Gage, derives from Spanish renaissance and baroque architecture, an influence rarely seen in New York City.

Limestone on the lower two floors and buff brick on the upper three,

the 32-foot-wide 1020 contained "every convenience and perfection" and was "more convenient and livable" than the typical New York row house, according to the *Record and Guide*.

The house was sold to Richard Trimble, secretary-treasurer of the United States Steel Corporation, whose family turned out to be its only residents. Trimble, with his wife and three children, moved to the row house from Long Island in 1914. They installed a paneled library with curved corners that still survives on the second floor in the present Givenchy men's shop. Mr. Trimble died in 1924, and his wife continued to occupy the house until her death in 1946.

The house was then sold and converted into shops and offices. In 1948, the corner house, 22 East 79th, was demolished and replaced with the present two-story taxpayer.

In 1977, the Landmarks Preservation Commission, then headed by Beverly Moss Spatt, designated a Metropolitan Museum Historic District including the entire Cook block—except for 22 East 79th and 1020 Madison. Although the 79th Street building is undistinguished, 1020 Madison is no less significant or intact than other buildings in the district.

The owner in 1977, Rafael Aryeh, still owns the property and his son, Benjamin, says that they did not oppose designation at the time. He said the building is included in a historic district, even though the district maps clearly show it is not.

Ms. Spatt does not recall anything specific about the boundaries, only that "the commission was very professional about its evaluations." A similarly unusual boundary in the same district was drawn down the middle of a group of identical row houses on Madison Avenue between 84th and 85th Streets after which the excluded buildings were demolished by a developer.

In 1979, the much larger Upper East Side Historic District was proposed and the initial boundary was extended to meet the Metropolitan Museum Historic District and include 1020 Madison Avenue. But that boundary was later redrawn and the last private house to be built on Madison Avenue remains an anomaly, orphaned by the landmarks process that protects its neighbors.

THE LEONORI

A Building That Recounts the Multiple-Dwelling Story

MUSEUM OF THE CITY OF NEW YORK

Leonori, on southeast corner of Madison Avenue at 63d Street, in 1905.

WORKMEN ARE PUTTING finishing touches on the new marble in the lobby of the turn-of-the-century Leonori, at the southeast corner of 63d and Madison Avenue, a building whose successive alterations document both the history of the multiple dwelling and of the Upper East Side.

Since the 1880's, Madison Avenue up to the 59th Street area had served as a locus for large apartment houses, and perhaps a dozen had gone up by 1899. In 1900 the 10-story 667 Madison Avenue went up at 61st Street and in 1901 Maximilian Morgenthau filed plans for the 12-story Leonori, the avenue's tallest.

The developer was not building an apartment house in the present sense of the word, but an apartment hotel—typical for its time but a rarity today. The Leonori had 10 parlor-bedroom suites per floor, which could be taken separately by singles or thrown together by families. None had kitchens, but meals were available in a rooftop dining room.

Apartment hotels offered residents not only doormen, superintendents and handymen, but also chambermaids. They also sweetened the pot for the owners.

"An apartment house is an investment, an apartment hotel is a business," noted the *Real Estate Record and Guide* in 1901. "The proprietor can make money out of tenants in many ways." The *Record and Guide* calculated that of the 46 hotels for which plans were filed in 1901, 40 were apartment hotels.

Morgenthau hired as architects Buchman & Fox, who designed a neoclassic facade of limestone, with a copper cornice at the roof and a modest projecting portico at the ground floor along Madison Avenue.

The building was completed in the summer of 1902 and leased to Charles L. Leonori. Leonori moved to the building to which he gave his name, and rented its suites for about $40 a room a month—plus the dining package and other services as desired.

The apartment hotel appealed to "families in easy circumstances, who like to live the untroubled life," according to the *Record Guide*. About half of the early tenants have no occupation following their names in city directories—suggesting that they were either retired or of independent means.

The Leonori originally had its entrance at 701 Madison Avenue and it retained it for two decades. But by 1907, increasing traffic and stores on Madison induced builders seeking cachet to take side street addresses, like 32 East 64th Street, one block north, begun in that year.

To take advantage of the rising retail leasehold values on Madison, the Leonori was one of the first large buildings to convert space for stores. In 1922, the grand Madison Avenue lobby was demolished and replaced by a lesser one on 63d Street, and the new address became 26 East 63d. Jardine, Hill & Murdoch installed the present iron storefronts with Ionic pilasters, the best work of its type on the avenue.

In 1925, the dining room was moved to the ground floor and opened to the public as a restaurant, freeing space for penthouse apartments, then coming into vogue.

By this time the major elements in the building had been changed, except for the rooms and the late Victorian finishes—sliding doors, dark wood trim, heavy ornamentation—now out of fashion in an era of light colors and neo-Georgian detailing.

More importantly, the apartment-hotel concept was losing out to the standard "housekeeping" apartment formula of the 1910's, with kitchen. With few exceptions, the apartment-hotel format acquired a slightly seedy reputation in the 20's and 30's and in 1937, a new owner rebuilt the interior with entirely new layouts, including kitchens. After this alteration, only the facade remained of the original building.

In 1981, a real-estate investment group headed by David Berley bought the Leonori and converted it to condominium ownership in 1983. By this time, the building had been included in the Upper East Side Historic District and what was left of it was protected from demolition, unlike 667 Madison Avenue, a block away and outside the district, which was demolished for an office building in 1985.

The condominium association has now put about $2 million in improvements into the building—about three times the cost of construction in 1901. Most of this was put up by the sponsor, which owns 36 of the 68 apartments.

WEST 83d STREET "TENEMENTS"

Is the Perspective Changing on Old Middle-Class Housing?

Middle-class tenements at 167–173 West 83d Street in the 1930's.

"THEY'RE JUST SOME old tenements," said Harold Pinc, the owner of 167 West 83d Street, referring to his building and its neighbors at 169, 171 and 173. "There's nothing special about them."

But, special or not, the Landmarks Preservation Commission has gone beyond its usual practices and included these and 75 other "tenements" along Amsterdam Avenue on its proposed Central Park West Historic District. If they are retained in the final district, it would indicate a new view of middle-class housing by the preservation community.

The buildings are not obviously special at first glance, only a bit more refined than the usual walk-up. Romanesque in style, they have smooth brownstone bases and deep red brick and terra-cotta ornament on the four floors above.

But the buildings were put up in 1885 by one of the city's most prominent developers, David H. King Jr., and designed by architects he regularly used, better known for grand buildings like the Villard houses and the old Penn Station—the firm of McKim, Mead & White.

When King acquired the West 83d Street property, the block was largely vacant and other West Side blocks were beginning to fill up with row houses for the prosperous. King served as contractor for the Washington Arch, the 1891 Madison Square Garden and the base of the Statue of Liberty.

His West 83d Street "tenements" were in fact "flats" to New Yorkers of the time, a slightly improved shading. Instead of two to four working-class families to a floor—the typical tenement density—these buildings had floor-through apartments and were designed for professional and business people of modest means. One of these was Royal Cortissoz, the influential art critic for the *New York Tribune*, who lived at 169.

"Tenement" is now the popular terminology for practically any walk-up apartment house. But the 83d Street buildings have many touches that are well beyond those in normal working-class accommodations. The original vestibule flooring is pink, white and gray marble in an elaborate interlocking design, now heavily worn but still handsome.

At least one apartment is more or less in its original condition, with raised decorations on the ceiling, stained wooden wainscoting and paneled doors and an original set of pantry cabinets which the occupant is about to junk to make way for a closet.

Other owners have covered over three of the four original marble vestibule floors and the facades of two buildings have been garishly painted within the last year.

If King thought that his flats would be surrounded by polite row houses, he was soon disappointed. For 83d Street became one of the West Side's occasional "stable streets," and the construction of a firehouse, stables and related structures discouraged row house builders. By the 1950's, many of King's apartments had either been subdivided or were serving as rooming houses.

In 1986, Landmark West!, a preservation group, proposed a Central Park West historic district running west from Central Park West and Columbus Avenue. Most other historic districts in Manhattan have concentrated on elite housing—private houses and luxury apartment buildings. But Landmark West! proposed to include not only the row houses in the blocks west of Columbus, but also the flats and tenements of Amsterdam Avenue itself. These tend to be of a fairly high caliber, approaching the quality of the 83rd Street buildings.

The Landmark West! proposal wraps around, but excludes, the McKim, Mead & White buildings—and all of 83d Street between Amsterdam and Columbus—because "the block wasn't cohesive enough," according to Andrew Dolkart, a board member of Landmark West! The group's proposed boundaries exclude the McKim, Mead & White buildings, while including a fairly ordinary tenement next door at the northeast corner of 83d and Amsterdam, whose cornice has been sheared off.

But in 1987 the Landmarks Commission itself went beyond the Landmark West! boundary and included the block—as well as much of Amsterdam Avenue—in its proposed district, and its final decision will be a bellwether of preservation attitudes.

The final district included the buildings.

SPUYTEN DUYVIL SWING BRIDGE

Restoring a Link in the City's Lifeline

Swing bridge at juncture of Harlem and Hudson Rivers, stuck in open position since 1983, in 1984 view.

SINCE TRAINS STOPPED running across it in 1982, the Spuyten Duyvil swing bridge has been stuck in the open position, like a faucet that cannot be turned off.

But the turntable railroad bridge, which was erected in 1899 and connects the northern tip of Manhattan to the Bronx, is scheduled for rehabilitation by mid-1990, although budget overruns may push the date back. When the bridge is repaired, it should be able to resume its back-and-forth sweeps across the Harlem River.

The history of the bridge is intertwined with the history of the New York & Hudson River Railroad, established in the mid-1840's with tracks extending north along the West Side from a terminal at Chambers and Hudson Streets in lower Manhattan.

The line ran along the Hudson River north of 72d Street and crossed Spuyten Duyvil Creek, now the Harlem River, on a wooden drawbridge. The bridge was built no later than 1848, when service was extended to Fishkill. Later, service was extended to Albany, and points west and north.

The early railroad had freight and passenger service. President-elect Abraham Lincoln used the line as he traveled to his inauguration in 1861, and his funeral train passed that way again in 1865.

A merger in 1869 with the New York & Harlem Railroad to create the New York Central & Hudson River Railroad shifted passenger service to Grand Central Terminal, but a shuttle ran from the old Hudson River line passenger station at 30th Street and 10th Avenue to the Spuyten Duyvil station in the Bronx.

At some point, the wooden bridge was replaced by an iron one, certainly by 1895 when the Spuyten Duyvil Creek and the Harlem River were widened and joined as the Harlem River Ship Canal, linking the East and Hudson Rivers. In 1899, the present bridge, called the Spuyten Duyvil Improvement, was erected by the railroad.

The 610-foot bridge, which was designed by Robert Giles, a staff engineer for the railroad, consisted of three fixed sections—two on the Manhattan side, one on the Bronx. They are connected by a 290-foot-long center section that pivots on a central tower and rotates almost 65 degrees to open a 100-foot channel on either side.

The truss systems of the bridge were not unusual, according to the

Engineering News of June 14, 1900, but the bridge was of "considerable interest" because of the shallow turntable construction to keep the bridge close to the existing railroad grades and thus close to the water. Today, depending on tides, there is often only five feet of clearance from the water line to the bridge.

Passenger shuttle service across the bridge continued until 1916, when all passenger service was shifted to Grand Central Terminal, but the New York Central & Hudson River Railroad played an increasingly important role in feeding New York.

In the 1920's, when other rail lines were closed in labor disputes, the West Side line was called the "lifeline of New York City," bringing in almost all of the city's food.

By 1934, according to Thomas Flagg, an industrial archeologist, 70 trains a day crossed the Spuyten Duyvil Bridge. But rail service declined after World War II and so did the use of the aging swing bridge, which began to have maintenance problems.

In 1963, the steam-operated motor was replaced with an electric one. Three years later, a tug maneuvering an oil barge hit the bridge, jamming it in the open position. Repairs took two weeks, and Harlem River shipping had to be rerouted around the Battery.

In 1983, a hit-and-run collision again left the bridge in the open position, but repairs were not undertaken. Regular freight service on the rail line had stopped a year before.

Since then, the Spuyten Duyvil swing bridge has been rusting slowly, as tidal currents and Circle Line boats pass by.

Now, as part of a plan to restore passenger service on the West Side, the bridge will be rehabilitated in a joint project of Amtrak and the State Department of Transportation. Passenger trains from Albany, the Great Lakes and Canada now go into Grand Central Terminal, but after the project is completed they will go into Pennsylvania Station, which will permit connections to points south.

There were concerns whether the swing bridge could be rehabilitated to operate as frequently as the new service requires, but Amtrak determined that it can be repaired and the original bridge retained.

Back in operation.

WEST 80th STREET DAY CARE CENTER

A Bright Hope for Children Giving Way to Office Condo

T HE PHYSICAL REMINDER of a dream that blazed briefly, but died, stands vacant and grimy today on West 80th Street, waiting for a new incarnation.

The dream began in the 1960's when the drive for low-cost day care for children of all economic classes was a vibrant movement, bringing together feminist, minority and antipoverty activists.

At a time when there was a "war on poverty," it seemed that day care that would mix young children of all classes and races might be an important element in eliminating discrimination and injustice in future generations.

Dorothy Pitman-Hughes, a working mother, founded a day-care center in 1966 after she had trouble finding someone to care for her own children. She charged a flat $5 a week for a child, regardless of family income.

By 1970, when "universal day care" was a major political issue, she was able to make up the bulk of her budget from Federal, state and city funds earmarked for day care, and in short order, Ms. Pitman-Hughes said, she dispensed with the child-care fee entirely.

There was not really a national consensus that day care was desirable—there was frequent criticism that the "mother's place" was with her child until regular schooling began—but many politicians were convinced to support day-care funding with the idea that mothers on welfare would take jobs if freed from child care.

While occupying rented quarters, Ms. Pitman-Hughes dreamed of owning a building for her nonprofit center. Somehow she managed to scrape together nearly $350,000—from fund-raising events and from contributions from prominent, wealthy West Siders—to buy and completely renovate a three-story building built in 1926 at 223 West 80th Street, between Broadway and Amsterdam Avenue.

The new West 80th Street Community Child Day Care Center opened in 1971, serving 125 children. If the interior—four classrooms, a roof play deck, a kitchen and a nursery—was not remarkable, the exterior was. The old brick facade was stuccoed over, the windows recessed and the roof line built up in an irregular form.

The facade was painted in a playful red-and-blue scheme and a brilliant yellow plastic tube ran from bottom to top, forming little play spaces inside. Ms. Pitman-Hughes recalled the tube as a reference to the space program, which captured children's imaginations at the time, and there is definitely a "space age" modernity to the building.

But Wallace Kaminsky, whose firm, Kaminsky & Shiffer, designed the renovation, said the idea was "a facade that could have been put together by children out of colored blocks."

"When they came down the street they could see *their* building," he said, and even see children playing inside—in contrast to the buttoned-up architecture of most schools.

New York magazine complimented the building in 1972, saying it "makes most of the midtown boutiques look tacky by comparison."

But in the center's first year of operation the movement for universal day care foundered. In 1972, the Federal Government cut New York's day-care funding by three-quarters. As a result all day-care funds were restricted to children of low-income families, a move that eliminated the economic and racial mix of most day-care programs.

In 1973, the *New York Times* said in an editorial that "if integration—socioeconomic as well as racial—is truly to remain the country's goal, the time to begin is when the children are still too young to have been inoculated with a virus of society's suspicions and hostilities." The government remained unmoved.

Then the city's fiscal crisis of the mid-70's reduced its own funds to a trickle and the West 80th Street Center limped along, finally relocating to Harlem in 1983—where most of the families on welfare had been moving, as low-cost housing on the West Side was renovated for families of greater means. Two years later, the day-care center closed its doors.

Community Child Day Care Center at 223 West 80th Street, in 1972.

In 1983, a group of doctors bought the building for $650,000 and later announced plans to replace it with a 12-story medical condominium. But work has never begun. Now Christopher Pendarvis, project director for the owner, 223 West 80th Corporation, says demolition will begin in June.

Purchased by Phoenix House, a drug-treatment program, which is repairing the interior and leaving the facade alone.

312–314 EAST 53d STREET

Twin Clapboard Row Houses, but Just One Is Landmarked

Twin clapboard houses at 314, left, and 312 East 53d Street in 1932.

AMONG THE FIRST buildings to be considered for designation by the newly formed New York City Landmarks Preservation Commission in 1966 were two identical clapboard row houses at 312 and 314 East 53d Street, between Second and First Avenues, built a century earlier.

The one at 312 was indeed designated, but its twin was not, a curious lacuna in the list of New York City landmarks.

In October 1865, Robert Cunningham, a builder and barrel maker, and James Cunningham, a contractor (it is not known if they were related), bought the land at what was later 312–316 East 53d Street and by mid-1866 had erected two three-story frame houses at 312 and 314, in front of an existing stable and workshop complex. The two houses are Italianate in style with simple moldings, plain wooden cornices, a common mansard roof and, for fire safety, brick sidewalls.

Fire protection has been a major concern of New York City building regulation since the 17th century, when "wooden chimneys" were outlawed. In the 19th century, new frame buildings were successively prohibited below "fire lines" at 14th, 23d, 32d, 42d and 52d Streets—river to river.

The Cunninghams completed their clapboard buildings just in time because in 1866, as the Department of Buildings called for the prohibition of all frame construction in Manhattan, the fire line was moved north to a point between 86th and 87th Streets.

In 1867, the first tenants moved in—Charles Nanz, a notary and minister, at 312, and Thomas Taylor, a contractor, at 314. The rear buildings may have doubled as a dormitory for the Cunninghams' or Taylor's workmen; the 1870 census lists 20 occupants in the rear structures.

In 1871, the Cunninghams built a tenement at 316 East 53d Street, preserving a vehicular passageway to the rear buildings. In 1872 Francis Lahey, a milkman, bought 314 and 316, occupying 314 and operating his business out of the rear buildings. In 1883, he sold his buildings to Bernhard Kolb, a Second Avenue undertaker who kept his horses and wagons in the rear building and occupied 314.

This section of East 53d Street had had light industry since the 1860's—including a foundry and factories for shirts, buttons and cigars. But by the 1920's genteel development from the central midtown sections spilled over toward the river, like the apartment house at 320 East 53d Street built in 1928.

Around this time the rear buildings were removed, making a large rear yard for 312 and 314. Muriel Draper, who was at the center of an art and dance circle, moved into 312 in the late 1920's. For a time, Lincoln Kirstein, the founder, with George Balanchine, of the New York City Ballet, also occupied 312, according to an article in the *New Yorker* in 1986.

The literary critic Edmund Wilson rented 314 in the 1930's for $60 a month, writing to F. Scott Fitzgerald in 1933 that he liked his offbeat neighborhood—"no doorman, no telephone"—and telling John Dos Passos that the large garden was coming to life.

In 1965, the Landmarks Preservation Commission was set up and the East 52d Street Association proposed 312 and 314 for designation. The commission was considering the matter as a developer began to assemble the southeast corner of 53d Street and Second Avenue for an apartment house.

The owner of 314, Donald Parson Jr., wrote the commission that he was not interested in designation since he sought "to sell the property as expeditiously as possible." But John Schaffner, owner of 312, asked for designation, saying he was not sure how he could "continue to resist financial blandishments." He said he had been offered $185,000. The panel designated 312, effectively blocking the complete assemblage, but never designated 314, which at the time was in nearly identical condition. It was later covered in aluminum siding to imitate clapboard and it is now owned and occupied by RKM Enterprises, a real-estate concern.

Frank Gilbert, secretary of the commission at the time and now senior field representative at the National Trust for Historic Preservation, recalled that the commission designated many buildings over the objections of owners, like Grand Central Terminal. "The enthusiasm of Mr. Schaffner allowed us to go ahead" with the designation of 312, he said. But as for 314, "in large cities, landmark commissions have a tremendous job, and we just never came back to it," he said.

GENERAL TIRE BUILDING

"Gas Station" Style: An Overlooked Gem of the 1930's

The General Tire Company Building at 602 West 57th Street as it appeared in 1935.

For the last several years, only an architectural detective would have noticed the building. Since the early 80's it has been boarded up, completely concealed under a uniform coat of white paint. But in the last year or so, the paint has peeled off, revealing a minor masterpiece of the 1930's, the Art Deco General Tire Building at 602 West 57th Street.

Apparently passed over by the Landmarks Preservation Commission, the one-story building occupies a large site in the middle of a 45,000-square-foot assemblage of garages and other low buildings, only a few blocks from the sites of such major projects as the huge office building planned for Columbus Circle.

Carriage makers and automobile companies first clustered along Broadway in the Times Square area, but by the 1910's, the pressure of theater development forced them north on Broadway, and in some cases west. By the 1920's, General Motors, Peerless, White and Republic all had service stations or workshops on 57th Street between 11th and 12th Avenues.

In 1927, the General Tire and Rubber Company signed a 10-year lease, with options to renew, with the Appleby Estate, the owner of an L-shaped plot wrapping around the southwest corner of 57th Street and 11th Avenue. General Tire, founded in 1915 in Akron, Ohio, entered a field of more than 300 tire-producing companies by supplying replacement tires rather than original equipment.

It is not clear how the company first used the site, but it apparently occupied several existing structures. The Depression slowed business everywhere, but by 1932, General Tire celebrated a return to full production in its Akron plant. In 1934, it opted to sell to vehicle manufactures in an agreement with International Harvester. And in July 1935, General Tire filed plans for a one-story shop at 602 West 57th Street.

The engineer-architects, Francisco & Jacobus, had developed a scheme for a reinforced concrete building with a great expanse of factory windows, unusual in only one respect: The exterior was covered in colored enameled metal panels.

Like terra-cotta and glass tile, metal-panel construction was a logical outgrowth of curtain-wall techniques oriented toward providing decorative effects with the least cost and wall thickness.

Completed in October 1935, the General Tire building was deep blue with contrasting elements in mustard, a rich visual combination impossible to obtain with conventional masonry materials. Four fluted pilasters divide the 57th Street facade, each supporting a panel enameled with a stylized capital, which, in turn, supports a frieze of fanshaped details.

Various streamlined elements—like stainless-steel bumpers at the driveway passage—give the building an Art Moderne flavor, but neither Art Deco nor Art Moderne completely describes the General Tire building. It is really more "gas station" than anything else. The rich colors, the integration of the sign into the facade, the clearly utilitarian character of the building and its taut two-dimensional look—designed to appear as a constant to an observer in motion—all are trademarks of commercial roadside architecture. It is unusual to find an example in such good condition anywhere, especially in Manhattan.

The interior was plain factory space, and period photographs show equipment for repair, testing and installation—and thousands of tires. Although the main facade was on 57th Street, the main entrance was on 11th Avenue; the separation of the principal facade from the actual entrance is characteristic of roadside buildings.

There have been few changes in the area since 1935. General Tire closed operations at the site around 1982, the same year its huge Akron plant shut down. Now used for automobile painting and engine repair, the interior has been subdivided, the great factory windows covered with plywood, and the facade given a coat of white paint, now largely peeled off from the shiny enameled panels.

In 1979, the staff of the Landmarks Preservation Commission called the building "extremely attractive," rating it on the same level with the Rodin Studio Building, at 200 West 57th Street, which has recently been designated a landmark. But it never acted on the General Tire building.

Chase Manhattan Bank represents the owner of the property, still the Appleby Estate, and a spokesman for Chase, Kenneth Mills, said there are no plans for redevelopment. But major projects like Television City and the proposed Westway replacement are brewing for the area, and a coat of paint may soon be the least of the General Tire building's problems.

FLATBUSH AVENUE TERMINAL

The Final Weeks for a Neo-Renaissance Grande Dame?

The Flatbush Avenue Terminal of Long Island Rail Road in Brooklyn, in a 1910 photo.

THE BATTLE TO save the Flatbush Avenue Terminal, the city's second most impressive rail station after Grand Central, was supposedly lost in 1980 when both the National Register of Historic Places and the Landmarks Preservation Commission declined to designate the 1906 structure.

Now the city's Public Development Corporation has announced that demolition of the neo-Renaissance structure—including its great waiting room—is only weeks away, to allow it to begin construction on its huge Atlantic Terminal project. But problems with anchor tenants for the new project may still yield a short reprieve for the old terminal, and for historic buildings short reprieves can sometimes flower into more permanent ones.

By the late 1890's, the Long Island Rail Road had outgrown its 1877 terminal on the block bounded by Flatbush and Atlantic Avenues and Fort Greene and Hanson Places. According to Vincent Seyfried, author of a seven-volume history of the Long Island Rail Road, planning for a new terminal began in 1902. It was designed to connect with the extension of the IRT—the city's first subway—to the site in 1908, as well as to existing el lines.

The new terminal, Brooklyn's only major rail facility, opened in 1906 and presented "nothing very new to the engineer," according to the *Railroad Gazette* of 1907. But architecturally, the station is rather grand, especially since the new East River tunnels leading to Penn Station promised to diminish the importance of the Flatbush Avenue Terminal.

The terminal is two stories high, faced with deep red brick trimmed with terra-cotta in a rich umber. A balustrade at the top of the building has been removed but the rest of the facade is largely intact, with great round portals at major entrances and ornamental swags on the frieze.

Designed by H. F. Saxcelbey, the exterior is, if not inspired, a perfectly competent building, its multi-angled facade appropriate for a complex transit hub.

But it is the interior, the main waiting room, that seems so remarkable—a great double-height space in tile, painted wood and plaster relief decoration.

About 80 feet on each side and 50 feet high, the room was originally lit by a giant coffered skylight, and glass insets in the floor below let light down to the lower level.

A second-floor gallery leads to office spaces, and the ensemble has the implicit drama that large rail-station waiting rooms share. It is a surprising and charming little brother to Grand Central—just the kind of feature that some redevelopment projects proudly use as a focal point.

While the waiting room has been closed to the public since 1985, it is entirely intact, if deteriorated, except for a new concrete floor and changes in doors and other minor elements.

The station seems to have had poor maintenance after the 1920's, and as Brooklyn lost ground relative to Manhattan, the fortunes of the Flatbush Terminal also declined.

In 1947, the *Brooklyn Eagle* called the building an "antiquated eyesore," quoting a commuter as saying: "They ought to frame this joint and put it with other relics of yesteryear."

Proposals to demolish the building were put forward in the 50's and 60's and in 1980 the Metropolitan Transportation Authority proposed to replace it with a new terminal complex. The Coalition to Save Brooklyn's LIRR Terminal Complex, a local preservation group, protested the demolition and preliminary staff reviews at the Advisory Council on Historic Preservation and the state Office of Historic Preservation indicated that the building would be protected.

But the nomination was finally rejected and although the M.T.A. project did not go ahead, a larger mixed-use project proposed by the city's Public Development Corporation in 1984 centered on the terminal site.

The National Register and the Landmarks Commission again declined to designate the Flatbush Terminal—although they did protect the Pioneer Warehouses, a fairly ordinary white-brick complex on the fringe of the project area.

While the new Atlantic Terminal project has had trouble securing major office tenants, demolition of the old terminal—which occupies only a small part of the project site—seems to have taken on a symbolic value. But in its eight decades, it has never been so close to the end of its line.

Terminal demolished, project under way.

CLAREMONT STABLES

An 1892 Survivor of Close Calls with Demolition

The Claremont Stables at 175 West 89th Street in the 1930's. The building was put up in 1892 by Edward Bedell as a public stable.

BUILT IN 1892, Claremont Stables at 175 West 89th Street in Manhattan has twice escaped demolition. Now the city, which had condemned the site for housing in 1965, has both offered to sell the building back to the family that has operated it as a riding academy since 1943 and proposed the building for landmark designation.

In the late 19th century, no one wanted stables on his block. Gradually, informal agreements by builders set aside certain streets in residential districts for stables and light industry.

In 1892, Edward Bedell, who had built the Cedarhurst Stable at 147 West 83d Street in 1887, put up three two-story private stables at 167–171 West 89th Street and a five-story public stable at 175 West 89th Street. The private stables were sold off to local families—167 to George Legg, an importer who lived at 25 West 81st Street—and Bedell sold the public stable for $90,000 to Charles F. Havemeyer, heir to the sugar-refining business his family established in 1828.

Havemeyer, operating with his brother-in-law, William B. Duncan Jr., net leased the building to Lee and Darius Tallman, who had been operating the Cedarhurst. The Tallmans ran the Claremont as a boarding stable, where West Side families kept their own carriages and horses.

Designed by Frank A. Rooke, who specialized in stables and factories, the Claremont has five floors, including a cellar. The main floor has a rectangular riding area originally used to store carriages and to hitch them to horses for their owners.

The cellar and second floor contain 135 stalls, and are connected to the main floor by cleated ramps for the horses. The third and fourth floors were used to store additional carriages, brought down by elevator, and hay dropped from chutes.

The Claremont was up to date, with scored concrete floors instead of wooden ones, extra ventilating flues serving the stall floors and drain piping from each stall dropped below the ceiling of the floor underneath for easy access.

The Claremont is now a kind of working museum of equine transport. Old carriages and sleighs are strewn about the upper floors, along with old tack, ancient hay and other stable detritus. A thick, rich lacework of cobwebs is strung across the beamed ceiling.

The exterior is a tame Romanesque Revival design in buff brick, although the Flemish-style stepped central arch—with a horseshoe carved into its keystone—and the paneled frieze of brickwork at the top are nice touches. The three private stables are similar in style.

After Claremont, other stables went up on 89th Street, along with tenements, a telephone company building and a public school. In 1907, the Monterey Automobile Garage was built at 139 West 89th Street, reflecting the increased popularity of the automobile.

Gradually, other stables were altered to garage use—the Cedarhurst by 1910—and although horses were still seen on the city streets, the demand for public stables had vanished. Around 1927, Claremont Stables was changed to the Claremont Riding Academy, apparently by a new owner, Emil Wellner, who had sought to serve those using the Central Park bridle paths.

In 1937, Wellner filed plans for a five-story garage to be built on the site. Irwin Novograd, who worked as a bookkeeper for Wellner, said the garage application was rejected by the city because it was too close to the public school across the street.

In 1943, Mr. Novograd purchased the Claremont and today it is the only public, as well as the oldest operating, stable in Manhattan.

In 1956, the city published an urban renewal plan for much of the Upper West Side showing large-scale public-housing construction on the blocks between Amsterdam and Columbus Avenues from 87th to 97th Streets—including the Claremont site. The city acquired the property by condemnation in 1965 and, although much of the projected housing was built, the Claremont building remained, with the academy, on a month-to-month lease.

But around 1977, in the midst of its fiscal crisis, the city retreated from its housing program for the Claremont site, although it did not specifically propose the preservation of the stable. In 1979, Paul Novograd, whose father had purchased the Claremont in 1943, asked that the Claremont be listed on the National Register of Historic Places in a further attempt to thwart demolition.

Paul Novograd said that the city has offered to sell the building back to the academy, and that a price is being negotiated. If the sale is consummated, and the Landmarks Preservation Commission designates the building, the Claremont Stables, the oldest in Manhattan, stands a good chance of reaching its centennial.

Designated a landmark.

GENERAL THEOLOGICAL SEMINARY

Restoration Drive Begun for Chelsea Landmark

The General Theological Seminary at Ninth Avenue and 20th Street in 1910's.

THE GENERAL THEOLOGICAL Seminary, on the block bounded by 20th to 21st Streets, Ninth to 10th Avenues, is a surprise to most New Yorkers who come suddenly upon the great green double quadrangle hidden by a perimeter of century-old dormitories and classrooms.

The seminary considered abandoning its landmark campus, but decided in 1986 to stay put and to restore its aging buildings.

Now, to support that decision, the theological institution has begun an ambitious $68 million, 10-year fund-raising program, and a historical exhibit and tours of the quadrangle are to open on May 25.

In 1817, the General Convention of the Episcopal Church established a "general Theological Seminary, which may have the united support of the whole church" instead of just the backing of a particular state or diocese.

Clement Clarke Moore, a Chelsea landowner (and author of "A Visit from St. Nicholas" in 1823), in 1818 offered as a gift to the as-yet-unbuilt seminary a full city block, part of his estate. Although the seminary began classes in 1819 with six students, it was not until 1826 that the first building opened, on what came to be known as Chelsea Square.

By 1836 a near-twin had joined it, to make a pair of rough stone Gothic Revival buildings. The two isolated structures were far from the established part of the city—Greenwich Village to the south was still just a nascent suburb—and the seminary first served as a sort of rural outpost.

But continuing financial troubles kept the seminary on a shaky footing and by the 1870's the rural outpost was surrounded by Chelsea row houses, with shipping and industry to the west and the Ninth Avenue elevated on the east. The shopping and theater districts along Sixth Avenue and Broadway in the 20's and 30's offered worldliness and even temptation to the students.

In 1879, Eugene Augustus Hoffman, who had both old money and solid connections to the city's Episcopal elite, was installed as dean. After briefly considering a move—one proposal was to situate it on some Trinity Parish land at 79th Street and the East River—Dean Hoffman retained architect Charles Coolidge Haight to develop a plan for what remains Manhattan's oldest large institutional complex.

Haight was already familiar with the seminary—his father taught

there in the 1840's and 1850's and he had altered the 1836 "west building" in the 1870's.

He was already at work on a plan for an academic complex for Columbia College on the small block bounded by 49th to 50th Streets, Madison to Park Avenues. At the seminary block, he had a much larger area with which to work.

Working in the collegiate Gothic style for which he became famous, Haight designed a double quadrangle, with four- to six-story buildings on the Ninth Avenue, 10th Avenue and 21st Street sides enclosing a great grassy space interrupted only by the chapel, which divided it in the middle.

The buildings are matched, but very slightly, in red brick trimmed with brownstone, "half monumental and half domestic," according to the *Southern Churchman* in 1884.

At the 10th Avenue end, there is a great refectory, a paradigm of the collegiate dining hall—a great oak-paneled space with a musicians' gallery, cathedral ceiling, leaded glass and portraits of professors ringing the room.

The main entrance to the grounds was from Ninth Avenue, through a low portal under a library/administration building, like a castle gate.

Hoffman's building campaign—funded in substantial part by his own money—continued from 1883 to 1902. By the end the seminary had become an urban retreat, the sounds of the city filtering in over the surrounding walls or on 20th Street, the 10-foot-high embankment that puts the seminary grounds above grade.

Some changes to the seminary have been happy, some not. Alfred Githens's Seabury Hall (1932), next to the chapel, is a brilliant infill work, mixing Gothic and Art Moderne design. But O'Connor & Kilham's new Ninth Avenue front (1961), which replaced the old library, looks naïve and ridiculous in its tentative Gothic appliqué to a plain box. Still, it is the Victorian architecture in combination with the quadrangles that makes the seminary so special.

As an 1893 guidebook put it, the "velvety green lawns . . . make a charming oasis of verdure and peace in the vast whirl of the city's secular life." If the seminary is successful in its restoration goal, this "oasis" should survive in good condition for another century.

THE RUSSELL SAGE FOUNDATION BUILDING

From Rentals to Cooperatives: Reconverting a Grand Palazzo

Russell Sage Foundation Building on the southwest corner of 22d Street and Lexington Avenue in 1915. Conversion to co-ops is under way.

N OT ALL PRESERVATION in New York is the result of noisy hearings before the Landmarks Preservation Commission, for most old buildings fall or survive without controversy, as the result of coincidence or chance.

The Russell Sage Foundation Building, built in 1915 at the southwest corner of 22d Street and Lexington Avenue, was converted to rental apartments in 1975. Its facade was preserved. Now the building is being converted again, to cooperative apartments, and the converter, Michael Beloff, the president of Beloff Properties, said he is pleased that he has such an impressive structure, nine stories of rough sandstone, but disappointed that the original interiors were mutilated beyond restoration in the rental conversion.

By the turn of the century, the area around Gramercy Park had acquired a marked institutional character. The National Academy of Design, the Free Academy (later City College), the Y.M.C.A., the Society for the Prevention of Cruelty to Children and a dozen others had settled around 23d Street and what is now Park Avenue South. By 1910 commercial buildings began to replace some of the low-rise institutions.

An exception was the building of the Russell Sage Foundation, erected at the southwest corner of 22d and Lexington from 1912 to 1915. Sage was a financier known for, among other things, his successful attempt, with Jay Gould, to gain control of the city's elevated lines.

He died in 1906 and left his $63 million estate to his widow, Margaret Olivia, who was named executor. Mrs. Sage, who had published an article entitled "Opportunities and Responsibilities for Leisured Women" in 1905, established the Russell Sage Foundation, dedicated to the improvement of social and living conditions.

She endowed the foundation with $15 million and by 1912 its offices were spread out over several locations in the 23d Street area.

In that year it filed plans for a new nine-story headquarters at the southwest corner of 22d Street and Lexington Avenue. Designed by Grosvenor Atterbury, the building is unusual in that its facade is entirely of rusticated stone.

Elements like the deep rustication—the rough texture of the stone—and the grand arches of the first-floor doors and windows are similar to those on Florentine palazzi of the Renaissance. Other typically Florentine elements are the elaborate grillwork over some of the windows and the use of decorated shields—with labels like "service," "play," "work" and "study"—at the second-floor level.

The original plan had the entrance to the offices on 22d Street, with a great vaulted lecture and exhibition hall on Lexington Avenue. Offices were on floors two through seven. On the eighth and ninth floors there was a double-height library with leather doors, tile floors and leaded-glass windows.

The Foundation examined and tried to solve the causes of social problems. It built the famous Forest Hills Gardens subdivision in Queens, also designed by Atterbury, in an attempt at a model housing enclave.

In 1949, the Sage Foundation sold its headquarters to the Roman Catholic Archdiocese of New York, which operated it as the Catholic Charities Building.

Twenty-five years later, the building was sold to a developer who converted it to 166 rental apartments. Although the exterior was left largely intact, the grand lecture hall was subdivided into shops, the office floors were totally rebuilt and the great library was divided into a warren of small duplex apartments with modern spiral staircases.

The grand building became just an elegant skin covering an interior of rental apartments, where some of the new flooring is already beginning to shrink and come apart. Only a few portions of vaulted ceilings, library fittings and other elements have been haphazardly left intact. In 1985, a new developer, Michael Beloff, bought the building and is converting it to a co-op.

"We would never have done the kind of conversion now that they did in 1974," said Mr. Beloff wistfully. "We've resurrected all that we can," noting that his firm was able to uncover the grand vaulted lobby ceiling, which had been covered by a drop ceiling but not destroyed.

But restoring the original spaces was too costly, and the building will probably remain as one with a split personality.

THE AVERY LIBRARY

FRANKLIN D. ROOSEVELT DRIVE

Institutions Use Air Rights Over a Multilevel Marvel

Franklin D. Roosevelt Drive, looking north from 81st Street and the East River; Triborough Bridge and Queens, in background.

NEW YORK CITY and the state are jointly rehabilitating the Franklin D. Roosevelt Drive, a project expected to be completed by the mid-1990's. Widely known as the East River Drive, it is certainly one of Manhattan's great public works, particularly the section between 53d and 92d Streets, a dizzying stretch of dips and rises, views and tunnels, sun and shadow.

But another more fundamental change is under way, for the institutions along the drive are just now beginning to make what has been a sunny boulevard between 62d and 71st Streets into a half-mile-long tunnel, using air rights transferred to them back in 1973.

When the East River Drive south of 53d Street was completed in 1939, it was a fairly ordinary waterfront highway. But for the section between 53d and 92d Streets, completed in 1942, unusual site conditions and imaginative design produced "one of the world's most thrilling stretches of multilevel highway," according to *New York 1930* by Robert A.M. Stern, Gregory Gilmartin and Thomas Mellins.

This stretch was constrained by the bulkhead line on the waterside—beyond which fill could not be placed—and the building line on the shore side, where there had been substantial apartment construction along Sutton Place and East End Avenue.

Walter Binger, the Commissioner of Borough Works, was able to make private agreements with most of the riparians, among them Lilie Havemeyer, for whom he demolished and then completely rebuilt a private house at 16 Sutton Square. But some parts were so narrow that his engineers and architects—Lester Hammond, J. C. Collyer, Harvey Stevenson and Eastman Studds—had to develop novel solutions.

In these sections, the sunny side-by-side highway was split in half with the northbound lanes on the bottom, the southbound lanes above those, pedestrian and garden decks above that and, at the Brearley School at 83d Street, a play deck forming a fourth level.

The East River Drive experience is one of sudden shifts from light to dark, open to tunnel and rising to falling, with changing views of the river and a changing waterside perspective of Manhattan.

The tunnel entrance on the drive at 92d Street is about as official a gateway as one finds in New York City. Two pylons stand before it, and sea gulls and dolphins and the legend "East River Drive" are rendered in concrete relief on the tunnel itself, which is flanked by a pair of blue-glass, nautical light assemblies.

Suddenly it is dark, in part because grime obscures the original white concrete walls. The road pitches right, then up, then down and a screen of concrete columns on the left reveals the river in a cinematic blur. Below 81st Street the opposing northbound traffic becomes level with the southbound lanes and the drive becomes a sunny boulevard, passing fragments of genteel apartment houses, industrial buildings and the rough-stone retaining walls of Rockefeller University.

Although flat, this open stretch retains drama with the water close by at left, views of midtown at right, and the spiky 59th Street bridge directly ahead.

Near the bridge the road swerves and rises precipitously again and then continues under the Sutton Place Gardens, where vines trail down beside speeding cars. The tight curves and grades of the Sutton Place tunnel are as exciting as their Gracie Square counterparts. Morris R. Werner, writing in the *New Yorker*, described the drive as "a carefully constructed and absolutely trustworthy roller coaster."

Architectural Review stated in 1944 that "a specifically American idiom is developing" and compared the drive's bold scale and complex rhythms to recent dam construction by the Tennessee Valley Authority.

While the drive has remained largely unchanged, two major Sutton Place South apartment buildings were erected on platforms over it in the late 50's. In 1973, Gov. Nelson A. Rockefeller arranged the transfer of air rights over the boulevard section, from 62d to 71st Streets, to Rockefeller University and New York Hospital. Now the first university building has gone up, bridging the drive at 62d Street and blocking out the Manhattan tower of the 59th Street Bridge, and New York Hospital is studying the use of its air rights. The agreement has a cutoff date of 2003 for new construction.

This section of the drive is probably eligible for landmark designation—it is more than 30 years old and other roadways like Riverside Drive and Eastern Parkway in Brooklyn have been designated.

But landmark regulation would not be received enthusiastically by the city and state, which have to maintain the drive, and certainly not by the institutions themselves.

Don't hold your breath for historic preservation to encompass our historic highways; it's easier to ignore the topic entirely.

LONG ISLAND CITY POWER STATION

A 1906 Railroad Landmark on the Queens Shoreline

Long Island City Power Station on East River above Newtown Creek, 1907.

THE CITY'S HUNTERS POINT development project—a combination housing-retail office complex for the Queens shoreline just above Newtown Creek—will begin its preliminary reviews in June.

The project is a joint venture of the city's Public Development Corporation and the Port Authority, and their environmental consultants are now scouring the 92-acre area for possible landmarks, like the Pepsi-Cola sign, so they are aware of potentially significant buildings.

But the area's most prominent waterfront landmark, the 1906 Long Island City Power Station, lies just outside the project boundary. Although the huge red brick complex and its four great smokestacks are not in the way of any planned development, unusual structural conditions may make it an attractive site for private development, if the city's project actually gets off the ground.

The Penn. Central Railroad and the Long Island Rail Road long envied the New York Central's in-town terminal, Grand Central; their own passengers had to transfer to ferries at Jersey City and Long Island City, respectively, to get to Manhattan.

Plans were proposed in the 1880's and 1890's to remedy the situation, but it was not until 1900, when the Pennsylvania took over the Long Island Rail Road, that a terminus in Manhattan actually materialized. The Pennsylvania's directors decided to bring their trains under the Hudson by tunnel to the new, grand Pennsylvania Station—and then keep on tunneling under the East River to connect with the Long Island Rail Road.

To supply electricity for tunnel service, the railroad built a power plant in Long Island City between Second and Fifth Streets, from 50th to 51st Avenues. Completed in 1906, the Long Island City Power Plant consisted of two sections, one with coal-fired boilers producing steam, and the other with turbines to convert the steam to electricity. The power plant was built on a bed of over 9,000 piles, covered by a layer of concrete six feet thick.

The boiler house, with four 275-foot-high smokestacks that still dominate the Queens shoreline, held two levels of coal-fired boilers, 64 in all. The steam was piped to the adjacent engine house, where three turbine generators produced over 16,000 kilowatts.

Coal was brought to the boiler house by barge, scooped up at the shoreline by large clamshell buckets to a great overhead rail line, 100 feet up. Small coal cars ran on the rails and entered the boiler house at its peak, dumping their coal into a huge attic coal pocket for the boilers below.

The mechanical systems were designed by Westinghouse, Church, Kerr & Company, but the exterior was designed by McKim, Mead & White, who were also at work on Penn Station. The exterior is imposing, but not inspired, a solid first floor of rock-faced stone, with the upper walls of deep red brick. "Pennsylvania," in terra-cotta letters, is really the only decoration.

On September 8, 1910, "Tunnel Day" was observed, and a new era in rail service for New Jersey, Manhattan and Long Island was inaugurated, although Penn Station itself would not be completely operational until 1911.

But even on opening day, advances in electrical generation by the Edison Company were beginning to render private power plants obsolete. According to the Long Island Rail Road historian, Vincent Seyfried, the Long Island City Power Plant was shut down in the early 1920's, and the boilers, turbines and elevated railway were later removed.

In the 1950's, the railroad sold off the vacant boiler house to the Metropolitan Plumbing Company and the turbine house to the Schwartz Chemical Company.

The Schwartz Company occupies the ground floor of its section, but it leases out the vast turbine floor to a tennis operation. Lessons are given there under an 80-foot-high ceiling with a traveling hoist, installed for the repair of the giant turbines, still in place.

The engine house is used by Metropolitan as a gigantic storehouse for plumbing parts, from small faucets to eight-foot-high gate valves. The upper two floors are each about 100 feet by 200 feet by 45 feet high. Above a great carpet of plumbing fittings rises a rain forest of columns, girders, catwalks and, at each corner, a huge black smokestack base. Spidery stairways take you up as high as you dare to go.

Carl Schwartz, president of the company, thinks the power plant site would be a good one for a building like the one Citibank is building several blocks away, 46 stories high. "The midtown and the railroad tunnels run on either side of the area," Mr. Schwartz said, and driving new foundations would be extremely complicated. But the power station foundation, cleared of its buildings, provides another opportunity. "This foundation," he said, "could support the World Trade Center."

PUBLIC SCHOOL 72

A Big, Solid Centenarian That Still Exudes Potential

Public School 72 on 106th Street and Lexington Avenue in Manhattan.

SCHOOL BUILDINGS HAD been put up in the village of Harlem as early as the 1840's. But by the 1870's the arrival of the elevated lines on Second and Third Avenues encouraged tenement and row-house construction, and in 1879 the Board of Education filed plans for a school stretching along the entire blockfront on the west side of Lexington Avenue from 105th to 106th Streets, the first such in the city.

David I. Stagg, then Superintendent of School Buildings, designed a symmetrical structure to be erected in two parts; the south half was completed in 1881, the north half in 1882. Stagg had begun his career as 1834 as carpenter for the city's schools, and at his death in 1887 the *New York Tribune* wrote that every one of the more than 300 school buildings in the city had been designed or altered by him.

His manner, according to the *Tribune's* obituary, was "somewhat austere with strangers," a habit it said he adopted because he was often approached by contractors seeking to bribe him. There is at least presumptive evidence that he did not enrich himself: the 1880 census shows that he and his wife took in six boarders in their house on St. Luke's Place.

The new school, Public School 72, accommodated 1,800 elementary school students. There were four floors of classrooms, with a janitor's apartment in a penthouse in the center of the fifth floor.

Education officials were concerned about the danger of fire, and the new P.S. 72 had seven slate-and-iron stairways in enclosed stair towers. Later, two additional exterior staircases were added to serve the second floor on the south end.

Today the interior of the building, now vacant, appears largely intact. There are 36 large, square classrooms on either side of a wide north–south corridor, all with 14-foot-high ceilings and high windows both to the outside and to the hallway; the ones on the hall are set higher.

The finishes are simple—plaster walls and bits of stained wood—and the ceilings are covered in pressed tin.

At the south end of the building, on the second and fourth floors, were large assembly rooms. The structural columns in these areas are fluted and carry elaborate composite capitals in cast iron. Originally these larger rooms were used for indoor play, recitation and evening lectures, but they have rolling wooden partitions that could change them into individual classrooms. Bathrooms for students appear to have been only on the ground floor.

The exterior of the building has elements of the neo-Grec and the mid-19th-century version of the Renaissance style often seen in municipal architecture. But the overall symmetry, the regularity of the window openings and the absence of any element that says "school" also impart a near-industrial air.

Indeed, in June 1887, a month after Stagg's death, the *Real Estate Record & Guide* called the city's school buildings "a shame . . . the same old stereotyped boxes." Later writers often compared schools of this era to factories, and by the turn of the century Stagg's work was in low repute.

A red-brick addition went up on 105th Street in 1912, but otherwise very little changed about P.S. 72 as long as it was a school—it still provided large classrooms, high and light, with good ventilation. But in 1975 the Board of Education surrendered the school to the Board of Estimate. The city leased it to a variety of community groups, and minor changes were made to allow office use.

The building was vacated last year to make way for a proposed 48-family "transitional shelter" sponsored by the city, but the plan was defeated by the Board of Estimate in December, and today the building remains vacant. Though there are signs of neglect in old P.S. 72— pigeons that are working their way downstairs through broken windows at the top—the simple, functional elegance of the building is unimpaired.

With its high windows, broad corridors and tin ceilings, it is as delicious an artifact as a century-old brownstone that has escaped modernization.

Fitting practical new uses to old buildings is always a chancy thing, but this structure cries out for an imaginative recycling. It could be converted into artists' studios, or even reconverted into a school.

SEAMAN-DRAKE ARCH

Encrusted Relic of a Mid-19th-Century Inwood Estate

The Seaman-Drake Arch on the west side of Broadway at 215th Street, circa 1908.

IT IS ONE OF the most unusual structures in upper Manhattan, a 35-foot-high, 20-foot-deep marble arch on the west side of Broadway at 215th Street. Built as the gateway to a hilltop estate in 1855, it is now surrounded by one- and two-story structures concealing most of its lower portion.

The soft marble is gradually deteriorating and the structure's roof is gone, leaving its interior open to the sky. But the Seaman-Drake Arch retains much of its original grandeur, and it can still provoke amazement in passersby.

In 1851, the Seaman family, whose forebears settled on Long Island in 1653, bought a commanding hilltop site a half-mile north of the Dyckman family home at 204th Street and Broadway, which was built in 1783. Directories and other sources indicate that in 1855 the Seamans built a great marble house on the site, using stone from a quarry at the foot of the hill along Broadway. Near the quarry site they also erected a marble entrance arch set back from the street, with a winding drive up to the house itself. According to Sidney Horenstein, a geologist with the American Museum of Natural History, this vein of marble extends all the way to quarries at Tuckahoe, which supplied the marble for St. Patrick's Cathedral.

The arch's 40-foot-wide street facade had two large niches for statuary and two plain inset panels flanking a central barrel-vaulted archway. A projecting cornice, still intact, across the top of the arch is supported on carved acanthus-leaf modillions.

Iron pivots for what must have been a huge iron gate across the vaulted passageway still survive, but the door and window openings on the ground-floor level are blocked up. On the upper section of the rear of the arch are a half-dozen window openings, apparently original, suggesting that it was once a gatekeeper's quarters.

From the tops of adjacent buildings the remains of stairs and plaster walls can be seen in the arch's interior; a fire in about 1970 left it open to the sky.

The marble house on the hilltop was apparently intended as a country residence for seasonal occupancy, and the Seamans are only irregularly listed as having lived there rather than at their downtown addresses. The principal occupant apparently was James F. Seaman, a merchant, who married Ann Drake. In an 1883 will she bequeathed "my marble house, grounds and outbuildings . . . furniture and plate" to her nephew, Lawrence Drake.

The extent of Drake's occupancy is not clear, but the grounds remained intact until the turn of the century. In 1897, the main house was occupied by the Suburban Riding and Driving Club, of which Drake was a member.

In 1905, the house and arch were sold to Thomas Dwyer, a contractor who had built the Soldiers' and Sailors' Monument and part of the Metropolitan Museum of Art. Dwyer occupied the house and used the arch for his business, adding a story to it and attaching painted signs. In 1912 the first of a series of low brick buildings began to surround the arch, forming a kind of compound; photographs of the period show this compound occupied by a succession of car dealerships, which used the arch as an entranceway.

Dwyer sold the main house and the property for apartment development in 1938; only the arch has survived.

Since the 60's it has been occupied by Jack Gallo Auto Body, and dented cars now rest under the arch, awaiting entry to the main shop just behind it.

The marble is decaying, depositing small piles of silvery grains where water drips, and the entire structure is as worn as the steps of an ancient cathedral. The owner of record of the arch is Glendale Management Corporation, in care of Joseph Mantione Jr., who declined to discuss the property.

There is not much real-estate development in Inwood, and nothing left to burn inside the arch itself; the main threat to the arch's survival seems to be New York's acidic atmosphere and rain. Until it falls or is taken down, the venerable Seaman-Drake Arch will probably continue to serve as a gateway, though of a quite different sort than that originally imagined.

The author married a Drake in 1980 and has enjoyed many happy visits to the Jack Gallo Auto Body Shop.

MANUFACTURERS HANOVER TRUST AT FIFTH AND 43d

A Convertible Bank Adrift in a Landmarks Limbo

Manufacturers Hanover Bank branch on Fifth Avenue at 43d Street in 1954.

DURING THE DEPRESSION, the sight of defunct banks—the padlocks on their doors belying what had been a long reputation for reliability—bothered Horace Flanigan. He wondered whether bank buildings could be designed so as to make them convertible to other uses if need be.

When Mr. Flanigan became president of Manufacturers Trust Company in 1951, he had a chance to do something about it. A new branch at the southwest corner of 43d Street and Fifth Avenue was to be constructed and he called on Skidmore, Owings & Merrill to design it.

The firm held an in-house competition for a design for a building that could be converted to other uses and Charles E. Hughes 3d won the contest—and $50.

To make sure of its adaptability, he showed the model to a publisher and a department-store president, according to a 1957 article in the *Saturday Evening Post*. The publisher offered to take the building off his hands before ground was broken.

The design, refined by Gordon Bunshaft, a partner in the firm, and others would express openness and accessibility where other bank buildings had expressed solidity and safety. Construction was completed in 1954 and the building received enthusiastic reviews and awards from the Muncipal Art Society, the American Institute of Architects and other organizations.

It was notable on several accounts. At five stories, it was dwarfed by the surrounding 1920's skyscrapers, like the 60-story 500 Fifth Avenue next door. Instead of the customary skin of brick and stone, the new bank had a wall of aluminum and glass, with some panes 9 by 22 feet, the largest ever installed in a building.

The bank's ceilings were made of translucent plastic panels, above which was placed cathode-tube lighting. The glow gave the building volume and eliminated the reflectivity that makes other glass buildings simply black, mirrored facades.

Inside, it was more like an airline ticket office than a traditional bank, with wide-open spaces, escalators, no teller cages and, on the second floor, a great, golden steel sculpture by Harry Bertoia.

The main floor, originally designed for briefer banking transactions, like check cashing, was of regular height. The second floor was really the main banking space, nearly twice the height of a regular story, resting on a cantilevered floor set back from the outer wall. This

setback, the thinness of the aluminum mullions and the glowing ceilings led writers to describe the building as a floating bank.

Only one element identified the building as a bank—a great 30-ton Mosler safe with a seven-foot-wide door that stood a shockingly small distance behind the Fifth Avenue plate-glass window. The safe, whose door was kept open during the day, signaled a revolution in banking symbolism. The *AIA Guide to New York City*, by Norval White and Elliot Willensky, said that the Manufacturers Trust Company building "led the banking profession out of the cellar and onto the street."

The bank merged with the Hanover Bank in 1961 to form Manufacturers Hanover Trust Company, but changes to the building have been minor. Signs and an automatic teller machine now block part of the Fifth Avenue windows and additional furniture and some office dividers on the first and second floors detract from the original expansiveness of the interior.

In 1979, the Landmarks Preservation Commission called the building "a classic of the International Style" but noted that it had "not yet reached the 30-year minimum age required for designation." But the commission held hearings on the building in September 1985 and others that November and December and a final one in March 1986.

Both the owner of the land, Mutual Life Insurance Company of New York, and the bank, which has a leasehold agreement, opposed designation. Under existing zoning regulations, and free of other constraints, the site could be redeveloped with a tower of about 30 stories.

According to a 1981 letter written by Kent Barwick, chairman of the commission until 1983, the Landmarks Commission had long observed a "two-year rule" for designations—dropping the proposal for a property "if no action has been taken within two years of the original hearing."

But Lillian Ayala, a spokeswoman for the commission, says there is no such rule, just a vague guideline of "about two to three years" and no specific cutoff. On September 11 three years will have elapsed from the original hearing. The bank is now "neutral on designation," according to John Meyers, a vice president, but Mutual Life Insurance of New York would not comment on its position and the designation remains in limbo.

By 1990 the bank was opposed to designation.

CITY AND SUBURBAN HOMES

East Side Women's Hotel
Built Among Tenements

The Junior League Hotel for Working Women in 1913.

EVER SINCE PETER S. Kalikow bought the City and Suburban Homes buildings in 1984, tenants and community groups have been fighting his announced plans, first to replace all, and then only part of the complex with high-rise luxury apartments. The buildings cover the whole block between 78th and 79th Streets, the East River Drive and York Avenue.

As part of that battle, the Coalition to Save City and Suburban Homes asked the Landmarks Preservation Commission to save the assemblage, and now the commission has announced that it will hold a hearing, probably in September, on a proposal to designate the complex of model tenements for historical and architectural significance.

The complex, although not really elegant, does have a certain harmony, even though its one distinctive building was completely rebuilt in 1979 by a previous owner.

The block was, at the turn of the century, a vacant island in a sea of tenements, factories and light industry. The City and Suburban Homes Company, founded in 1896 by philanthropists seeking to demonstrate that humanely designed tenements could produce an attractive financial return, began constructing their 13 model tenements on the York Avenue end of the block in 1901. Building in groups of two or three, by 1913 they had covered most of the block with six-story apartment houses that yielded a return of 4 percent on their investment.

But for one lot, at the northwest corner of 78th Street and the East River, City and Suburban joined with the Junior League of New York to erect in 1910–12 an unusual residence specifically for single women. The League, which was founded in 1901 to encourage young women of privilege to engage in charitable work, supported and supervised the social-service project, called the Junior League Hotel for Working Women.

Like the rest of the model tenements, the new hotel was a plain buff Milwaukee brick with marble trim but with neo-Renaissance touches, such as rusticated piers and Florentine arches at the fifth floor. The entrance was in a central archway now on the noisy East River Drive but originally facing quiet Exterior Street. The building was designed by Philip Ohm, who also designed many tenements on the site.

Its distinctive features were a series of great open balconies in the middle and pergolas on the roof. With the exception of private residences like Gracie Mansion, the Junior League Hotel was apparently the first riverfront building on the East Side to acknowledge its unusual siting.

The hotel contained 102 apartments, most with two and three rooms, and the communal facilities included a dining room, sewing and typewriting rooms, an electric piano, and basketball and tennis courts on the roof. There were also "beau parlors" where woman could entertain male guests with some degree of privacy.

In 1913, there were 317 residents including 40 stenographers, 32 dressmakers, 18 librarians, 14 milliners and 5 telegraphers, among other occupations. They paid from $4 to $7 a week including board. The

Evening Post (whose lineal descendant, the *New York Post*, is now owned by Mr. Kalikow) was impressed by the Junior League's work on the project, editorializing: "We commend their activities to those pessimists who are convinced of the degeneracy, selfishness and general uselessness of the rising generation of the well-to-do."

Sometime in the 1920's the Junior League severed its connection with the project, but it was still operated as a women's residence, the East End Hotel.

In the 1940's the East River Drive, an express highway, put an end to the quiet "dead end" character of the block. The hotel remained largely unchanged until 1979, when a subsequent owner completely rebuilt it into 184 apartments. In the process, the public rooms were eliminated, the main entrance was replaced with one on 78th Street, the riverfront balconies were filled in and the majestic rooftop pergolas were shorn off, replaced by an additional story.

What had been an unusual, if plain, building became simply plain. In 1984, Mr. Kalikow acquired the block, ran into opposition to its demolition and subsequently announced plans to raze only the four easternmost buildings—including the former hotel—and replace them with a residential tower. Nikki Henken, a spokeswoman for Kalikow 78/79th Associates, which owns the complex, said that the old Junior League Hotel is now 60 percent vacant, and that the company still hopes to redevelop the site.

Landmark protection has already been extended to an unusual arts-and-crafts style group of model tenements between 77th and 78th Streets. At the adjoining City and Suburban Homes block, the commission will have to weigh the historical and social significance of a less distinctive assemblage.

While searching for an old photograph to go with this story I made repeated calls to the preservation group. Over a dozen calls and a letter to their putative archivist went unreturned—which struck me as strange, considering that they were hungry for press coverage. Finally I was told, abruptly, that they had no old photos whatsoever. This seemed really bizarre, since what was described as a major research effort had been underway for several years. Soon they published their own history—with plenty of old photos—and the truth came out. Despite the fact that mine was the first letter in the Commission's file to support landmark protection, and that I had declined the request of the owner's architect to serve as the owner's expert against designation (this was before I worked at the Times), my article was perceived as potentially hostile and they thought that by denying me information they could kill the article. This pretty much sums up the problem of depending on our preservation community for neutral historical inquiry.

The Commission designated the entire block, but the Board of Estimate vetoed coverage of the riverfront parcels, and the matter is still the subject of litigation by the preservation group.

GAINSBOROUGH STUDIOS

The Restoration of a 1908 Co-op

The 30-unit, 16-story Gainsborough Studios at 222 Central Park South, in 1908.

TRADITIONALLY, CONTRACTORS AND vendors are wary in responding to initial inquiries from co-op boards, who represent shareholders wanting to keep costs down. But an object lesson that confounds this truism is now nearing completion at the art-encrusted Gainsborough Studios at 222 Central Park South.

For in the last eight years, the 80-year-old co-op has elected to spend more than $1 million on essentially cosmetic restoration.

Co-ops and artists' studios had enjoyed a symbiotic relationship since the first co-op, the Rembrandt, was built at 154 West 57th Street in 1881, the result of a joint venture among several artists. By the early 1900's, artist-entrepreneurs were erecting studio-cooperatives as a serious business.

But the facade and interior of the 30-unit, 16-story Gainsborough, between Seventh Avenue and Broadway, are anything but businesslike. The ground-floor exterior is an ornate, but not remarkable, arrangement of white terra-cotta and granite Ionic columns. Above this ran a frieze, now removed, by Isidore Konti, representing a procession of people bringing gifts to the altar of the arts. In the middle, in a shallow niche, was a bust of the painter Thomas Gainsborough above a palette.

Starting at the second floor are two bays of large studio windows, with elaborate detailing, flanked by three brick piers. At the seventh floor, the brick piers are faced with multicolored tiles in a geometric design. The roof is crowned not with a projecting cornice, which would cut down on the light for the studios facing north, but with a restrained treatment of shell forms in terra-cotta.

It is difficult to say whether Mr. Konti or the building's architect, Charles W. Buckham, was primarily responsible for the exterior, but the interior plan was no doubt Mr. Buckham's work.

While there are conventional apartments at the rear, the front apartments are all duplexes, each with a two-story living room overlooked by a sleeping balcony. Many of the duplexes—with art tile fireplaces, leaded glass cabinetry and mahogany and oak woodwork—were apparently custom-designed for their initial occupants.

While Mr. Buckham, who died in 1951 and was considered a pioneer in designing duplex apartment houses, was responsible for at least two others, only his Gainsborough survives in New York City.

Although studio co-ops were already attracting nonartists in 1908, the Gainsborough had only a sprinkling of others among its initial residents.

Research by Virginia Kurshan at the New York City Landmarks Preservation Commission indicates that August Franzen, president of the original building corporation, was a prominent Swedish-born portrait painter—and an admirer of Gainsborough. Other residents included Elliott Daingerfield and Montague Flagg, both artists; William Ordway Partridge, a sculptor, and Thomas Janvier, a travel writer.

Over the years, the building was sandwiched between taller structures that were built on Central Park South. In the 1950's, Donald Deskey, an interior designer who lived in the building, oversaw a lobby modernization that, among other things, replaced the original elaborate iron doors with modern aluminum ones.

But the clock was turned back in 1981, when the corporation spent about $100,000 to restore the lobby, including reproducing new doors modeled from old photographs. Then, the condition of the facade prompted a five-year project, not just to make it safe, but to actually restore it.

The face of the tiles at the top had cracked off beyond the point of salvage, so new tiles to match the old ones have just been installed. The bust of Gainsborough and the frieze, severely deteriorated, have been removed, and reproductions will be installed in August or September. The building was designated a landmark early this year, but only after the work was near completion.

Simply making the exterior of the building safe would have cost about $50,000. But Tod Williams, an architect and shareholder who has overseen part of the project, said the restoration had cost in excess of $1 million.

Adelaide de Menil, president of the Gainsborough's board of directors, explains that the owners wanted to take "the right way as opposed to the cheap way." Referring to a nearby hotel on 62d Street and Central Park West, which was stripped of its ornament early in the 1980's to widespread dismay, she said:

"Everyone in the building felt strongly about the Gainsborough. We didn't want it to be like the Mayflower."

BRONX BOROUGH COURTHOUSE

For an Abandoned Civic Landmark, a Second Life?

The Bronx Borough Courthouse, Third Avenue at 161st Street, in 1914.

IT IS NOW not much more than a huge pigeon coop—abandoned and windowless. But the grandeur of the Bronx Borough Courthouse still comes as a surprise as a motorist rounds the bend of Third Avenue heading toward 161st Street in the Melrose section.

Built between 1905 and 1914 and abandoned in 1978, the building is one of many empty shells in a neighborhood with vacant lots and fire-damaged apartment houses. But the Borough President, Fernando Ferrer, hopes to renovate it as part of a larger program of courthouse construction. The pigeons may soon have to roost elsewhere.

In 1903, the newly consolidated City of New York filed plans for a new $800,000 courthouse on the trapezoidal block bounded by 161st and 162d Streets and Third and Brook Avenues, part of a larger citywide movement for new municipal structures.

A prime force in the movement was Louis Haffen, whose family had long operated a neighborhood brewery, and who had become the first Borough President of the Bronx in 1897.

Mr. Haffen retained as architect Michael J. Garvin, described by the *New York Tribune* as "a close personal and political associate of the Borough President." Mr. Garvin left his job as Commissioner of Buildings for the Bronx to take the courthouse commission, and around the same time, designed the Jefferson Tammany Hall at the southwest corner of 159th Street and Elton Avenue for the local Democratic organization.

Mr. Garvin proposed an all-granite building, four stories high, in the Beaux-Arts style, called at the time "modern French." But as soon as construction began in 1905, Oscar Bluemner, an architect and artist, sued Mr. Garvin for $20,000, alleging that Mr. Garvin had retained him actually to design the building, promising money and recognition.

But when the plans were approved, Mr. Garvin "turned the cold shoulder to me," Mr. Bluemner told the *New York Times*. Mr. Garvin "couldn't draw the plans for a big thing like the new courthouse to save his life," Mr. Bluemner was quoted in the *Times*. "He is a fairly good architect of tenements, but that is all."

Mr. Garvin denied Mr. Bluemner's assertions, but in 1906 a court found in Mr. Bluemner's favor, awarding him $10,201.

The courthouse was supposed to take two years to build, but when it finally opened in January 1914, the *Times* reported that by then the project had become a standing joke "with two or three laborers digging when they were not engaged in lighting their pipes and smoking."

There had been public protest meetings over the delays, Mr. Haffen was forced out of office in 1909 amid charges of corruption, and even at the official opening many rooms were incomplete. Invited guests had to stand, as only a table and chair had arrived.

The completed structure was the most imposing municipal building in the Bronx—a great angular block of granite with a marble statue representing Justice in a central bay. Although generally Beaux-Arts in style, it had elements of the sophisticated Art Nouveau style that was sweeping Europe at the time of the design.

The huge hemisphere-topped finials at the roof, stone balusters at the first floor in a similar style, and the unusual handling of the window enframements are so original as to corroborate the claims of Mr. Bluemner, who was a medalist of the Royal Academy of Berlin.

The building housed three courtrooms, a coroner's office and cells, all organized along a great east–west hallway with leaded glass walls at each end, of which only occasional shreds now survive.

In 1934, the Bronx County Courthouse was built at 161st Street and the Grand Concourse, and the older building continued to be used as an adjunct courthouse until 1977, when all court operations moved elsewhere. The Bronx Borough Courthouse was sealed on the first and second floors in the early 1980's, and isolated fragments of the iron trim of the doorway project like forlorn skeletons beyond the cinderblock.

In 1981, the building was designated by the Landmarks Preservation Commission, making demolition very unlikely, but without assuring any reuse.

But in 1987 Mr. Ferrer proposed a renovation of the structure as part of a larger courthouse-construction program now under way.

A new roof was installed to stop water damage, and the Department of General Services has determined that the building can be economically rehabilitated.

The New York State Office of Court Administration is studying how best to reuse the structure, and Mr. Ferrer is seeking $6 million to bring Mr. Garvin's—or perhaps Mr. Bluemner's—"big thing" back to life.

116 JOHN STREET
Déjà Vu in Zoning Dispute

Office tower at 116 John Street, center, built in 1931, rising above 111 John Street, right, in a photo made in 1951.

THE ARGUMENT OVER the height of 116 John Street, which was built 58 years ago, sounds just like the current zoning dispute case at 108 East 96th Street, a dispute that has caught the public's attention because it is so unusual.

In the current case, a 31-story apartment building developed by Albert Ginsberg appears to have 12 illegal floors, a situation that the Board of Standards and Appeals will consider again on August 9.

In both cases, neighbors complained that the buildings were too tall, even though they had initial approval from the Department of Buildings. The owners continued construction, even though there was a possibility that any illegal portion would have to be demolished. In the case of 116 John Street, the Board of Standards and Appeals upheld the validity of the building permit. At 108 East 96th, the final decision is still pending.

There was a similar controversy over the legality of the office tower at 116 John Street, built in 1930 by the Platt Holding Corporation.

At first glance, 116 John Street, which also fronts on Pearl and Platt Streets, is no different than other downtown office buildings of the same period. It has a mild Art Deco facade that rises 22 stories along the building line wall with setback floors extending to the 35th story.

The lobby has some nice touches—dark-veined marble and metalwork around the doorways—but it is otherwise just an average office building. But looking west on John Street there is a noticeable difference between 116 and its neighbor, 111 John Street, which was built only a year earlier.

The 111 building, then owned by 111 John Street Corporation, begins its setback at about 120 feet, at the 11th floor. But the setbacks on 116 begin about 250 feet up, at the 23d floor. To the builders of 111 John, the zoning law required setbacks to begin at 129 feet for structures at the northwestern corner of John and Pearl Streets. With setbacks beginning at this level, the total height of 111 John Street was kept to 26 stories.

But a year later, the builders of 116 John Street at the southwestern corner of Pearl Street came up with a novel interpretation of the zoning law—yes, the 129-foot setback was required for a building at that corner, barring other considerations. But John Street becomes Burling Slip as it crosses Pearl Street. If the slightly wider Burling Slip, 600 feet long, could be considered a public place, as if it were a park, then the setbacks could begin at the 23d floor, producing a correspondingly higher building—35 floors, in fact.

The architect in charge of the project, Charles Glaser, later testified before the Board of Standards and Appeals that he reviewed the "public place" idea with the chief engineer of the Department of Buildings, Charles Bastress.

"I didn't want to prepare plans for a 35-story building and have fault found with them," Mr. Glaser said. Mr. Bastress approved the concept and construction began in July 1930.

The owner of the neighboring property, the 111 John Street Corporation, first became aware of the higher setbacks being used next door in late September, when they received a renting circular showing the actual configuration of the building. Noting that they, 111 John Street, had 638 windows facing John Street and would receive less sunlight if the extra floors were allowed, they began an appeals process in early October that culminated in a Board of Standards and Appeals hearing in November 1930—when the steel framing on 116 John Street was substantially complete.

In the minutes of the meeting, the board seemed particularly sympathetic to the plight of the owners at 116 John Street, but did not delve too deeply into the concept of a street being considered a park or public place.

It upheld the validity of the building permit, and 116 John Street was completed in accordance with its original designs.

John P. Comer, in his book *New York City Building Control* of 1942, said he believed that there was no merit to the public place interpretation and that the board did not "dare to risk the enforcement of the law against such a costly fait accompli."

In 1931, Mr. Bastress was indicted for taking a bribe to approve a building permit at 280 Madison Avenue, and later convicted of that charge amid a wide-ranging investigation of Mayor Jimmy Walker's administration.

Buildings Commissioner Charles Brady—who had strongly defended the public place theory before the Board of Standards and Appeals—disappeared from New York City as other criminal indictments were handed down, although no one ever specifically asserted that 116 John Street received illegal favors.

The Department of Buildings was reorganized, and Mayor Walker resigned under a cloud in 1932, in part because of irregularities in cases like 116 John Street.

CBS STUDIO ON 52d

At One Time, the "Last Word in Broadcasting Design"

Right: Vanderbilt guest house, 49 East 52nd Street, in 1910. Far right: The building in 1940, after CBS renovated it.

THE MUSEUM OF THE CITY OF NEW YORK

AVERY LIBRARY

FOR NEARLY 50 YEARS it was one of the most unusual buildings in midtown, with a seven-story-high modernistic facade, blank except for a strip of windows at the top. But earlier this year the ground-floor studio space in the CBS Studio Building at 49 East 52d Street was taken over by a Duane Reade drugstore, and a storefront has now replaced the ground floor's 50-foot expanse of gray and blue terra-cotta blocks.

The CBS Studio Building began life in 1908 as a guest house for the Vanderbilt family; they built it as a supplement to their Victorian mansions along Fifth Avenue. Guests were apparently not forthcoming because in 1924 the giant English Renaissance style building—designed by Warren & Wetmore—was sold to the Juilliard Musical Foundation as auxiliary space for its school, then at 120th Street and Clermont Avenue.

In 1927, the Columbia Broadcasting System, following the National Broadcasting Corporation by a year, organized a second nationwide broadcasting network.

CBS made its quarters in an otherwise unremarkable office building at 485 Madison Avenue, at the southeast corner of 52d Street. It was from this building that Orson Welles broadcast his famous *War of the Worlds* radio program in 1938. Broadcasting facilities were carved out of the building, but the continuing growth of the radio industry required more technologically advanced studios, and CBS bought the old Vanderbilt Building from Juilliard, completely renovating it in 1939–1940.

Designed by Fellheimer & Wagner, the new studio building was "the last word in broadcasting design" according to an article in *Architectural Forum* in 1940. The building contained seven studios—including two double-height ones—control rooms, equipment rooms and areas for sound effects, testing and acoustical research.

The larger studios could seat 300 people and accommodate live, network-organized symphony and orchestra performances, which were standard radio fare for the period.

The latest soundproofing techniques were employed—perforated asbestos wall panels, faceted ceilings, nonparallel studio walls and a special system of Acoustivanes, fields of movable, winglike vanes that could be pivoted to form a flat, hard surface, or be opened to reveal more absorbent surfaces behind them.

Because of the soundproofing requirements, the CBS building had few windows, and the facade was almost entirely a vast expanse of white stucco with a ground-floor wall of terra-cotta blocks. The only outright decoration was a simple neon sign, "CBS," above the main entrance.

It was a striking Modernist statement sandwiched between a 1920's office building and some 1850's row houses; the absence of windows proclaimed the strange new arts practice inside.

But by the 1950's the tradition of live studio broadcasts had dwindled and the Records Division of CBS began to use the building for recording. Among the many artists who have used the building are Frank Sinatra, Barbra Streisand and Paul Simon—whose father had been a violinist for Arthur Godfrey's radio show in the same building in the 1940's.

In 1965, CBS moved into its new corporate headquarters at 51 West 52d Street, diminishing the importance of the East 52d Street building. In that year CBS sold the building, but remained as a lessee, and in 1979 the Fisher Brothers—planning their massive Park Avenue Plaza office building at 55 East 52d Street—acquired the site in part to protect the sunlight that would reach their new building.

Now the CBS building is a shadow of its former self. The studios are filled, not with performers—not even recording goes on there now—but with file cabinets, and are used by CBS as office and technical space. Receptionists sit incongruously in windowed control rooms.

The white stucco has been painted a chocolate brown and the neon tubing of the CBS sign is broken; it hasn't been lit in years. The Duane Reade drugstore—with its massive roll-down gates—further compromises the stark simplicity of the facade.

But there are still enough flourishes to attract the informed observer—an amazing streamlined stairway to the basement with chrome accents and recessed lighting, the irregular curving hallways upstairs, hugging the asymmetrical studios, and the remaining terra-cotta and stainless-steel detailing at the entry. Despite the changes, the CBS Studio Building has not entirely lost the power to startle and please.

MARINE ROOF, HOTEL BOSSERT

Famed Nightclub, Long Adrift, Sinking into Oblivion

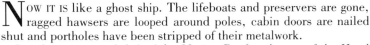

The Marine Roof atop the Hotel Bossert in 1916.

Hotel, in 1909, at Montague and Hicks Streets, Brooklyn.

Now IT IS like a ghost ship. The lifeboats and preservers are gone, ragged hawsers are looped around poles, cabin doors are nailed shut and portholes have been stripped of their metalwork.

But there is enough left of the Marine Roof at the top of the Hotel Bossert to hint at the lost magic of what was once one of Brooklyn's premiere nightclubs. The Watchtower Bible and Tract Society is completing an extensive renovation of the building, the crowning touch of which will be an elaborate copper mansard addition that will wipe out the last traces of the Marine Roof.

By 1908 Louis Bossert had become rich from the lumber business he started in 1868 and he decided to build a modern hotel for Brooklyn comparable to those in Manhattan. The site he chose at Montague and Hicks Streets, on the southeast corner, was in what the *Brooklyn Eagle* called "the most aristocratic section of Brooklyn." Designed by Helmle & Huberty, the new hotel was in the Italian Renaissance style, with a great limestone Doric portico on Montague Street and an elaborate cornice with "HB" emblazoned on shields at the corners.

The ground floor contained a grand lobby and a Palm Room and, after an extension in 1912–1913 doubled the size of the building, a ballroom and dining room. On the upper floors were 375 rooms leased out on an annual basis.

Mr. Bossert was proud of his hotel and its place in Brooklyn. "It is his desire to retain it in his family as a permanent investment," said the *Real Estate Record and Guide*. The *Eagle* later called it "the Waldorf-Astoria of Brooklyn."

Mr. Bossert died in January 1913 aboard the liner *Cleveland* at the beginning of a projected four-month world cruise. His son Charles completed the extension, and the family indeed retained ownership.

Charles Bossert and his brother, John, were both avid yachtsmen—Charles was at one time commodore of the Bayside Yacht Club—and in 1916 they opened an unusual addition to their hotel, the Marine Roof.

Just as the original Bossert had been a notable improvement for Brooklyn, the Marine Roof was the first attraction of its kind for the borough, according to the *Record and Guide*.

The Marine Roof was a two-level restaurant–dance floor at the very top of the building. The restaurant ran along the Hicks Street side and had a panoramic view of the harbor and of Manhattan. In the rear, up half a flight of steps, was a rectangular dance floor with views of New York Bay and downtown Brooklyn.

Paul Schleich and John Smeraldi, who had designed other specialty rooms like the elaborate Japanese Tea Garden on the roof of the old Ritz-Carlton in Manhattan, designed the Marine Roof in a nautical theme, with smokestacks, life preservers, deck chairs and even lifeboats and davits. There were red and green running lights, a great searchlight and canvas roofing. It was meant to simulate "the promenade deck of a palatial private yacht, the height of comfort for a land-loving sailor," said the *Record and Guide*.

The Marine Roof was a success, attracting such notables as Jimmy Walker, Pola Negri, Al Smith and Rudy Vallee. The plan for the WQXR radio station was conceived there in 1935, Elliot Willensky wrote in his book *When Brooklyn Was the World*.

At some point the Marine Roof was glassed in and the sailcloth roofing replaced with galvanized iron, but it was still an important attraction.

The hotel had originally cost $1.5 million but in 1937, when the Bossert family lost it at foreclosure, it sold for only $200,000.

In 1948 the Marine Roof operation lost $30,000 and it closed in 1949. There were repeated attempts to reopen the roof "to entertain a new generation of romantics," according to one article, and it did apparently operate in the 1960's.

But by this time the Bossert was no longer a first-class hotel; it had a growing number of transients and elderly residents on limited incomes. In 1984, with the Marine Roof long closed, Watchtower bought the building as it expanded its world headquarters, located in the area since 1909.

The Watchtower is renovating the entire building, which is in the landmark Brooklyn Heights Historic District, and has carefully restored the lobby and rebuilt the deteriorated cornice.

It has also proposed a magnificent two-story-high copper mansard roof to enclose the old Marine Roof space, which it will totally rebuild. The Landmarks Preservation Commission rejected the original design in July as too prominent for a rooftop addition, but seems likely to approve a revised version and with that the old Marine Roof will disappear.

The Landmarks Commission approved a revised, more modest addition and the Marine Roof went to the bottom in 1990.

THE CENTRAL PARK STABLE

For a Police Station, Restoration of an 1870 Jewel

Drawing of the Central Park Stable in Central Park at 86th Street in 1870.

WHILE IT IS one of Manhattan's great Victorian Gothic buildings, generations of neglect and decay render it nearly invisible to the thousands who pass it every day on the 86th Street transverse in Central Park. But now restoration is planned for the 22d Police Precinct station house, erected in 1870 as the Central Park Stable, and the low brick-and-brownstone gem may finally emerge from its obscurity.

In designing Central Park, Frederick Law Olmsted and Calvert Vaux had to accommodate two large reservoirs north and south of the present transverse. That road and three other east–west transverses were brilliantly conceived, apparently based on English precedents, where depressed roadways screened urban traffic from park surroundings.

Service buildings, too, were meant to be screened from the park itself, and from 1869 to 1872 three structures, including the stable, went up in the relatively hidden space at about the center of the park between the transverse and the southerly reservoir. One is a workshop for repairing park equipment, with an exterior that mixes brick, cast iron and stone.

The middle structure—on the site of the present parking lot—was a reservoir-keeper's house, demolished in 1935. To the east of the house, squeezed by the curving transverse on the north and the sloping wall of what once was a reservoir on the south, is the station house, a low, triangular complex with the gateway facing the transverse.

The stable was built to accommodate 30 horses used to maintain the park, which by 1870 was nearing completion. Horses pulled wagons of earth and plants, were used to power winches for crude derricks and drew grass-cutting machines.

The stable is sometimes credited to Vaux but it is primarily the work of his associate, Jacob Wrey Mould, according to Joy Kestenbaum, who has studied the careers of both architects. At the time of its construction, Mould was chief architect of the Department of Public Parks.

It was actually three connected structures—open sheds backing up against the reservoir and a tiny supervisor's cottage and the stable itself on either side of an entry gate on the 86th Street transverse. At the center is a courtyard, originally containing a manure pit and two turntables for wagons. The wagons were stored in the open shed area.

The cottage is the most highly decorated structure in the stable complex, with inset multicolored tiles. But the buildings are largely similar in execution—a rough base course of granite, walls of random blocks of brownstone interspersed with brick and peaked roofs with low dormers and deep-set windows. Some of the original heavy paneled wooden doors survive and the dormer windows, which led to haylofts, have jerkin-head gables, some with hooks for hoisting hay up for storage.

The varied roof lines, the way the buildings follow the curve of the transverse and the rich contrasts between chocolate-colored brownstone, gray granite, deep red brick and color tile work make it a memorable structure once noticed.

In 1915, the open sheds on the south side were closed up but it was not until the South Reservoir was replaced by the Great Lawn in 1934 that the stable complex saw other major changes.

At that time, Robert Moses, then the city's Commissioner of Parks, needed more room in the arsenal building for the army of draftsmen busy with his various building campaigns and he decided to move the police station house—in the arsenal since before 1910—to the old stable. The building was gutted and the 22d Precinct moved into its new quarters early in 1936.

The reservoir-keeper's dwelling was demolished, and the present large parking lot was created. A second opening to the courtyard, from the parking lot, was also cut through.

Police station houses never seem to get careful maintenance, and the old stable building continued to deteriorate—doors sagged, windows rotted, roofs leaked and the brownstone blocks on the facade began to crumble.

In 1966, the city held a competition for a new public stable complex to occupy the parking lot site. Peter Samton, whose firm, Gruzen Samton Steinglass, won the competition, says that the old stable was slated to become a horse museum—but that the project died amid public controversy and the death of a private backer.

The Police Department planned to renovate its station house in the early 1970's and the project slowly moved forward.

In 1985, the city, in conjunction with the private Central Park Conservancy, commissioned a restoration study. Now design work is under way for a complete restoration of the exterior and renovation of the interior in 1990; the total cost is set at $4.7 million.

Project is now delayed for years.

THE RUSSIAN TEA ROOM

Sweet Deals Fail to Tempt
a West 57th Street Fixture

The Russian Tea Room, center, at 150 West 57th Street, in 1930's. Buildings on each side of it are gone.

WITH A KNIFE edge of Harry Macklowe's 78-story Metropolitan Tower on one side and the rising superstructure of Carnegie Hall Tower on the other, the Russian Tea Room on West 57th Street east of Seventh Avenue is Manhattan's newest holdout, a five-story, brownstone peanut of a building whose owner has so far resisted temptations to sell out.

Built as a private house in 1875 by a tea and coffee merchant, it was later converted into apartments and stores and since the 1920's it has housed the Russian Tea Room. The current proprietors declined to sell either air rights or the building itself—noting that the site could be rebuilt to a height of 18 stories.

John F. Pupke was living in a row house at 31 West 56th Street when he bought the lot running through the block from 153 West 56th Street to 150 West 57th Street in 1873. In that year, he built a two-story stable and coachman's dwelling on the 56th Street side. In 1876, he built a four-story brownstone on the 57th Street side of the lot.

Born in Germany, Pupke came to the United States in 1835, worked in the tea and coffee business and ultimately became president of Eppens, Smith and Wiemann, an importing firm on Washington Street.

Period photographs show a typical Italianate brownstone. A high stoop on the right led up to a columned portico at the parlor floor. The building was designed by John G. Prague, who specialized in row houses.

In 1886, Pupke built a conservatory in his larger than average garden, which extended to his stable.

He occupied the house with his wife, four children and three servants. By the time he died in 1898, this section of 57th Street had passed through a residential to a semipublic phase. Carnegie Hall, at Seventh Avenue, was built in 1891 and other artistic and cultural enterprises began to sprout on the street, some in the shells of the aging brownstones.

The Pupkes moved out of 150 around 1900 and the building was occupied by Mrs. William Eustis Munroe's School for Girls for a few years and then studio apartments. In 1919, the year the Pupke estate finally sold the house, the stoop was removed to allow for stores on the ground floor.

Although the date of the establishment of the Russian Tea Room is usually given as 1926, the business does not appear in directories until 1929. The founder is often considered to be Polish-born Jacob Zysman,

who operated a chocolate shop in a store at 145 West 57th Street, moving to 150 West 57th Street in 1929. But in that year a corporation directory gives Albertina Rasch as the president and her name appears along with "Russian Art Chocolate" and "Russian Tea Room" in early photographs of the shopfront.

The restaurant was indeed a tea room in its earliest days with wicker furniture, a light menu and silhouettes of ballet dancers on the walls. By 1933, Alexander (Sasha) Maeef was running the Russian Tea Room and the Siberian emigré was for the next 15 years the main personality associated with the restaurant.

In the 40's, said Rosalie Maeef, the restaurateur's widow, Georges Balanchine would arrive "with a ballerina on each arm." "The applause of an especially brilliant performance is often resumed at the restaurant," according to a pamphlet, "for more often than not the artist will come to the Russian Tea Room Restaurant straight from the performance, flowers and all."

Although in its earliest days the restaurant was a modest operation—sharing its storefront with Dale's Hosiery Shop—by the 1940's it had become a striking collection of rooms stretching back into the old stable—the Empire-style Casino Russe, the mural-covered Boyar Room, a nautical-style bar and the Moroccan-style Baghdad Room, with striped upholstery and columns, which opened for business at 2 A.M.

Maeef sold the business—including recipes for the Volga Cocktail and other specialties—in 1948 and the operation has passed through a series of owners. The building and business are now owned by Faith Stewart-Gordon. None of Maeef's unusual décor survives intact but upstairs changing rooms for the staff still contain woodwork and marble fireplaces from the Pupke era.

In 1981, as midtown development began to shift west, Faith Stewart-Gordon announced that the restaurant would add three floors and completely reface its building, but the project was never carried out.

By that time the assemblage for what became Harry Macklowe's Metropolitan Tower at 142 West 57th Street was under way but the developers were unable to buy the Russian Tea Room site or even its air rights. In May of this year foundations were completed for Carnegie Hall Tower at 152 West 57th Street on the other side of the Russian Tea Room; again the Tea Room had declined to sell its site or its air rights. "We could build up to 18 stories," said Mrs. Stewart-Gordon, adding that she had no plans to do so at the moment.

THE 125th STREET STATION

Metro-North Plans New Makeup, Not Plastic Surgery, for a Beauty

Stairway to rail platform at 125th Street station at Park Avenue.

IT HAS BEEN so neglected that it has the air of an abandoned building, even though 3,400 passengers use it daily. But now the Metro-North Commuter Railroad has put out to bid plans to renovate its 125th Street station at Park Avenue, which was built in 1897. Sometime next year the exterior will emerge from decades of neglect, but the long-hidden golden oak interior will simply get another coat of paint.

There was a low, turntable railroad bridge crossing the Harlem River at Park Avenue as early as 1840. After 1875, most of the grade-level tracks were sunk into an open cut at the center of the avenue and a modest station—really only waiting areas recessed under the flanking roadways—was built at 125th Street.

As river and rail traffic grew, the conflict between train schedules and waterway rights increased, and the low bridge delayed both types of traffic. The bridge was owned by the New York Central Railroad, but another competing line, the New York & Northern Railroad, had leasehold rights to use it for its own operations.

In 1890, as its trains were delayed more and more frequently, the New York & Northern told the War Department, which had authority over navigable waterways, that the bridge's clearance made it hazardous. The New York Central was forced to rebuild the bridge, and at first it promised to build a new station at 125th Street, under the new elevated tracks leading to the new, higher bridge. But neighboring property owners threatened to sue and succeeded in delaying construction, and the railroad threatened to eliminate the stop altogether.

"The Harlem station has never paid," Chauncey Depew, the president of the railroad, told a protest meeting called by local businessmen and residents like the impresario Oscar Hammerstein and the importer Cyrus L. Sulzberger.

But Harlem got its station, which opened in 1897 when the new bridge and viaduct went into service. It was designed by New York Central's principal architect, Morgan O'Brien, and was made up of three levels—a basement consisting of a section of the old cut between 125th and 126th Streets that had not been filled in, a street-floor waiting room and open-air platforms above, at the level of the track on the station's roof.

The exterior is a modest affair, white brick and terra-cotta beneath

years of paint. There is some competent iron detailing, but the building is otherwise indistinguishable from a very large public comfort station.

It is the street-level interior that is most striking—and most abused. "The interior is finished throughout in antique oak," the *New York Times* reported in 1897. "The ticket agent's box is an elaborate piece of furniture in carved oak and ground glass. The main entrance is guarded by handsome steel gates of unique design. . . . The new station is one of the finest in the city."

The station contained a gentlemen's smoking room, telegraph office, bicycle room, a vault for storage of railroad records and a baggage room with an elevator to the two platforms above.

The platforms themselves—raised three feet in the 1970's—are roofed over with simple sheds with decorated iron supports, but have dramatic views of the city. Outside stairs leading directly to the street have elaborate curved ironwork, but now tilt crazily to one side.

The basement, which is closed to the public, contains an archeological surprise: the original 1875 station platforms and column footings for the 1897 station above, made up of dressed stone copings salvaged from the original wall of the open cut.

Time and human agency have not been kind to the 125th Street station, which has been slowly tortured rather than quickly killed. The oak woodwork now peels off in great strips, and is nearly drowned in layers of paint. Windows are boarded up, and whenever it rains outside, it rains inside.

There are a few touches that suggest a grander state—elaborate art-glass light fixtures above the ticket windows, an old railroad bench with a few brass armrests still in place, elaborate cast-iron radiators and an old railroad clock at the stairway that station personnel keep in operation.

Metro-North projects about $1.2 million for the station's renovation. But Wayne Ehmann, its architect, said that the golden oak interior would be repainted rather than stripped. "We want to keep it a minimum effort at this time," he said.

How 125th Street could shine with just the barest hint of sensitivity to its historic buildings! What a lost opportunity!

THE LANE THEATER

In a 1930's Movie Palace, the Stars Still Come Out

The interior of the Lane Theater in New Dorp on Staten Island in 1938.

THE ART MODERNE Lane Theater in New Dorp has an unusual decorative scheme, but most of it has been painted over. It is also the last single-screen movie house on Staten Island, at a time when the multiplex theater dominates movie-house economics.

The Landmarks Preservation Commission, which considered the building for interior designation at its September 6 meeting, must weigh these two factors when it decides on the Lane's designation, sometime after next Tuesday.

By the 1920's, movie-palace construction was in full swing, with huge theaters like the 6,200-seat Roxy, on West 50th Street near Seventh Avenue, setting the standard. Most of these vast rooms were "hard tops," hugely inflated versions of Renaissance and baroque interiors, with elaborate gilt and chandeliers. But another approach, the "atmospheric" interior, developed in opposition to the hard top.

First used in 1922 by the architect John Eberson for the Majestic Theater in Houston, the atmospheric interior sought to give the illusion of presenting a film outdoors. The auditorium ceiling was a smooth surface, often light blue, decorated with stars and projections of moving clouds.

The Depression ended the construction of large theaters in center-city locations, but movie houses still went up in developing neighborhoods.

Charles, Lewis and Elias Moses, who operated theaters on Staten Island, filed plans in 1937 to build a new one on New Dorp Lane at the southeast corner of Eighth Street at a cost of $100,000.

The Lane, named after the street, opened on February 10, 1938, showing Deanna Durbin in *100 Men and a Girl*. Also designed by Mr. Eberson, the Lane is L-shaped, wrapping around corner stores that were part of the project. The outside is little more than an entryway with a streamlined marquee.

But it is the interior that is of real interest. A flowing serpentine corridor leads to a 550-seat auditorium in the Art Moderne style. There is stepped paneling on the ceiling and streamlined bands on the walls like those on a 1930's radio. The original carpet and stage curtain had zigzag patterns.

The most striking element of the interior is the painted ceiling. Large areas of plum, green and blue are bounded by rainbows of color and decorated with random designs that seem patterned after stellar explosions but bear an abstract resemblance to the masks of comedy and tragedy often used in theater decoration.

Period photographs also show unusual painting schemes along the walls, including four large areas with more stellar designs set against black fields. According to the yearly *Theater Catalogue* for 1948, the Lane was one of the first theaters to introduce fluorescent murals using black light.

The walls were painted over in 1976, but the recessed black lighting still survives, as do other, exposed lighting fixtures. These range from unusual Buck Rogers–style aluminum affairs to Empire-moderne chandeliers, which mix classical metalwork with modernistic glass tubing.

According to William Trapani and Maryanne Ranieri, who organized the drive to designate the Lane's interior a landmark, the Moses brothers at first planned to name the theater the Astro. But Jane Preddy, an architectural historian who has studied the career of Mr. Eberson, says the original plans call the theater the Globe. In either case, the space-travel implications of the design are clear: If Mr. Eberson's earlier theaters were atmospheric, this one is galactic.

Decorative murals in the lobby have also been painted over, though they could be restored, and there is water damage in the auditorium and other parts of the theater. But the biggest threat to the Lane is the changing nature of movie-house economics.

Large single-screen theaters typically produce too little income to justify their operating costs, and the Lane must deal as well with competition from a tenplex not far away. Even charging $4.50 for admission, the lowest price in the city for a first-run house, a recent weeknight had only 17 patrons seated at the beginning of *Married to the Mob*.

Henry Picciurro, one of the partners who own the Lane, said the current operator, the L.M.S. Theater Corporation, had a month-to-month lease, and he would like to re-lease the space to them.

But Meyer Ackerman, president of L.M.S., said the Lane was no longer viable in its present form and he would like to divide it for multiple screens.

The Landmarks Preservation Commission, after the public hearing earlier this month, promised not to act before Tuesday. Its decision will be complicated by knowing that much of the theater's unusual paint scheme is concealed—but only by the 1976 coat of paint.

Designated a landmark—and vacant since that time.

THE OLD SQUIBB BUILDING

"Restoration" Is Adding Color to Original All-White Design

The Squibb Building at 745 Fifth Avenue in 1939. Bergdorf Goodman is at right, Savoy-Plaza Hotel, now gone, at the left.

A LTHOUGH THE 1930 Squibb building at Grand Army Plaza was built to the architect's original design, renovations meant to make up for what had mistakenly been thought to be cutbacks brought on by the crash of '29 are still being carried out.

Scaffolding covers the first six floors of the building, which is at 745 Fifth Avenue, at 58th Street, and new colored marble panels and gleaming metalwork are being installed.

The current owners originally announced that their renovations would make up for economies necessitated by the market crash of October 1929, when the building was under construction. The architects, Hammond Beeby & Babka, however, said they learned that there had been no such change.

Ely Jacques Kahn, who designed the 32-story Squibb building, built his reputation as the preeminent architect of office buildings in the 20's on his use of color. Buildings like his massive 2 Park Avenue, at 33d Street, are distinguished by their careful but exhilarating application of polychroming, usually in glazed terra-cotta.

But Kahn gave the Squibb building a totally white facade. He was designing for Abe N. Adelson—for whom he had also done 2 Park Avenue—and Adelson wanted the building "harmonized with the other buildings in the square," according to an article in the *New York Times* in 1930.

These were generally white, some in marble, and without any color decoration, like the Plaza Hotel, the Metropolitan Club and Bergdorf-Goodman.

The lack of color was certainly not because of budget constraints. A giant Art Deco nickel-steel screen was installed over the Fifth Avenue lobby portal, and a Viennese sculptor, Valley Wieselthier, was hired to model the elevator doors.

Arthur Covey, president of the National Society of Mural Painters, was retained to paint a lobby ceiling mural; it shows stylized airplanes flying over a map of Manhattan bounded by emblems of the city's activities—fine arts, music, drama and others.

The lower facade was executed in marble with subtle fluting and scalloping, the upper floors in white brick with abstract Art Deco ornament.

Kahn was proud of his all-white design and in his unpublished autobiography called it "one of my cherished creations."

"No alterations to the facade were permitted without my consent," he wrote.

Construction proceeded despite the crash and the building opened in 1930 with E. R. Squibb & Sons, the drug company, as the prime tenant, on the top 12 floors.

The Depression deepened and Adelson lost his project in foreclosure in 1933. Over time, the building experienced the usual minor indignities of any commercial property: The marble front was painted, the giant portal screen was removed and ventilation ducts punctured the lobby mural—one right in the middle of the fine-arts emblem.

Squibb moved to a new building at 40 West 57th Street in 1972 and in 1985 F. A. O. Schwarz, the original corner-store tenant, moved to the General Motors building.

Kahn's "cherished creation" was largely intact, one of those sleeping midtown masterpieces awaiting restoration. In this case Hexalon Real Estate, a Dutch investment group, bought the building in 1986 and began to plan a renovation of the mechanical systems.

In 1987, after a year of study, Hexalon also announced that Hammond Beeby & Babka of Chicago would remodel the exterior of the lower six floors.

This was to include ripping off much of the old white marble and putting on huge new panels of green, pink and black marble and gleaming metalwork trim.

The stated rationale was that the building had not been carried out according to the original, presumably highly colored, designs because of cutbacks after the crash of 1929.

But the building was executed exactly according to its July 1929 drawings. These are on file and can be seen at Columbia University's Avery library. The all-white facade was considered an elegant gesture, not just a cost-saving measure.

Charles Young, the principal design architect on the renovation, says his firm is continuing its original plan with only minor revisions because "the owners came to us and said they didn't like the facade." His firm, Mr. Young explained, developed a design to suit the client's tastes.

The lower floors were toned down to accommodate the new store tenant, Bergdorf-Goodman, but the entire episode is an example of the mangling of history by our "artchitects."

THE HIGH BRIDGE WATER TOWER

Fire-Damaged Landmark to Get $900,000 Repairs

The granite High Bridge Water Tower rising over High Bridge and the Harlem River in 1895.

SINCE 1872, THE High Bridge Water Tower, on the Manhattan cliffs at 174th Street, has dominated the Harlem River Valley. But the granite landmark has been a civic embarrassment—visible from several major highways—since its peaked roof caved in after a fire in 1984.

Now the Department of Parks says that roof repairs will begin next year but that the tower's magnificent interior will stay closed.

The Croton Aqueduct of 1842 brought the first dependable supply of fresh water into New York City. A 40-mile-long line connected the Croton Lake in Westchester to Manhattan and crossed the Harlem River on an elevated aqueduct built in the Roman style. But increasing water demands—particularly for the newly developed flush toilet, according to Sidney Horenstein, a geologist   strained a system that had not been designed to serve Manhattan's higher ground.

This need for "high service" moved the State Legislature to authorize a new waterworks on the Manhattan side of the High Bridge Aqueduct in 1863. From the aqueduct, water would be pumped up nearly 100 feet to a seven-acre reservoir at ridgetop and also to a 47,000-gallon tank in a 200-foot-high tower. Completed by 1872, the entire project was designed by John B. Jervis, an engineer who had worked on the Erie Canal and had supervised the original Croton Aqueduct, including the High Bridge Aqueduct itself.

Although iron framing technology was fairly advanced by then, Jervis designed the tower with bearing walls of stone, mixing elements of the Romanesque and neo-Grec styles. Its rock-faced granite gives the tower a chunky, fortified appearance, as if it were a lookout for a much larger castle complex that was never built.

The tower's octagonal shaft rises to an upper section with paired windows concealing the water tank itself. When completed, the tower had a peaked copper roof with a lantern that doubled as a lookout and a large weather vane. The granite is competently handled, but the details are not very inspired or elegant. The tower is more picturesque than beautiful.

But the interior is more impressive. An iron stair, decorated with quatrefoils and other designs, circles the interior walls, and perforations in the stair—presumably to save weight—give the huge column of interior space an airy quality.

There are six landings, and windows at several points give an expanding set of views. The ironwork is so nicely detailed, the stairways so wide and the landings so commodious that they seem to have been designed to permit regular public access.

There is no evidence that the tower was ever open to the public, but the surrounding High Bridge Park—established in 1849—was a destination for day trips from the city for much of the 19th century and other elements in the Croton system accommodated the public.

Even with the High Bridge improvement, the existing aqueduct was at full capacity by 1875. In 1890, the New Croton Aqueduct supplemented it. Reliance on the High Bridge Aqueduct and Water Tower gradually decreased; it was redundant enough to be shut down entirely during a sabotage scare in World War I.

In 1934, the reservoir was converted to the huge public High Bridge Swimming Pool and in 1949 the tower was removed from service entirely. In 1958, the Altman Foundation donated a carillon to be installed in the water tower, and for years the sound of bells rang through the neighborhood.

For a structure without a specific function, the water tower remained in remarkably good condition. But in 1984, someone set fire to the timber framing of the roof, and it collapsed inward in a heap; it now rests on the top of the empty water tank. Charred timbers are littered about the upper sections of the stairway and to get to the paired windows a visitor must now step across a three-foot-square void, about 125 feet straight down.

Once beyond that, though, the view is exhilarating. The tower is perched on the edge of the steep river valley, and there is nothing else of comparable height in the vicinity.

Richard Schwartz, chief of staff for the Division of Capital Projects of the city's Department of Parks, said the roof area will be cleaned up in the next few months. And the department has retained the William A. Hall Partnership to supervise the structure's rehabilitation. Deteriorated granite will be removed, the exterior will be cleaned and a new roof and a carillon will be installed at a total cost of perhaps $900,000.

Because of security considerations in a high-crime area, however, the interior will remain closed and the views will be of, not from, the tower.

A new cupola was installed in 1990.

45 EAST 66th STREET

For a Jewel on the East Side, a Loving Facade Restoration

Apartment house at Madison Avenue and 66th Street in 1908.

IN THE MIDDLE of a three-year, $900,000 restoration and still swathed in scaffolding, the 80-year-old apartment house at 45 East 66th Street has undergone a cleaning that has removed decades of grime that hid its unusual red-and-white French Gothic design.

Now that the cleaning is done, the laborious restoration of the deteriorated terra-cotta work will begin in earnest and the scaffolding probably will remain up for another year.

In 1905, Charles F. Rogers, who had built the Prince George and other hotels, bought the All Souls Church site at the northeast corner of Madison Avenue and 66th Street. Rogers, the son of the sculptor John S. Rogers, lived at 60th Street and Madison Avenue and was an All Souls parishioner.

In 1906, he retained the architectural firm of Harde and Short to design a 10-story, $1 million apartment house. The firm had been active in housing design and had recently completed an unusual six-story French Gothic-style building at 350 West 85th Street.

The new building dominated the Madison Avenue brownstones, and its distinctive round corner tower was unusually prominent.

The square-doughnut structure has a central light court, but the majestic multipaned windows—framed in white terra-cotta and rising to overhanging, screen-like assemblies of Gothic ornament—are what catch the eye. They are bordered by deep-red brick with recessed, blackened mortar. A copper cornice, now deep green, crowns the building.

Madison was still a residential street in 1906, and the original entrance, of carved marble with elaborate iron doors, was right at the corner. The building was divided into only two apartments—with 12 and 13 rooms—on each floor. Only a handful survive intact, still grand and elegant but with most of their unusual woodwork painted over.

The building opened in 1908 as 777 Madison Avenue. Harde and Short went on to design the Alwyn Court in a similar plan, at 58th Street and Seventh Avenue; Rogers lost his 66th Street building in a foreclosure in 1912.

By the 1910's, the fashion for flamboyant design had passed and subsequent apartment buildings were typically in the more reserved Renaissance and Georgian styles, leaving the 66th Street building a high-water mark in early apartment styling.

In the 20's, growing demand for stores along Madison Avenue led the owners of 45 East 66th Street and other buildings to convert ground-floor apartments to retail space. Thus in 1929 the entrance was moved onto East 66th Street, giving the building its present address.

Starting in the 30's, most apartments at 45 East 66th Street were gradually subdivided. The exterior remained in fairly good shape except for a gradual buildup of grime from engine exhaust (Madison Avenue streetcars were replaced by buses in the 1930's). From 1928 to 1973, the building was owned by the Bing & Bing real estate company.

Major change came after the mid-50's, with most of the overhanging decorative work at the sixth and 10th floors either cut back or stripped away entirely.

In 1973, 45 East 66th Street was acquired by a builder, Sigmund Sommer, who cut back some services, discharged the elevator attendant and replaced incandescent lighting with fluorescent in the hallways. Tenants conducted a rent strike, picketed a new Sommer building at 425 East 58th Street and even demonstrated at Belmont Race Track, where Mr. Sommer had two horses in the field.

They ultimately won most of their battles and the Bing interests took the building back in the spring of 1977, just as a tenant effort for landmark designation was starting.

The Bing interests asked the architect Percival Goodman to present an opinion to the Landmarks Preservation Commission. He said the building was representative of "the shoddy, spectacular, speculator ways of a particularly shoddy period in our history." Nevertheless, the commission designated the structure a landmark in 1977.

In 1987, a partnership managed by M. J. Raynes bought the building and began a cooperative conversion plan that was completed last month. As part of the conversion, the owner hired Vincent Stramandinoli, an engineer, to supervise a restoration of the facade. He said the task would be completed next fall.

LONDON TERRACE

Time Erodes Unity of a 1,665-Unit City Within a City

London Terrace, 1931, from 10th Avenue at 23d Street.

LONDON TERRACE, THE huge apartment development on the block bounded by 23d and 24th Streets and Ninth and 10th Avenues, was built as a self-contained urban community in 1929–31 with an elaborate array of services. Time and other elements have gradually compromised the special unity of London Terrace and now a partial co-op conversion is testing even further the cohesion of the venerable complex.

It was not until after World War I that Manhattan saw the rise of planned residential enclaves like the Sutton Place town houses in 1920, the Tudor City apartments of 1925–28 and London Terrace in 1929–30.

In 1929, Henry Mandel leased the London Terrace block and began a two-phase building operation. In 1929–30 he built two rows of five 16-story apartment houses facing 23d and 24th Streets and in 1930–31 pairs of 18-story apartment houses at each end of the block facing Ninth and 10th Avenues. It was the largest apartment development ever built in New York City, according to Andrew Alpern, an architectural historian.

The completed buildings—with 1,665 apartments—form a perimeter wall with burnt-orange brick with corbelling and other details in various Romanesque styles. While each has its own entrance and elevators, the block-long, ground-floor, east–west corridors create interior sidewalks.

The basement has even more elaborate passageways—permitting residents to walk from 24th Street and Ninth Avenue to cash a check at a Chemical Bank branch at 23d Street and 10th Avenue without ever stepping a foot outside the enormous complex.

Mandel's original concept included a variety of services to unite the project into "one great community, quite self-contained and with every accommodation for modern urban life," as the magazine *Architecture & Building* put it in 1930.

The Marine Roof—decorated in a nautical theme—permitted sunbathers to observe passing ocean-liner traffic. Staff in the complex stood ready to babysit, clean, cook, run errands, fix toasters, refinish furniture and perform other chores, in some cases without charge. There was a large dining room along Ninth Avenue and, on 10th Avenue, an indoor 75-foot-long swimming pool that served all the tenants. And all the doormen were dressed as London bobbies.

The ads read not only "Swim before Dinner" but also "Live like a Prince at Popular Prices" for these apartments of one to four rooms renting for around $30 a month.

Why Mandel began the second phase after the stock market crash of 1929 is not clear, but the complex was only just completed when he declared bankruptcy. In 1935, London Terrace was foreclosed.

It was at this time that the first cracks in the city within a city began to appear. Different parties had different claims on the 10 midblock apartments and on the four end buildings; in the foreclosure process the ownership of London Terrace was split between two groups.

Business Week wrote in 1934 that the complex was "in a London fog of scrambled titles. . . . Its bobbies now direct a traffic stream of tenants down the scale of living." The ownership of the corner buildings included the pool, that of the midblock buildings the garden, but both amenities were still open to all residents.

Gradually other services were cut back. The restaurant was converted to retail space, page boys no longer ran errands and the Marine Roof was stripped. In 1952, the garden was largely paved over and interrupted by a north–south walkway in a sort of zigzag modern style, an early, unusual work of the architect Philip Birnbaum. Later the western half of the walkway was walled off for offices, effectively eliminating access to that half of the garden.

Last year, apartments in the four corner buildings were converted into a co-op and the sponsor began a $10 million renovation including new windows, restored masonry decoration, new water piping and a restoration of the pool. The corner buildings now look fresh and spiffy while the midblock buildings seem a bit tired, with areas where the cast stone detailing has been crudely shorn off and with windows in varying states of repair.

With the change in the character of ownership have come new pressures. A new health club is being built in conjunction with the pool restoration and the question of whether the co-op will restrict the pool to the tenants of its four-building complex is in the air.

Andrew Hoffman, general manager for the owner of the midblock buildings, London Terrace Gardens, declined to comment on the issue. And Marc Portnoy, president of the co-op corporation, London Terrace Towers Owners, calls it an open question. "The structure of the complex is changing within such a short period of time that it's hard to predict where it will end up," he said.

Mr. Hoffman reports that all tenants are welcome at the pool. And I forgot to mention Farrar & Watmough, the architects of this bland complex.

THE CHILDS BUILDING

Fast Food, Then and Now, on Stylish Fifth Avenue

The Childs Building at 604 Fifth Avenue near 48th Street in 1925. Collegiate Church of St. Nicholas was at left, Goelet residence at right.

I T'S ALMOST A reenactment: A fast-food restaurant moves to elegant Fifth Avenue, to the dismay of the Fifth Avenue Association. But although the 1925 version resulted in good feelings and cooperation all around, the 1988 replay has left the parties at loggerheads, and the Roy Rogers/Pizza Hut restaurant in the Childs Building, 604 Fifth Avenue, is likely to remain a sore point for years.

William and Samuel Childs established the Childs Restaurant chain in the Financial District in the 1880's, emphasizing spare, sanitary surroundings and quick, modest lunches for office workers. Their distinctive, white-tiled chain was a success and by the 1920's competition from imitators forced William Childs to consider other markets.

At the time, Fifth Avenue south of 59th Street was just recovering from two controversies. Around 1900, the Vanderbilts and other householders north of St. Patrick's Cathedral began a pitched but unsuccessful battle against the invasion of their neighborhood by expensive shops and even lofts. And farther south, retailers had successfully fought off loft and garment-factory buildings. The Fifth Avenue Association was established in 1907, in part because of these battles.

In the developing shopping district on Fifth Avenue, eating establishments were generally limited to clubs, large restaurants or hotels. But as expensive shops brought crowds of patrons, the patrons sought nourishment—not always expensive—and it was here that William Childs saw his opening.

He arranged to lease the Russell Sage residence on the west side of the avenue between the Collegiate Church of St. Nicholas on 48th Street and the Goelet residence on 49th. Although the Sage house was, by then, a flower shop, Childs was the closest thing to fast food and thus a distinctly new, even undesirable, element for Fifth Avenue.

Foster Ware and Brock Pemberton, writing in the *New Yorker*, said that the Fifth Avenue Association got wind of the Childs plan and "had its misgivings. Would a nickel-plated lunch place go well along the avenue housing Altman's and Tiffany's?"

William Childs took their concerns seriously, interviewed a score of architects and hired the Modernist William Van Alen, who in 1929 designed the Chrysler Building.

Van Alen produced a five-story limestone building reserved in style but still a shocking intrusion between the old brownstones. Inside, he did away with the signature Childs white tile, substituting Caen stone and bronze trim. The most striking element was the curved glass at the southern corner, where the facade was brought around to face the church on its south side.

G. H. Edgell, in *American Architecture of To-Day* (1928), said, "When viewed from slightly uptown each story seems to be supported at the edge only by the frail, curved pane below. The effect is rather terrifying and fascinating at the same time."

Terrifying or not, Childs opened on Fifth Avenue in 1925 as a success, and even the Fifth Avenue Association was pleased. There were soon nine Childses on the avenue. By 1927 the chain had expanded to 108 restaurants in the United States and Canada.

Childs remained at 604 Fifth into the 1960's with only one major change. When the church on 48th Street was replaced by an office building in 1950, the curved glass at the corner was blocked off by the new building and replaced with glass block.

The Childs chain was acquired in 1961 by the Riese Organization, and within a decade most of the Childs restaurants had been replaced with more modern food operations, like Chock Full O'Nuts. In 1981, Riese acquired the 604 Fifth Avenue building and this fall opened a Roy Rogers/Pizza Hut restaurant in the old Childs space. This time, fast food and the Fifth Avenue Association have reached no accommodation.

"We don't like them," said Michael Grosso, executive vice president of the association, referring to fast-food operations. "An elegant boutique will not go on a block with a fast-food restaurant any more than one with a shop with a 'going out of business' sign."

"Fifth Avenue is an institution," said Mr. Grosso, who is retiring this December after 43 years with the association. "We have to maintain it. It will never be duplicated."

But Vin Rosa, executive vice president of the Riese Organization, said that he takes "some offense that they would not want working people to have a place to eat. We put a lot into the restaurant so that it would not detract from the community and the public seems to be very happy."

WASHINGTON MEWS

Gates for Protection Against the Threatening City Beyond

Washington Mews seen through the University Place gate in 1928.

THE COBBLESTONED WASHINGTON MEWS is one of the most unusual lanes in Manhattan, its converted two-story stables making it a sort of retreat from the hustle and bustle of the city. Originally open, then later closed by gates, the Mews was open again after 1916.

Now concerns about crime have provoked a new plan for gates for the private Greenwich Village street—destroying its open, serendipitous character.

When Capt. Robert Randall died in 1801, he left his large farm north of Washington Square to be improved with a home for elderly and disabled sailors. But Sailors' Snug Harbor, as the institution became known, never followed Randall's plan for the property; instead, it leased the land for long terms to people building their houses and used the income to support its huge complex in Staten Island.

Various lessees, working under a uniform master plan, built the row of houses along the north side of Washington Square from Fifth Avenue to University Place. They established a back alley for the row, dedicating it to two-story stables.

According to Luther Harris, who is preparing a history of the area, private streets for stables are common in other cities like London but very rare in New York. Over time the simple brick stables served families like those of Richard Morris Hunt, the architect, John Taylor Johnston, first president of the Metropolitan Museum of Art, and Pierre Lorillard, the tobacco entrepreneur.

An 1879 view of Washington Mews shows the small street completely open. But in 1881 the New York City Department of Public Works ordered the building of gates at each end, apparently to distinguish the privately owned Mews from public streets.

Around the same time, as the center of fashionable residences reached as far north as Central Park, the first artists invaded the area; the house and stable at 3 Washington Square North was demolished for a studio building in 1884.

By the 1910's the motorcar was rapidly replacing the horse and carriage and in 1916 Sailors' Snug Harbor announced a remodeling plan for 12 of the stables. Dr. William T. Manning, rector of Trinity Church and a trustee of Sailors' Snug Harbor, said that "the little stables of the Mews, whose usefulness has long since passed away, will be transformed into airy and light studios for artists who are making Washington Square one of their favorite centers."

Architects for the alteration were Maynicke & Franke, who covered the brick stables with light stucco and decorative tiles. The firm also took down the old iron gate at University Place, replacing it with an elaborate Mediterranean-style brick-and-stucco gateway with lanterns. But at the Fifth Avenue end the old iron gate was replaced with a simple chain between two posts, apparently to permit easy access by automobile.

Artists, like the sculptor Paul Manship, did in fact occupy studios in the Mews. By the 20's the growing Bohemian attractions of Greenwich Village created a residential building boom, with buildings like the huge apartment house at 1 Fifth Avenue, at the corner of Eighth Street. But the Mews retained its character, even after 10 new two-story houses masquerading as converted stables were built on it across from 1 Fifth Avenue in 1939.

At some later point the gate on University Place was rebuilt in plain red brick, and around 1950 New York University leased the entire property from Sailors' Snug Harbor. Some artists remained—like the painter Edward Hopper, who died there in 1966. But gradually, the buildings were taken over for offices and faculty housing.

For years, tourists have casually wandered down the quaint Mews, guidebooks in hand, oblivious to the fact that it is nonetheless a private street. But residents of the Mews have been complaining of increasing numbers of burglaries, and now New York University has retained the architect Abraham Bloch to design a new six-foot-high gate for the Fifth Avenue end.

The gate will be unlocked during the day, but will still create a sense of privacy and might just permit residents to leave radios in their cars. But the informal, open quality of the Mews will disappear as yet another barrier goes up in an increasingly guarded city.

The gate is now in place.

TURTLE BAY GARDENS

The Fate of "a Beautiful Whole" Hangs on Talks on Restrictions

Turtle Bay Gardens row houses on East 48th Street in 1920.

TURTLE BAY GARDENS, a row-house enclave between 48th and 49th streets and Second and Third Avenues, was completed in 1920 with a great common garden at midblock.

The garden and the character of the surrounding houses had always been protected by property restrictions agreed to by all the owners. But the restrictions lapsed in 1983 and have not been renewed, and the future of one of Manhattan's most unusual communal residential projects is unclear.

Architects and critics have been lambasting the mean little backyards of the typical brownstone plots since the mid-19th century. In 1893, the *Real Estate Record & Guide* described the typical midblock collection of backyards as "a dreary monotone of gray board fences, ash and garbage barrels, slop pails and clotheslines."

In the article, Charles Judson, a row-house builder, advocated property restrictions to merge the rear gardens into a larger common one, as was frequent in England. But he allowed that "the American opposition to cooperation" made such an effort nearly impossible. His dream could be realized, he said, only if "some rich individual" took matters in hand and built a block of dwellings based on the plan, including a common garden and architectural controls.

Such an individual did not emerge until 1918, when Charlotte Hunnewell Sorchan bought out 21 adjoining householders and established Turtle Bay Gardens.

The architects Edward C. Dean and William L. Bottomley altered the brownstones in two major ways: They shaved off the old facades, replacing them with light, pastel stucco in a variety of Flemish and Regency styles facing the street and Mediterranean styles facing the interior. And they reoriented the houses, placing the service areas on the street and the principal living and entertainment areas facing the garden.

The garden itself became a single great green room of shrubbery, flowers and mature trees. The backyards are separated only by brick walls, perhaps three feet high, and all share a common path down the center of the block, with fountains, statuary and picturesque details. The low walls present a sweep of private space almost unparalleled in Manhattan neighborhoods.

In a 1920 article in *Architectural Record*, Arthur Willis Colton praised the laying aside of private interests for a larger, communal one. "Each owner has, visually speaking, surrendered a part and received back a beautiful whole," he wrote.

To regulate this "beautiful whole," Mrs. Sorchan—by 1921 Mrs. Walton Martin—established restrictions limiting roof additions, regulating architectural changes and preventing anyone from reerecting high walls in the garden area. One owner, at 240 East 49th Street, held out and Mrs. Martin erected a high brick wall around his garden to shut it off from the larger one. In 1947, a new owner put the property under the garden's restrictions. A plaque in the garden calls it "a fine example of cooperation and understanding among neighbors."

Among the first purchasers in Turtle Bay Gardens were artists, writers, professionals and business people, of whom only Maria Chapin, founder of the Chapin School, is widely known today. Later owners and occupants have included many active in the arts and letters—June Havoc, Ricardo Montalban, Henry Luce, E. B. White and Garson Kanin.

Turtle Bay Gardens was the first of several such enclaves, like the houses on Sutton Place between 57th and 58th Streets, most of which relied on property restrictions as a unifying force.

The original Turtle Bay restrictions had been set to expire in 1939, but were successively renewed four times until 1983. In 1964, the restrictions were revised to allow garages, but otherwise they remained largely unchanged.

But 1983 came and went without renewal, as have the succeeding years. It is not clear whether the restrictions lapsed because of a lack of interest or because of actual disagreements about them.

Julian Bach, a spokesman for Turtle Bay Gardens, would comment only that "there are discussions" about renewing the restrictions, but he would not disclose their nature. The exteriors of the houses are now well kept, but the common garden has been neglected. Most trees carry some dead limbs.

Turtle Bay Gardens is protected by landmark designation, so demolition of any buildings is unlikely, even in the absence of property restrictions. But the lapse of the communal impulse is a troubling chapter in the history of what has been one of Manhattan's first-class residential enclaves where "the beautiful whole" has always taken precedence over individual interests.

Julian Bach says that renewed convenants are "about to be signed."

THE CENTURY ASSOCIATION CLUBHOUSE

Richardson's Lost Work Discovered Housing a Travel Agency on East 15th

THE ALL-MALE CENTURY ASSOCIATION has been in the news recently because of its decision to admit women as members to its 1889 clubhouse at 7 West 43d Street. But there is news of a different sort about the venerable club: Its earlier clubhouse on East 15th Street, thought to have been demolished, is not only still around, but also seems likely to be a hitherto undiscovered work by H. H. Richardson, one of the greatest American architects.

The association was founded in 1847 for professionals and amateurs in the field of arts and letters. In 1857, after occupying various quarters, it bought an old building on the north side of 15th Street between Union Square and Irving Place, then numbered 42 East 15th Street, but later renumbered as 109.

Membership doubled to 500 by the late 1860's and, amid controversy over whether the club should move to larger quarters, a $21,000 program was approved to add a new facade and new interiors.

By this time the Century was "the most unspeakably respectable club in the United States," according to Mark Twain, with members like Albert Bierstadt, William Cullen Bryant, Frederick Church and Henry Hobson Richardson, then just beginning his architectural career.

In 1867, Richardson formed a partnership with Charles Gambrill, who had proposed Richardson for membership in the club the year before.

Although Gambrill had also had professional training, later scholars all either questioned his talent or indicated that "Gambrill served primarily as the business manager of the firm," as Jeffrey Ochsner writes in his 1982 book *H. H. Richardson: Complete Architectural Works*.

For the 1869 reconstruction, the club retained Gambrill & Richardson and work was carried out over the summer of 1869. The new facade was designed in the neo-Grec style with a mansard roof, red brick and chunky limestone detailing, all still remarkably intact.

Richardson did several works in the neo-Grec style in the early years of his practice, when it was considered avant-garde for the United States.

The first-floor interior has been radically changed, but large portions of the second-floor interior survive intact, apparently from the Gambrill & Richardson work: burled-walnut bookcases, a musician's gallery, a stained-glass skylight and elaborate carving and lacy trim.

The Century has always been a strictly social club, but Richardson nevertheless made or confirmed some valuable business connections there.

Frederick Law Olmsted, William Dorsheimer, John Lafarge, Joseph H. Choate and other club members were later either clients or collaborators on some of his most important commissions.

In the 1870's, Richardson developed his signature round-arch Romanesque style, which came to be considered the first authentic American-based architecture, and created his reputation as one of the foremost American designers, along with Louis Sullivan, Stanford White, Frank Lloyd Wright and a few others.

Club records mention Gambrill in connection with the 1869 work, but he was more active in Century affairs than Richardson and may only have been the firm's liaison with the building committee. The Gambrill and Richardson partnership continued until 1878.

But the Century Club commission, perhaps because of its earlier styling and uncertain authorship, was forgotten. Modern researchers, like Ochsner, in part because of the change in street numbering, have assumed that the old clubhouse had been demolished.

However, the building indeed remained standing after the club moved to its present home on 43d Street.

The old clubhouse went through a succession of owners and is now occupied by a travel agency and owned by the Ponti Realty Management Corporation. The property manager, David Lee, said he has always been

Century Association clubhouse, East 15th Street, 1892.

told that the building was built by a Mexican ambassador to the United States.

But it is now not only the only work connected to Richardson in Manhattan—the architect's house survived, although altered, in Staten Island—it is also the oldest surviving private club building. The second-oldest is the New York Racquet Club of 1876, at the northeast corner of 26th Street and Avenue of the Americas.

Although discoveries like this one may not increase the value of the property, they do set in motion other changes. Daisy Yau, an officer with Ponti, says that plans for the property are not certain, although a condominium tower on the old clubhouse site is possible.

But the Landmarks Preservation Commission has heard, but not designated the Racquet Club Building, and is likely to consider any intact Richardson building of importance, particularly one associated with so prominent an institution as the Century Association.

Subsequently heard but not yet designated by the Landmarks Commission. This must rank as the most important discovery of my working life as an architectural historian—a third-rate building by a first-rate architect.

PARK AVENUE

A Grand Residential Boulevard or Just Monotony Lane?

Park Avenue, looking north from 86th Street, in 1930.

THERE ARE TWO ways for a commissioner at the Landmarks Preservation Commission to look at Park Avenue—as the grandest residential boulevard in Manhattan or as a waste of time, with a monotonous collection of similar buildings and constant window replacements and air-conditioner installations.

It now looks as if there will be a verdict on Park Avenue between 86th and 96th Streets in the next few months, because the panel is considering proposals to include all, part or none of it in an expansion of the existing Carnegie Hill Historic District.

Park Avenue in the Carnegie Hill area developed much as it did in the lower sections. After the railroad tracks were covered in 1875, flats and tenements went up on most blocks. But the really high ground around 93d Street attracted generally modest row-house construction. By the turn of the century, Park was almost fully developed as a boulevard of the bourgeoisie.

But construction of town houses for the gentry was moving up Fifth and Madison Avenues and there was some spillover to Park, especially after the railroad converted from steam to electricity in 1903. That year, Elihu Root built a house at the southeast corner of 71st Street, and Amos Pinchot built one at the northeast corner of 85th Street in 1906. Above 86th Street, Francis F. Palmer built a house at the northwest corner of 93d Street in 1917.

But luxury-apartment-house construction came to dominate upper Park Avenue beginning with 1155 Park in 1916 and 1049 Park in 1919. In 1922, the next four of what would become a nearly uniform wall of apartment houses from 86th to 96th Street went up: 1045, 1050, 1060 and 1105 Park Avenue, which was the first cooperative in the section.

In 1927, an article in the *New Republic* called Park Avenue "the end of the American ladder of success," noting that "higher one cannot go." Although its similar apartment buildings constituted an "unendurable monotony," the article noted that it was still "a broad and noble avenue."

The wave of construction continued through the 1920's, but the crash of 1929 left unrealized several major projects, among them a 52-story apartment hotel at 86th Street by Fred F. French and a 21-story setback apartment house by Rosario Candela at 1245 Park. After that, only a few later buildings—Brick Church at 91st Street and the modern 1065 Park—interrupted the line of red, gray and tan brick that stopped at 96th Street, where the end of the railroad tunnel established a social boundary.

Today the buildings do not seem quite so uniform as they once did. Delano & Aldrich's 1040 Park is an unusual mixture of Georgian and Art Deco, with Condé Nast's glassed-in penthouse still intact, the first such dwelling in New York.

William Bottomley's 1049 Park, although carelessly altered, is still a distinctive Italian Renaissance design. Mott Schmidt's 1088 Park has its genteel garden courtyard and unusual detailing. DePace & Juster's setback 1100 Park is in a warm Mediterranean style, with multipaned windows that are steadily being replaced by single panes. Schwartz & Gross's neo-Gothic, blockfront 1185 Park has an immense drive-in courtyard.

The original Carnegie Hill Historic District designated in 1974 has boundaries that have proved to be an embarrassment to the Landmarks Commission. They protect midblock, side-street buildings and are so irregular that the district was rejected when nominated to the National Register of Historic Places. The Metropolitan Museum Historic District of 1977, farther south, is still mostly side streets, but the Upper East Side Historic District, designated in 1981, includes most of Park Avenue from 62d to 79th Streets and the district report calls it "essential to the architectural fabric of the area."

Since 1980, Carnegie Hill Neighbors, led by Elizabeth Ashby, and other groups have been lobbying for an extension of the Carnegie Hill District. The Landmarks commissioners walked the area in November and are now examining the matter. They will almost certainly extend the district to include Fifth Avenue, and there are groups of row houses between Park and Lexington Avenues that are of fairly obvious architectural value. But Park Avenue itself remains a thorny question mark.

The most conservative approach would be to enlarge the existing district to the west to include Fifth and to the east just short of Park, covering the buildings east of Park by separate designations. But if the commissioners decide that Park Avenue is itself a feature worthy of protection, they will have to create a much larger district.

And if they do include Park from, say, 86th to 96th Street, many will then wonder why the avenue from 79th to 86th Streets, excluded from the Metropolitan Museum Historic District, is not similarly protected.

The new proposal for the extension of the Carnegie Hill District includes only a few blocks of Park.

THE PLAZA THEATER

Is the Reel Running Out for a Converted Stable?

The Vanderbilt stable at 42–44 East 58th Street around 1916.

DEMOLITION WORK HAS begun on a handful of small buildings on the north side of 57th Street between Madison and Park Avenues in anticipation of a new commercial project that William Zeckendorf Jr. is developing.

Mr. Zeckendorf and his partners control a plot of about 20,000 square feet, and are understood to be attempting to enlarge their zoning lot by acquiring nearby property or, perhaps, only the unused development rights from those properties. One such property is the 10,000-square-foot plot occupied by the one-story Plaza Theater, at 42–44 East 58th Street, which started life as Cornelius Vanderbilt 2d's stable.

The death of Commodore Cornelius Vanderbilt in 1877 dispersed his great fortune in several directions. A major beneficiary was his favorite grandson, Cornelius 2d, who inherited the family portraits and $5 million, according to John Foreman, who is writing a book on the Vanderbilt family houses.

In 1879, when the estate was finally settled, Cornelius 2d began construction of his mansion at the northwest corner of 57th Street and Fifth Avenue—one of several family houses that helped change Fifth in this section into "Vanderbilt Alley." He also built a grand stable at 42–44 East 58th Street, neither too close nor too far from his home.

Designed by George B. Post, the stable was French Renaissance in style, of brick and limestone with a peaked roof. Large central doors led to a storage area on the first floor for carriages and a ramp to the basement for the horses. Servants lived on the second floor.

The stable housed not only carriages but also sleighs for winter use in Central Park.

Elizabeth Lehr in her 1935 book, *King Lehr in the Gilded Age*, recalls seeing the Vanderbilt sleigh "flash by in a blaze of red—dark red liveries, red carriagework, crimson plumes, red and gilt."

Cornelius 2d died in 1899 and in 1916 the family converted the stable to a dance hall. The Vanderbilt house itself was replaced by the Bergdorf-Goodman store in 1928. The next year the Vanderbilts leased the former stable to a theater operator, Leo Brecher.

Brecher retained Harry Creighton Ingalls to design not a new building, but an alteration. The front wall was taken down and an auditorium was inserted in the first two floors. According to Brecher's son, Walter, the present central stairway to the basement lounge is a reworking of the old cleated horse-ramp, and the lines of brick arches that run through the lower floor are actually the remains of the original stall enclosures.

The 500-seat theater opened in January 1930 with an unusual policy. "Better a good old picture than a dull new one," the *New York Sun* quoted Brecher, who was competing against giant movie palaces like Proctor's at 58th Street and Third Avenue. The *Sun* reported that the Plaza "revived the old Chaplin two-reelers and had dowagers rolling up in limousines" to see them. Indeed, the intimate theater was designed to look antique to appeal to a more moneyed crowd "who didn't like to be part of a huge mob," according to Walter Brecher.

Tudor in style, the building has a rough stucco exterior with irregular stone trim, a small balcony over the marquee and six double doors of colored, leaded glass with insets of coats of arms.

The architect gave the lighting fixtures antique finishes, artificially aged the woodwork, installed a timbered ceiling and decorated the rough white walls with colored stencilwork.

In 1938, Gertrude Vanderbilt Whitney, founder of the Whitney Museum and the daughter of Cornelius Vanderbilt 2d, sold the building to Walter Reade, the theater-chain owner, although the Brechers continued to operate the theater through the 40's.

Now the building is owned by the family of Jules Stein, founder of the Music Corporation of America, known as M.C.A.—and leased to Cineplex Odeon of Toronto. The stencilwork has been covered with dark paint, but the theater is largely intact—the chairs and sofas in the downstairs lounge make it as inviting as a private club.

Representatives for the owner and the lessee would not comment on reported offers to buy out their interests. But Mr. Zeckendorf confirms that the 5,000-square-foot theater parcel would make a nice addition to his assemblage. The Stein family also owns another 5,000-square-foot parcel at 601–603 Madison Avenue—connected to the Zeckendorf site only by the Plaza Theater land.

Mr. Zeckendorf has not yet announced plans for the project he will build on his assemblage. And so the fate of a Vanderbilt stable converted to a mock-Tudor movie house that favored the old over the new remains undecided.

The building has survived the Zeckendorf project, which is now under construction.

THE STUDEBAKER BUILDING

Just Off Times Square, a Car Factory with Offices

The Studebaker Building at Broadway and 48th Street in 1903.

BUILT FOR THE venerable carriage manufacturer as it was entering the automobile business in New York in 1902, the Studebaker Building recently lost its elaborate cornice and with it, almost certainly, any possible landmark protection against demolition.

The building, at 1600 Broadway at 48th Street, is on a prime development site.

By 1900, the area in and around Longacre Square—now Times Square—had become the center of the carriage industry in New York and it soon attracted the automobile business. The 1908 New York–to–Paris automobile race began there, and around that time, Benz, Renault, Oldsmobile and other auto manufacturers were settled on Broadway between 42d and 50th Streets.

The Studebaker Brothers Manufacturing Company had been established in 1852 in Indiana and by the turn of the century was the largest vehicle manufacturer in the world. According to Michael Quinn, an editor of *Turning Wheels*, the magazine of the Studebaker Drivers Club, the company introduced an electric automobile in 1902 and its first gasoline-powered automobile in 1904 as part of an expansion program.

Studebaker first came to New York City in 1895, and in 1902 work began on its huge, 10-story factory/office building. Offices and sales rooms were on the first floor, but a huge elevator could shift automobiles between the battery-charging rooms, storage areas, assembly finishing and repair rooms on the other floors.

It is an unusual structure, a high-rise office-factory for both automobiles and carriages. Nothing else like it has ever been built in New York City.

The exterior is of red brick and terra-cotta with the repeated use of the anthemion motif in the terra-cotta and in the huge projecting copper cornice at the roof level. It was designed by James Brown Lord, who also designed Delmonico's restaurant on 44th Street and Fifth Avenue and the elaborate Appellate Courthouse on 25th Street and Madison Avenue.

According to Mr. Quinn, the early 1900's were boom years for Studebaker; in 1910 it received the largest request ever for automobiles, an order by Gimbel's for 150 delivery vehicles.

But the Studebaker Building's glory years were short-lived. In 1902, the huge Astor Hotel, at 44th Street and Broadway, had been started and in 1903 plans were filed for the Times Tower at 42d Street and Broadway. They presaged a totally new development of the area as theaters, restaurants and hotels displaced the older buildings.

In 1911, Studebaker deserted its recent building for space in one at 57th Street and Broadway, and its flagship building was reconstructed for office use.

Ironically, the wave of tall buildings did not materialize—at least not until recent years. Now high-rise building projects ring the old Studebaker Building and Cushman & Wakefield's *Directory of Manhattan Development* lists the site for future development by Sherwood Equities, the present owner.

In 1979, the staff of the Landmarks Preservation Commission included the building in a list of over 200 recommended for landmark designation or consideration, but the panel never acted on it. But the 1979 report missed the Studebaker identification, treated the structure as a standard office building, dated it as 1912 and attributed it to a minor architectural firm, all of which undercut the structure's significance. The errors had not been corrected as of late last month.

Last October, Robert Redlien, engineer for the owner, filed plans to "repair ornamental cornice." But Mr. Redlien now says, "We're just taking it off."

He and the owner say that the cornice is dangerous, that pieces have fallen to the ground. But no violations have been lodged against the cornice. And a facade inspection of 1987, filed with the city, called it "safe," according to Vahe Tiryakian, a spokesman for the Department of Buildings.

In a reporter's inspection last December, the supporting steel brackets all appeared to be free of anything more than surface rust. But the cornice did have large holes in it—made by the wrecking crew.

The thick copper cornice itself—there is evidence that it had been in disrepair—had been sawed into sections with the anthemion crusting cut into four-foot lengths, apparently for resale. The cornice still in place appeared to be as sound as many others of the period.

Alan Goncharoff, vice president of Sherwood, says that the consideration of landmark designation has never come up and declined to comment on the company's plans for the site. Only three buildings in Manhattan without their cornices have been designated as landmarks and the likelihood of landmark designation is now, at best, highly improbable.

Still standing, although horribly scalped.

RHINELANDER INDUSTRIAL SCHOOL

A $1.9 Million Effort to Rectify the Alteration of an 1891 Relic

The Rhinelander Industrial School in 1907.

THE TYPICAL RESTORATION story reads like a honeymoon, with a rosy aura of press releases, civic awards and back-patting. But the story of the Children's Aid Society's old Rhinelander Industrial School at 350 East 88th Street is more like a tale of child abuse.

Now near the end of a $1.9 million renovation, the 98-year-old gabled building was so damaged in a 1950's alteration that even the tenderest of loving care cannot reclaim its historic character.

The society was founded by Charles Loring Brace in 1853 to help the growing numbers of neglected and abandoned children in New York City. He established lodging houses, industrial schools and summer retreats in a variety of quarters.

A major building program began in 1880 with the East Side Boys' Lodging House at East Broadway and Henry Street. Others were erected in congested tenement districts, with later ones built farther uptown.

The 22d Children's Aid Society building, at 350 East 88th Street, its northernmost, served the growing Yorkville tenement district. Like most other buildings of the society, this one was individually sponsored, in this case by Julia and Serena Rhinelander, who presented it to the society in 1891.

Built to serve 300 children in eight schoolrooms with cheery fittings and plain finishes, it had narrow but definite playgrounds on three sides, a reflection of the period concern with light and fresh air.

It was designed by Calvert Vaux and George Radford, who had designed eight others for the society in Manhattan, like the 1888 Astor Memorial Building at 256 Mott Street.

The facade of the four-story Rhinelander building was red brick with stone terra-cotta trimming and a stepped gable fronting on the street. It was dotted with decorative panels: the letter "R" on a field of vines at the center, and the legend "Rhinelander Industrial School" on a giant oval cartouche on the left.

The society's buildings were a bit dour, but taken collectively they formed a distinctive network, demonstrating the citywide work of a great charity.

The late Dennis Francis studied Vaux's work in the 1970's, and according to his research, the gable-end form was dictated by Brace, who asked the architects to emulate a 16th-century building in Nuremberg he had seen on a trip.

Vaux's career will be the subject of an exhibition opening in April at the Museum of the City of New York.

By 1902, the Rhinelander Industrial School was serving 477 children, only up through age 12 because "the children go to work at the age of 13," according to the annual report of that year.

Boys were taught manual trades and girls were taught cooking to provide household economy to those who needed it most.

"People with small means are most apt to go to delicatessen stores for ready-made dishes, which prove to be expensive," as the annual report put it.

The school remained active, and a building campaign in 1958 even enlarged the charity's presence—an adjacent, five-story structure at the southwest corner of 88th Street and First Avenue was erected and a playground was cut through to 87th Street.

At the same time, changes were made in the old building and the entire facade was coated with stucco as an inexpensive substitute for repointing the brick joints. The newly stuccoed building was the same in form, but now had a ghostly presence.

In 1988, the Children's Aid Society sold the corner parcel and the 87th Street playground to General Atlantic Realty, which is now erecting a 46-story condominium on the site.

Peter Moses, a spokesman for the society, said that the organization can now "devote our resources to serve the poor and needy in a truly poor and needy area," and the society is seeking a building or site in Washington Heights.

The old building, retained by the society, will now house a performing arts center, a residence for six homeless infants who would otherwise have to live in hospitals, and a training center for the prevention of child sexual abuse and teen-age pregnancy.

But the architectural work on the exterior will not match the good works inside.

According to Anthony Caine, architect for the society, the stucco coating has proven impossible to remove, so the facade will be scored and tinted to look like brownstone blocks. The east wall has been mostly covered by a projecting cinderblock stairway tower, a jarring note.

But perhaps most insulting to the original building is the loss of its original easterly stepped gable wing with its giant memorial cartouche.

To gain a few extra feet for sale, the society decided to demolish the low, left-hand wing, a crucial and unusual element in the building's overall design.

Even with the best of intentions, all preservation stories do not have happy endings.

The society has decided against buying another building, and will put its money into a community schools program with the Board of Education.

THE UNION SQUARE THEATER

The Ghost Behind a Huge Sign

The Union Square Theater, 58 East 14th Street, circa 1875.

NOW COVERED BY a huge McDonald's sign, the old Union Square Theater at 58 East 14th Street—usually described as the oldest such surviving structure in New York City—apparently had an intact Victorian theater interior walled off in 1936, when stores were inserted in the ground floor. Now the owner, Philips International Realty, says the building will be demolished this year.

The theater was actually an alteration, an auditorium created in 1871 within the shell of the five-story-high Morton House Hotel between Broadway and Fourth Avenue in Union Square, which was emerging as a center of shopping and entertainment.

Among the offerings on East 14th Street were the Academy of Music, an opera house that opened in 1854 at Irving Place, and Steinway Hall, a showroom and music hall that opened in 1866, west of it near Fourth Avenue. At the southwest corner of Union Square was Tiffany & Company.

With a combination of burlesque, ballet, comedy and pantomime, the Union Square Theater was advertised as "the model temple of amusement," according to John W. Fricke's 1985 book, *New York's First Theatrical Center—The Rialto at Union Square*. Later, it was converted to legitimate productions, but in February 1888 a fire destroyed the roof and parts of the auditorium.

The theater reopened the next year, almost completely rebuilt to the designs of John Terhune and Leopold Eidlitz, although some of the design was by Charles P. Palmer, the manager of the property. Because of the cramped site, Palmer developed a horseshoe balcony, rising in the center, that made efficient use of the high, narrow space. The interior was painted in old gold and ivory and the proscenium arch had a large medallion with a painting of Shakespeare. The chairs were of handcarved cherry, upholstered in electric blue.

The opening show was *A Woman's Strategem*, which did not impress the *New York Times*'s critic, who called it "absurdly loud and disturbingly unintelligent." But the same anonymous writer called the auditorium "bright and cheerful."

In 1893, the theater was taken over by B. F. Keith and Edward Albee and converted to continuous vaudeville. One act was George M. Cohan, making his New York debut to an indifferent audience. In 1896, the theater exhibited some early motion pictures and in 1908 it was converted entirely to films, ultimately "dabbling in the most dubious activities that a picture house can indulge in," according to J. C. Furnas in the *New York Herald Tribune* of 1932, alluding to racy films and sex lectures. In that Depression year it was converted to all-Soviet films and

Furnas described the barker's cries: "Come and see the world ablaze! See the triumph of the working classes!"

These "triumphs" lasted only until 1936 when the theater operation was ended. The ground floor was divided for stores, destroying the orchestra section of the auditorium—but since that time theater historians have generally supposed that the hung ceiling above the first floor stores concealed intact tiers of balconies and boxes above.

Donald King, a theater historian, unsuccessfully tried to get access to the hidden spaces from the roof, sides and bottom in the 70's. Fricke's book states the survival of the upper portion as a fact, but no one has actually seen it in modern times.

The 1889 rebuilding complicates the theater's historic status, but with 1871 as the basic date of the structure, it contains the oldest surviving theater space in New York City. According to Michael R. Miller, the theater historian, the next later theaters are Carnegie Hall and the Bedford Avenue Theater in Brooklyn (both opened in 1891) and perhaps the old Sans Souci at 100 Third Avenue, which may be as early as 1877.

In 1986 the Philips International Corporation acquired the site and has almost completely vacated the buildings although it does not yet have specific plans for redevelopment.

Philips permitted a reporter access to the building this month on the condition that he go in unaccompanied; the company states that the building is unsafe. Beyond a vacant store, at the rear, there is a staircase leading to what was originally the stage area, a lofty, Piranesi-like space without ornamentation.

In the conversion to store use, a wall of firebrick had been erected across the stage opening, shutting off the auditorium from the stage itself. A light inserted through a small hole in the brick disclosed that the 1936 alterations had not simply covered the original auditorium, but also had removed almost everything below the ceiling. On the walls there are only occasional fragments of composite capitals and painted decoration, although the outline of the horseshoe balcony is evident.

The ceiling still has its old gold and ivory paint and two large cupolas, into which huge ventilation ducts have been inserted. The only part that is not visible is the proscenium arch, and it is conceivable that the arch and its Shakespeare medallion are still intact. Short of a serious documentation effort by the owner, only demolition promises a really complete view of what is left of the old Union Square Theater.

Still standing, as development plans for the site are on hold.

O'REILLY BROTHERS WAREHOUSE

A Marvel of Fancy Brickwork Awaits the Dawn of a New Day

The now-vacant and boarded-up O'Reilly Brothers Warehouse, at 123d Street and St. Nicholas Avenue, in 1938.

THE O'REILLY BROTHERS Warehouse is something of a one-note building, but the note is exquisite. Now vacant and boarded up, the nine-story structure at the northeast corner of 123d Street and St. Nicholas Avenue is fairly plain, without ornament, but it presents a rich interplay of orange brick and brownstone.

A private developer, Bluestone Management Inc., wants to renovate the building but will do so only if the city removes a restriction limiting it to nonprofit use.

Storage warehouse design benefited from advances in office construction in the 1870's and high-rise versions began appearing in the 1880's.

Cornelius O'Reilly had been a builder since the 1860's, when he put up a row of brownstones at the present site of the Museum of Modern Art on West 53d Street. In 1876, he and other family members began a storage business, O'Reilly Brothers, and by the 1880's they occupied a five-story warehouse on 44th Street near Lexington Avenue.

In 1890, Cornelius O'Reilly, who had been practicing as an architect since 1880, filed plans for a new building at the 123d Street site as West Harlem was being built up with houses and apartments.

The warehouse was completed in 1892 at a cost of $40,000 and towered over the row houses and a riding academy that occupied the rest of the block. In fact, it dominated the entire neighborhood, a broad plain at the foot of Morningside Heights.

The design is unsophisticated—undulating brick walls, with a peaked corner tower. Barred windows on the ground floor and a top-floor arcade, corbeled out beyond the building line, provide the fortified aspect favored by warehouse designers. But the large expanse of brick—light orange, with contrasting pointing and trim in salmon—and occasional use of a deep red brownstone make the building stand out.

The height of the warehouse, its low neighbors and the diagonal of St. Nicholas Avenue give the building full sunlight even in winter, and the setting sun gives it a rich golden color, like a log fire in cold weather.

The warehouse's position facing a small square, Hancock Park, gives it a memorable setting.

Vacant lots in the area were gradually filled in with low apartments and row houses until the early 1900's, when overbuilding caused a collapse in housing prices in Harlem and its emergence as a black enclave. The O'Reilly company continued in operation, although Cornelius O'Reilly was killed in a construction accident in 1903 at another building of his design, Our Lady of Lourdes Church at 467 West 142d Street.

Later, Harlem saw little new construction in this area except for the 10-story Sydenham Hospital, erected directly across Hancock Park in 1925.

The first black residents to move into Harlem apartments and houses had in quantity what had not been available to them before—good-quality housing, recently built. But without new investment and regular maintenance, conditions declined noticeably by the 1940's.

Now the O'Reilly Brothers Warehouse looks on apartments and houses that are in good shape, but it also backs up on abandoned row houses and a vacant lot.

The building, which later became known as the Dwyer Warehouse, was not sold by the O'Reilly family until 1959. The building went through a series of uses and was ultimately taken back by New York City for taxes.

In 1980, the city sold it for $47,000 to Our Families Protective Association Inc., a community organization, with a restrictive covenant stipulating a nonprofit use for the building after renovation.

But the organization's president, L. Kofi Brown, says it was impossible to raise construction money, and in 1985 Our Families sold it to Bluestone Management. Philip Levien, one of the principals there, says his group was unaware of the deed restriction at the time of the sale.

Mr. Levien, who says that the Our Families group is a limited partner in the project, plans a conversion to retail and commercial space and housing for artists if the city will remove the covenant.

The Department of General Services supports the plan and is sponsoring the change at the City Planning Commission and the Board of Estimate.

A buyout payment to remove the covenant has been set at $163,000, plus 8,000 square feet of space to remain for nonprofit use. The city is expected to make a decision sometime this spring.

Buyout completed—building still a derelict.

THE NAUMBURG BANDSHELL

Everyone but the Donor's Family Wants It Gone

Dancing at the Naumburg Bandshell in July 1961.

THE FUTURE OF the 1923 Naumburg Bandshell on the Mall in Central Park, while not exactly a controversy, presents a messy problem nonetheless.

It is a handsome structure in the classical style but apparently everyone wants it replaced by a modern structure. Everyone, that is, but the family of the donor.

The Department of Parks is now surveying other sites where it might move the stone bandshell—an undertaking it considers doubtful—and if no suitable site is found, it plans to demolish it.

Central Park's designers, Frederick Law Olmsted and Calvert Vaux, had always envisioned musical events in the park. In 1872, according to William Alex, an authority on Olmsted, the designers wrote: "The effect of good music in the park is to aid the mind in freeing itself from the irritating effect of urban conditions."

Although concerts were tried using a floating bandstand in the middle of the lake, the main spot for music was always the mall, the long row of walks and trees leading up to the Terrace and Bethesda Fountain. Originally, a small ornate bandstand, open on all sides, stood on the west side of the mall.

But in 1921 Elkan Naumburg, a retired merchant and banker, offered the city $100,000 to build an elaborate bandshell of Indiana limestone. The bandstand was torn down and the bandshell was opened in 1923, as the band concert movement was near its peak in America; five concerts a week in the summer drew audiences of up to 30,000.

The *New York Times* described the tall structure as "a sort of Roman temple cut in two" with an acoustic shell to amplify the music to the crowds. Designed by William Tachau, a nephew of Naumburg, the structure has a coffered half-dome, originally meant to be gilded. It is easily the equal of other park structures like the Soldiers' and Sailors' Monument in Riverside Park.

The bandshell, carrying the inscription, "Presented to the City of New York and Its Music Lovers," was built across the mall from the old one, but backed into the hill carrying the Wisteria Pergola, and a *Times* account of the design mentions that the point was to avoid "any interfering with the design of the mall in its relation to the original park plan."

But where the original bandstand had been open on all sides, the Naumburg had a single orientation, and a large area of the mall itself had to be clear for movable benches.

The arrangement served well enough and Elkan Naumburg's son, Walter, established a series of free concerts by the Naumburg Orchestra, which continued to play in the shell until about 1980. The acoustic shell itself was made irrelevant by electric amplication and, even more so, by a wider variety of events.

Joseph Killian, a Parks Department employee whose title is director of the bandshell, says that events now include jazz, rock, folk and classical music as well as opera, theater, and a broad miscellany from New York City Marathon events to a Guide Dog Walk. "It's a multi-art facility," he says.

Gradually, more and more of the mall was paved over and the bandshell area now looks like a parking lot without cars. The shell, too, has declined, its delicate Indiana limestone painted over, with individual blocks deteriorating or damaged by casual additions.

In 1985 the Central Park Conservancy, a nonprofit organization, in a restoration plan for the entire park, stated that the bandshell blocked the view of the mall from the Wisteria Pergola on the hill behind it and has "outlived its usefulness."

Since then the Department of Parks has received an offer of $500,000 from Mitchell Leigh, a theatrical composer and director, and his wife, Abby, to build a new, seasonal stage on the site of the original bandstand and demolish or relocate the Naumburg Bandshell.

The new stage would be equipped for all kinds of events and be stored off-season (the Naumburg shell is generally unused for nine months of the year).

The Landmarks Preservation Commission has approved the bandshell demolition and no preservation or park organization has questioned it. "We try to stay out of Central Park matters," says Allen Payne, a spokesman for the nonprofit Parks Council. "They've got the Central Park Conservancy."

But the Naumburg family is angry. Philip Naumburg, grandson of the donor and executor of Walter Naumburg's will, vows that the Naumburg Orchestra will never again give free concerts in New York City if the bandshell is demolished. The orchestra now gives two or three concerts a year in Damrosch Park, to which it moved, Mr. Naumburg says, because the city would not stop noise from drummers, radios and other sources around the bandshell.

Christopher London, a great-grandson of Elkan Naumburg, deplores the fact that the shell is used "for more and more nonmusical events, which it was never designed to serve."

As for having a new bandshell that would be up only a few months of the year, he said: "They've spent millions on the Wollman Rink, and that's only used seasonally too. I think they should be raising money to restore the bandshell, not demolish it."

Carter Horsley, for a subsequent New York Post *article, discovered that the Commission had indeed "approved the bandshell demolition" but that they had neglected to tell me that the approval was only given contingent on a restoration of the original Olmsted & Vaux bandstand—something the Leigh proposal certainly did not include. In any event, this column scored highest on the "reader outrage" meter of any I have published and the proposal has been dropped. This awful instance points up the need to change our Art Commission's purview. It has authority only over additions to the city architecture—but it also needs authority over deletions.*

THE INSPIRATION POINT SHELTER

Restoration for an All-but-Ruined Hudson "Temple"

Shelter on the Henry Hudson Parkway at 190th Street in the late 1930's.

THE ROADSIDE SHELTER at Inspiration Point, on the Henry Hudson Parkway and 190th Street, was built in 1925 as a destination point for promenaders and pleasure drivers.

But as Riverside Drive gave way to the present high-speed highway in the 1930's, the little Greek temple became a lonely vestige of a lost custom, deteriorating and barricaded, its roof collapsing.

Henry J. Stern, Commissioner of the New York City Department of Parks, says that the agency will restore the structure at a cost of $100,000 and perhaps the leisurely Sunday driver will again make an appearance at Inspiration Point.

Views of the Hudson and the Palisades made Riverside Drive an excursion spot in the 19th century for bicyclists and carriage parties.

The drive below the 125th Street valley, near the present site of Grant's Tomb, was opened in 1880 but the stretch above it was a discontinuous roadway broken by industrial complexes and estates.

In 1924, the city began work on the completion of Riverside Drive all the way to Inwood, a $1.45 million project. The drive stopped at Dyckman Street and was thus not a regional highway.

Near 190th Street the drive rounded Inspiration Point, an outcropping "long a popular resort for those who appreciate Hudson River scenery," according to the *New York Times* in 1924. "An elaborate shelter is being constructed there which will be the longest, largest and most attractive on the drive, 136 feet above the level of the river," the article explained.

The next year, the *Times* said: "The view here is perhaps the finest to be enjoyed anywhere in the city. The drive for a moment curves outward, giving an uninterrupted view to the north and south. On clear days, it is possible to see as far up the Hudson as Ossining and southward to the Battery and even beyond, a sweep of more than 30 miles."

The shelter—26 feet wide, 106 feet long and 16 feet high—is in the form of a covered peristyle, a rectangular screen of columns of cast stone.

Designed under the supervision of Gustavo Steinacher, chief engineer for the Department of Parks in 1924, the Inspiration Point shelter almost matches a similar structure built in 1910 at 122d Street designed by the parks architect, Theodore Videto. Both structures are open on the main level, working out over the river with stairs leading to public toilets below. In 1910, the *Real Estate Record & Guide* called the 122d Street building "a riverside ornament."

In both structures the Doric columns and coffered wooden ceilings lend a classical purity suitably inspirational.

The improved Riverside Drive and the shelter were opened in 1925 after a parade by 10,000 Fort Washington schoolchildren.

A two-way drive, it had a wide sidewalk on the river side; this was an environment where the automobile and the pedestrian were meant to mix agreeably. Drivers were encouraged to stop at the roadside in a large turnoff in front of the $150,000 shelter, the last stopping place before the end of the drive at Dyckman Street.

As the automobile changed from a pleasure vehicle to mere transportation, the pleasure drive lost its patron in road planners. The Miller Elevated Highway (or West Side Highway) below 72d Street of 1931 to 1933 was meant for moving, not inspiring, people. But it was Robert Moses' Henry Hudson Parkway of 1937—although an idyll compared to the modern interstate—that made the bed of the old isolated Riverside Drive a through highway, with a bridge crossing the Harlem River.

Gradually, increased traffic turned what had been a walking/driving experience into a no man's land for pedestrians. The walkway is now overgrown and concrete bumpers now barricade what was the original promenade.

The shelter at Inspiration Point itself now suggests despair. The doors to the toilets are walled up. Cast-stone copings, indeed whole sections of balustrade, have been pushed over, down the steep slope. The rotting wooden roof has miraculously escaped destruction by fire, but whole sections have fallen off or hang precariously at the edge. Water damage has buckled the elegant coffered ceiling and most of what remains looks like driftwood scavenged from a lost civilization.

Occasionally, an intrepid jogger navigates the deteriorating promenade, vaulting over the mounds of trash that the shelter has attracted. But the shelter itself has no visitors—it is merely a picturesque ruin, a blur to motorists fleeing the city. It looked as if the Inspiration Point shelter was headed for the same fate as other roadside antiquities, like the Art Moderne gas station south of the George Washington Bridge, demolished a few years ago. But now the Department of Parks has announced a stabilization campaign for the shelter, to begin later this year.

The restrooms will not be reopened, but the concrete bumpers in the area of the shelter will be removed, trash and brush will be cleared away and cast stone elements replaced. The roof will be taken down and replaced with an open trellis in a similar style to minimize maintenance costs.

Inspiration may once again be available at Inspiration Point.

Work completed.

THE LITCHFIELD VILLA

Back to the Past for a Landmark in Prospect Park

Rendering of Litchfield Villa in Prospect Park showing original 1853 stucco facade.

PERHAPS IT IS the granddaddy of all the exposed brick walls in renovated brownstone apartments, first popular around 1960. It has looked the way it does for so long that its original appearance has largely passed out of living memory.

Now the Department of Parks has proposed to restore the original stucco coating to the facades of the Litchfield Villa in Prospect Park, which have been red brick since the 40's. If the city's Office of Management and Budget approves the cost, a new stucco coat, scored and tinted to look like stone, could be put on the structure beginning in 1990.

Edwin Litchfield built his house along the Mount Prospect ridge in Brooklyn from 1853 to 1857. At the time, the area was largely farmland and his large tract ran down to the Gowanus Canal and afforded views of the Battery and New York Harbor.

Litchfield hired the architect A. J. Davis, who designed an asymmetrical, Italian-style villa with a variety of towers, bays and porches. A circular reception hall—with a floor of multicolored tiles—was surrounded by a second-floor gallery and illuminated by a skylit dome.

The house received unusual decoration—columns modeled after bamboo stalks, an elaborate ceiling mural and column capitals on the porch in the form of corncobs and wheat stalks.

The exterior was built of plain, unglazed bricks, which casual passersby now think are original but which were actually coated with stucco in imitation of stone. According to Jane B. Davies, a specialist in the work of Davis, this was common practice in the period and at the Litchfield house the stucco was scored and lightly painted to suggest stone blocks.

Litchfield, who was active in real estate and railroads, moved into the house with his wife Grace and three children in 1857. According to a report on the villa for the Parks Department by Patricia Florio Colrick, he soon became active in developing his land, especially along the waterfront, but reserved as an estate the property around his house.

Manhattan's Central Park had been designed in 1858 and a movement began in Brooklyn for a comparable work in the area of Mount Prospect. An early scheme approached but did not include Litchfield's house and he was an initial supporter of the project. But the landscape firm of Olmsted & Vaux revised the design to enlarge the park and include Litchfield's house.

Donald E. Simon was the Curator of Prospect Park from 1969 to 1975 and has conducted extensive research on Litchfield.

"He fought the enlargement intensively and had tremendous political clout in largely Democratic Brooklyn," Mr. Simon said. An 1869 article in the *Brooklyn Daily Eagle* states that Litchfield left for a European trip "convinced that his house was his castle" and would not be acquired. But according to Mr. Simon, the park project was controlled by the New York State Legislature, largely Republican, and Litchfield's house was condemned while he was abroad.

The Litchfields were granted a lease to expire in 1883, after which Litchfield left for Europe, where he died in 1885. The building then became a headquarters for Brooklyn's Department of Parks and has remained a park property to this day.

Later changes to the Litchfield house, which is a designated New York City Landmark, have been surprisingly minor; most of the original interiors survive under several coats of paint or, in the case of the mural, a tin ceiling. But the major change came in the 20th century with the removal of the stucco.

The conventional account is that it was taken off in the 1930's, but Clay Lancaster, curator of the park from 1966 to 1969, took photographs of the building in 1944 that show the stucco still in place, although quite deteriorated and about to be removed.

Mr. Simon interviewed workers who remembered the project and they all recall that the stucco was removed only so that an entirely new coat could be applied, but this was never done.

Now Tupper Thomas, Administrator of Prospect Park, says that money has been budgeted to completely rebuild the mechanical systems of the Litchfield house and to restore the original stucco treatment under the supervision of the architectural firm of Hirsch/Danois.

The change will be obvious and certainly logical. But there will still be a twinge of regret in some minds when the stucco is applied.

"I'm kind of charmed by the appearance of the building in its present state," said Elliot Willensky, co-author of the *AIA Guide to New York City*. "When I first saw it in the 1960's it never occurred to me to think that it had had any other surface, and I still have a warm response to the brick."

METROPOLITAN MUSEUM
A Diminished Garden Courtyard for an Old Facade

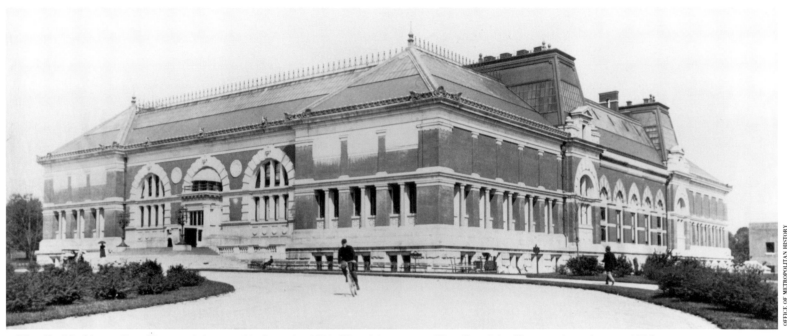

Wing B of the Metropolitan Museum, left, opened in December 1888. Wing A is at center, Wing C at right. They are shown here ca. 1895.

THE METROPOLITAN MUSEUM of Art is putting into place the last element of its master plan of 1970—a second garden court. But what was originally conceived as a vast, skylit garden court has now shrunk to a quarter of its original size and, inside, the museum's 1888 facade has been beautifully restored but been robbed of its perspective.

The museum's first wing in Central Park, built in 1880, was conceived as an inner element in a much larger complex and was given a modest entrance facing the East Carriage Drive.

The next building, later called Wing B, was designed as a principal facade in and of itself, with a entrance stair facing south to the growing city. It was New York's first really grand museum structure.

Built at a cost of $350,000, Wing B opened on December 18, 1888. The exterior continued the contrast of deep red brick and light stone of the 1880 Wing A, designed by the Central Park architects Calvert Vaux and J. Wrey Mould—Frederick Law Olmsted was a landscape designer—but with an important shift: Instead of continuing the Victorian Gothic styling of the earlier building, Theodore Weston designed a structure of grand, almost Roman proportions, incorporating decorative elements of the neo-Grec style.

The chunky quality of the stonework, the repeated use of the rondel motif and the polished granite columns of the main floor windows of Wing B are all elements found in other neo-Grec buildings, like Richard Morris Hunt's Lenox Library of 1877 at 70th Street and Fifth Avenue, later replaced by the Henry Frick residence.

As built, Wing B also had a high, rock-faced stone basement, a grand stairway with two elaborate torcheres and unusual, demon-like heads at the cornice line. Friezes of relief sculpture in the classical style at the second floor were never carried out.

The new wing was bold and vigorous in its color contrast and handling, and the classical elements lent it a sense of sophistication and antiquity appropriate for a major collection of art objects.

Weston, a Yale graduate, had written on topics like Roman waterworks. A founder of the Metropolitan Museum, he was obviously an educated man, but his career had been largely as a civil engineer, working on canal and sewer projects, and no other buildings from his hand have been identified. It is curious that he was responsible for such a major building.

Associated with him was Arthur Lyman Tuckerman, who published several histories of architecture and subsequently designed Wing C, an extension to the north. But he is also otherwise unknown as a practicing architect.

The main entrance of 1888 became secondary by 1902, when the first of the museum's buildings facing Fifth Avenue was completed. The subsequent massive limestone facade along Fifth Avenue, begun in 1902 and completed in 1926, made the old red brick complex seem dowdy by comparison. Eventually the area in front of Wing B became a parking lot.

In 1970, the Metropolitan announced a master plan to complete the museum, which had seen a number of such plans go unrealized. The centerpiece was the Lehman Wing, which covered the original Wing A facade and, in general, the museum was extended all along its western edge into Central Park.

An announcement by Thomas P. Hoving, then director of the museum, referred to "the delicate situation" of the landmark status of the complex. But, he added, the Wing B facade "is a landmark of such importance that it must be restored to its original grandeur."

The solution developed by the museum's architects, Roche Dinkeloo and Associates, was to reuse the main facade within a skylit garden courtyard, "available to the public as park land independent of the regular museum hours." There was controversy at the time about the museum's expansion into Central Park.

The Lehman Wing opened in 1975 and the *New York Times* architecture critic Paul Goldberger wrote in *New York: The City Observed* that the Wing A facade had been "overly cleaned up, sterilized."

Since that time construction on the master plan has continued and now the last element, the second garden court, is under construction and was roofed in last year.

But the plans have been revised to permit more gallery space and the original court has been shrunk to little more than a tall corridor along the Wing B facade.

The museum now says the court will be open only seasonally, during museum hours.

What remains of the old building has been cleaned, but a new, higher floor level has robbed it of its height and the narrower court design has removed any sense of approach. But even so diminished, it is still a powerful design and its return to the public domain will be welcome when the new courtyard opens in 1990.

603 PARK AVENUE

A Grand Mystery House
Up for Sale at $20 Million

The Thomas A. Howell residence at 603 Park Avenue at 64th Street in 1928. It has a 100-foot frontage on Park Avenue.

EDGELL, AMERICAN ARCHITECT

IT COULD ARGUABLY be described as the grandest single-family residence in New York, with a full 100-foot frontage on Park Avenue at the northeast corner of 64th Street. Such a claim may account for the asking price of $20 million for the old Thomas A. Howell residence built in 1920.

But it remains to be seen whether its prominent position at 603 Park Avenue will encourage or discourage its reuse as a private dwelling.

Private-house construction on Park Avenue above Grand Central Terminal began in the late 1870's after the railroad tracks were sunk and partially covered.

But cinders and steam still spewed out of the vents in the park-like malls in the center of the avenue and most houses were oriented to the street rather than to the avenue itself.

One such group was a row of houses at 101 to 113 East 64th Street begun in 1881, all with entrances facing on 64th. By the end of the 1880's, Park Avenue had developed into a boulevard of the bourgeois, a line of modest apartments and row houses which had to tolerate the train traffic.

But in 1903 the State Legislature mandated electric-powered trains in the cut and Park became attractive as an upper-class residential boulevard accommodating the spillover from Fifth and Madison Avenues.

Houses and apartments went up in relatively peaceful coexistence but after World War I construction of private houses was reduced to a trickle. One of the last was 603 Park Avenue, completed for Howell, a sugar wholesaler, at a cost of $65,000.

Howell's architects, Walter Lund and Julius Gayler, produced a trim, neo-Federal design that covered the entire 20- by 100-foot plot of the old 101 East 64th Street, with an entrance facing Park Avenue. It was in startling contrast to its heavy brownstone neighbors. Of variegated red brick, the house is decorated only with restrained marble detailing—a small, columned entryway at the ground floor, a Palladian window above that and other elements.

Inside, the great length of the house necessitated a long, half-elliptical stair hall, and every room looks out onto the avenue.

Howell suffered financial reverses shortly after moving in and had to sell the house in 1923. The next occupant was James W. Ellsworth, who had made a fortune in coal mining and then retired. By the 20's one of his major concerns was his son, Lincoln, who was dedicated to exploration, an activity his father did not appreciate. But he was able to introduce Roald Amundsen to his father in the house in 1924.

Amundsen had discovered the South Pole in 1911 and induced the senior Ellsworth into backing an aerial expedition to the North Pole in two seaplanes.

In 1925, members of the Amundsen–Ellsworth expedition made it to within 136 miles of the North Pole before they had to land. They were

stranded on the icecap for a month. The expedition party finally made it back, but not before the senior Ellsworth died of pneumonia without knowing of his son's fate.

The next occupants of the house were the family of Dr. James B. Murphy, later head of cancer research at Rockefeller Institute, who leased it from the Ellsworths in 1927 and purchased it in 1933. The Murphys made a minor but distinctive change, hiring Philip Johnson around 1932, "when I really hadn't done anything yet," the architect said in a telephone interview. He said he redesigned a small room on the third floor in the modernistic style, with veneered wood built-ins and streamlined leather upholstery.

Dr. Murphy died in 1950 and Mrs. Murphy, later Mrs. Ray S. Blakeman, remained in the house until her death in 1987. But after the 1950's, 603 Park Avenue took on the appearance of a mystery ship. Although the brass on the doors was kept polished and the house was in no disrepair, the windows were never washed and it seemed as if no one entered or left.

In 1988, the Kips Bay Boys' Club charity, with the permission of the Murphy family, had designers redecorate the rooms and opened the house to the public for two weeks at a $10 fee.

The building is now empty except for one of Philip Johnson's leather chairs and the intercoms which still bear the Howells' names. There is enough faux painting and mural work to stock a movie studio. The fresh paint, the clean floors, the sunlight flooding in, the rooms, all make it look like an elegant summer house that is just about to be reopened.

Now it is on the market for $20 million and most brokers agree that its conversion to apartments is unlikely, and that it will probably return to use as an embassy or private residence. According to Leslie Garfield, one of the brokers handling the sale, the previous high sale price for a Manhattan town house is $11 million, paid for 116 East 80th Street last year.

There are only three houses left on Park Avenue in strictly private occupancy—603, 711 and 1145 Park Avenue.

At one time, a prominent location on an avenue for a house was considered desirable. But 603 Park Avenue, which, as part of the Upper East Side Historic District, is protected from redevelopment, seems very exposed for the security-conscious 80's and it will be instructive to see who buys it and for what purpose.

Subsequently sold for $12.5 million and now again on the market for $19.5 million. The most rercent broker has comically attempted to promote the house as a "John Carere [sic] residence." Should someone tell him that architect Carrère died eight years before the house was designed? Leslie Garfield says the $12.5 million figure remained as a high from June 1989 until September 1989, when 9 East 71st Street sold for $13.2 million.

ST. THOMAS MORE ROMAN CATHOLIC CHURCH

A Touch of the English Countryside in Manhattan

St. Thomas More Roman Catholic Church at 65 East 89th Street, formerly the Episcopal Church of the Beloved Disciple, in 1890.

IT'S A SIGHT to make a preservationist's blood run cold—heavy scaffolding suddenly going up around a 119-year-old church in an area that has been proposed, but not yet accepted, for landmark designation.

"When you see scaffolding, you always hope they're restoring it," says Halina Rosenthal, president of the Friends of the Upper East Side Historic Districts, "but you are always afraid that the owner has something else in mind."

This time, there is no cause for alarm. The Roman Catholic Church of St. Thomas More at 65 East 89th Street, built in 1870 as the Episcopal Church of the Beloved Disciple, is just being repointed and the scaffolding should be down in time for June weddings.

The church was established in conjunction with St. Luke's Home for Indigent Christian Females, which occupied the adjacent lot at the northeast corner of 89th and Madison. Established by St. Luke's Episcopal Church near the church's own building at Hudson and Grove Streets, the home's relocation to 89th Street meant its elderly residents could no longer conveniently attend services.

The Rev. Isaac Tuttle, rector of St. Luke's, approached Caroline Talman—not connected with St. Luke's Church but active in Episcopal philanthropy—and explained the need for a new, separate church; she offered the money to build one.

According to a history of St. Luke's published in 1920, Miss Talman enjoyed watching the progress of the church's construction and would often go uptown from her Murray Hill residence to see it. Later, after losing substantial sums in poor investments, she thanked Dr. Tuttle for persuading her to make "an investment of which she could never be robbed."

The Gothic-style building has the air of a picturesque English country church, with a plot of green in front and a square tower rising in front of the sanctuary. According to Andrew S. Dolkart, an architectural historian specializing in church design, the building is closely modeled after Edward B. Lamb's Church of St. Martin's, Gospel Oak, London, built in 1865.

"It has almost every little quirky detail of the London church," says Mr. Dolkart. "The chamfered corners, the varying planes of the facade, the asymmetrical pinnacle at the top of the tower. It really captures your attention."

The exterior is executed in a beautifully soft, olive-gray sandstone identified by Sidney Horenstein, a geologist with the American Museum of Natural History, as quarried in Nova Scotia. The same stone is used in some of the walls surrounding Central Park and as trim on the Dakota apartment house.

A one-story chapel on the west was added in 1879, and a rectory and a parish house were added on the east side between 1880 and 1893, completing the complex.

When the church first rose it was in largely vacant territory; now it is the second-oldest church structure on the East Side, after the Church of the Resurrection at 115 East 74th Street, completed in 1869. The architects, Hubert & Pirsson, were later prominent in the syndication and design of early cooperative apartment houses and their 1884 Hotel Chelsea, at 222 West 23d Street, still stands.

Miss Talman died in 1897, leaving $5,000 to the home, which was moved to a new building at the southeast corner of 112th Street and Broadway in 1899.

But Beloved Disciple continued until the mid-1920's, when the Church of the Heavenly Rest, a much larger congregation then at Fifth Avenue and 45th Street, began its present building at 2 East 90th Street. Beloved Disciple agreed to merge with Heavenly Rest—retaining some identity in the form of an eponymous chapel in the new building. The old church was sold in 1929 to a Dutch Reformed congregation, and then in 1950 to the Roman Catholic Church of St. Thomas More, which is how most people know it today.

Tall apartment houses on Park Avenue shut off its east light in the 1920's and the 38-story apartment house at 45 East 89th Street, at the corner of Madison, blocked off the chapel's west windows in 1973. It now gets only raking light, morning and evening, and the deep shadows cast by the buttresses and other vertical elements, the darkened olive-gray stone and the striking tower all make it one of those midblock secrets missed by the guidebooks but savored by local residents. It's an English country church in Manhattan.

A Carnegie Hill Historic District was designated in 1973 but reached south only to 90th Street, excluding the church. Civitas, Carnegie Hill Neighbors and other community groups have been pushing to extend the district boundaries to include the church and other buildings, but the Landmarks Commission has yet to act on the proposal.

Samuel White, with the firm of Buttrick, White & Burtis, is serving pro bono as architect and says the work is strictly normal maintenance, repointing the stone, and only minor restoration of some elements will be made. Msgr. George F. Bardes, the pastor, says the work is part of a larger program to make the exterior sound. St. Thomas More has kept up its building very nicely, but Monsignor Bardes is nonetheless relieved that it is still not yet a landmark.

The facade was later given a disastrous cleaning.

SYLVAN TERRACE

Restoration Leaves a Lot of Unhappy Homeowners

The view west on Sylvan Terrace in upper Manhattan in 1905.

A RE THE RESIDENTS of Sylvan Terrace looking a gift horse in the mouth? Or have they just been taken for a ride?

The one-block landmark street of 20 wooden row houses connecting St. Nicholas Avenue and Jumel Terrace between 160th and 162d Streets got a facelift in 1979–1981 with $400,000 in Federal Community Development funds. But a few years later the homeowners complained of poor design and workmanship. To date, their complaints remain unresolved.

Sylvan Terrace was carved out of the estate surrounding the Morris–Jumel Mansion in 1882 by the developer James E. Ray, who had the architect Gilbert Robinson Jr. design two rows of high-stoop wooden row houses facing each other across a narrow private street leading to the mansion.

The buildings are often referred to as servants' houses built for the mansion, but period directories reveal that early occupants were solidly middle class. Among them were Homer Gilles, a feed dealer, at 10 Sylvan Terrace, and Thomas Ryerson, a grocer, at No. 17.

In the 90's, brownstones went up on the surrounding streets followed by small apartment houses. The city acquired the Morris–Jumel Mansion as a museum in 1903. The last major building in the area was in the 1910's when a few tall apartment houses went up.

By the 30's when the private-street status had lapsed, some decorative details, like the fancy door hoods, had been removed, but the houses were in good repair and some even had decorative painting.

After World War II, aluminum, asphalt and other siding swept the nation. On February 1, 1981, the *New York Times* quoted one resident as saying: "Johns-Manville sent salesmen in here and, one by one, the block got to be false brick of all colors." She also said that by 1978 only two of the original door hoods had survived. It had become hard to tell that the houses had been built as a group.

In 1970, despite the changes, the Landmarks Preservation Commission designated the Jumel Terrace Historic District, a two-square-block area around Sylvan Terrace.

Beverly Moss Spatt, chairman of the commission from 1974 to 1978, originated a program under which facades are restored on landmark buildings with Federal funds. Usually the owners pay a percentage, but at Sylvan Terrace—because of the owners' limited means, the unusual character of the street and the proximity to the Morris–Jumel Mansion, a National Historic Landmark—only consent, not contributions, was required.

Except for one stucco-front holdout at No. 16 Sylvan Terrace, the owners agreed. Work was completed in 1981 and the row was restored to something fairly close to its original appearance, yellow clapboard with green, brown and maroon trim—although it is uncertain whether the house colors were originally identical or varied.

The completed project was an improvement but there was a deadened homogeneity to the restoration. The backs of the rows were not done and the rear facades now form a catalogue of mid-20th century siding materials. The sole interruption to the new facade was No. 16.

"They tried to queue me in, to redo my steps and things, but I knew I was right," said Thelma Walker, the owner. "I didn't see why I should take off my good stucco front," which she had put on around 1950.

During construction, residents complained that paint had been applied in freezing temperatures, and it began to peel in places within a few years, according to Ruth Edwards, who organized a block association to address the problems. Some residents have since repainted their facades in similar but not identical colors, leavening the uniformity.

The windows—wooden ones, with double glazing—look good but many are balky, at best requiring delicate and regular adjustments and at worst basically inoperable.

But historic preservation and modern habitability collided on the wooden stoops. The stoops seem quaint and charming, but close inspection reveals inadequate drainage and rotting, buckling wood.

"The wooden stoops, even in 1882, were crazy," says Richard Ferrara, whose firm, Ferrara-Maruca, was the restoration architect. The stoops were not weathertight and were principally supports for the exterior stair. But later occupants took over the space underneath for storage and other purposes and what was once normal drainage is now a leak that must be plugged.

Ms. Edwards says the city has washed its hands of the matter and the Department of Housing, Preservation and Development, which actually organized the work, believes the problems are largely a result of inadequate normal maintenance.

The residents are still annoyed but seem to accept the reality that they, not the city, will have to resolve their complaints. Mrs. Walker, the holdout, feels vindicated.

"They say they restored it back to what it was but they only did the front—and it's just a cheap job," she said. "Now the other owners have the attitude that I was right."

THE CHAMBER OF COMMERCE BUILDING

New Owner for a 1902 Landmark

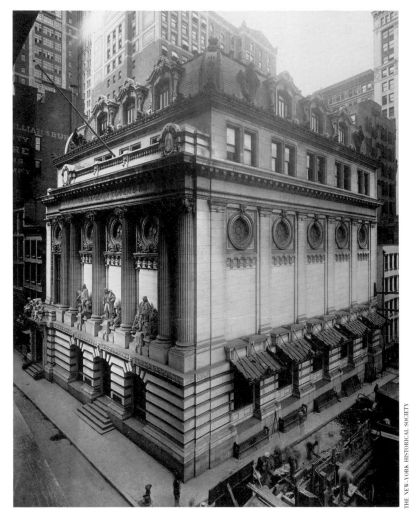

Chamber of Commerce Building at 65 Liberty Street, circa 1905.

THE OLD CHAMBER of Commerce Building at 65 Liberty Street is a little Beaux-Arts treasure dwarfed by later skyscrapers. But the chamber moved out in 1980 and the building has been in use only intermittently. Now a new owner, the International Commercial Bank of China, is ready to buy the building. Although the exterior is landmarked, the sumptuous Great Hall inside is not, and exactly how the magnificent room—90 by 60 feet and 30 feet high—will emerge, if at all, is not clear.

Established in 1768, the New York Chamber of Commerce was chartered by King George III in 1770 and claims to be the third-oldest such institution in the world after those in Marseilles, France, and the English island of Jersey. The chamber always was influential, but post–Civil War commercial expansion made it by 1900 the preeminent business organization in the city.

David Hammack, in his book *Power and Society: Greater New York at the Turn of the Century*, calls it "the most important organization" in the New York area in the 1890's. He ascribes to the chamber the beginning of the successful movement to unite Brooklyn, Queens and Staten Island with Manhattan and the Bronx, completed in 1898.

But since its founding the chamber had never occupied permanent quarters, carting its growing collection of portraits of business people and politicians from place to place as its leases expired.

In 1901 the chamber acquired a site at 65 Liberty Street between Broadway and Nassau Street. A member, James B. Baker, designed a four-story building of marble with a rusticated base, a giant screen of Ionic columns framing stretches of blank wall and a sumptuous terrace and mansard roof.

"Instead of a skyscraper," wrote the *Real Estate Record and Guide* in 1901, "to take all the light possible from neighbors to increase the rent roll, there will be a building which shows that the chamber recognizes there is something beyond revenue only."

There was a bit of revenue, from a banking room rented out on the ground floor. But the rest of the new building held the chamber's offices and the Great Hall, paneled in mahogany, with gilded decorations and a stained-glass ceiling. Lined top to bottom with the chamber's vast portrait collection, the room was "one of New York's greatest interior spaces," in the words of Robert Stern, Gregory Gilmartin and John Massengale in their book *New York 1900*.

The finished structure had a distinctly commercial air, but its size and blank walls suggested a very private club.

The dedication in November 1902 was attended by J. P. Morgan, Levi Morton, former President Grover Cleveland and President Theodore Roosevelt, who said that the Chamber of Commerce "has been able to show that the greatest commercial success can square with the immutable and eternal laws of decent and right living."

The chamber gained prominence as an organization of powerful individuals. But after World War I the rise of the modern corporation, where the stamp of the individual was less significant, was not consonant with the chamber's history as something of a private club. New York was growing in such a way that the influence of a small group of businessmen became blunted.

"After World War II it was all-volunteer," said Donald E. Moore, president of the New York Chamber of Commerce from 1978 to 1980, "very much run by its membership, and members still came together in the Great Hall and voted on issues of interest." But around that time, most operations were shifted to a professional staff, and the Great Hall did not see such frequent use.

In 1979, the chamber decided to sell its building and moved to a conventional office building at 200 Madison Avenue, as it merged with the New York City Partnership, an advocacy group involved in housing, education and other issues. Now the chamber still brings together its members, but uses outside meeting places, often those of corporations, said Ronald Shelp, president since 1987. The portraits were removed from the Great Hall when the chamber left in 1980.

The Landmarks Preservation Commission designated the exterior of the building a landmark in 1966, but as the chamber prepared to move, the commission decided to consider the Great Hall and related areas for designation. The chamber objected on the ground that the interiors were private—only interiors open to the public can be designated as landmarks—and the commission dropped the matter.

Two projected sales, in 1980 and in 1985, fell through. But the chamber now says it is about to sell the property to the International Commercial Bank of China, which will use it as offices later this year after renovation. L. C. Shu, a spokesman for the bank, said it is not clear what the new owner will do with the Great Hall.

The bank's restoration was finished in 1991, but the absence of the chamber's collection of portraits, which originally lined the walls, has drastically changed the Great Hall.

ALAN GARAGE–FRANKLIN HOTEL

Unusual Combination for Conflict

The Alan Garage on East 87th Street as it neared completion in 1930.

JEROME WEINSTEIN

ALTHOUGH THE BLOCK between 86th and 87th Streets, from Lexington to Third Avenues, has mostly unexceptional buildings, some big names in real estate—Norman Segal, Mark Perlbinder, Edward S. Gordon and William Zeckendorf—are involved in carving it up for development. Mr. Zeckendorf took title in April to the sprawling Loews 86th Street theater.

If there is a preservation controversy it will probably turn on two names otherwise unknown—Alan and Franklin, an unusual garage–hotel combination at 154–164 East 87th Street.

In September 1928, Stanhope Estates Inc. tried to file plans for a garage fronting 154 feet on the south side of 87th Street, just east of Lexington. Permission was denied because the zoning did not permit garages on the street and the owners went to the Board of Standards and Appeals for an exemption.

Various property owners protested the proposed variance, including Emanuel Ornstein, a local real-estate owner then preparing to build a 21-story hotel at the northwest corner of 87th and Lexington. Over their objections, the board granted a variance for the garage in January 1929.

But the board required that the garage be built no closer than 20 feet to the easterly lot line—bordering the Loews movie theater—and that it carry no more than one advertising sign.

Furthermore, it required that the "front elevation shall be designed in attractive architectural treatment . . . with face brick and architectural terra cotta."

The neighbors sued, but the Appellate Division of State Supreme Court confirmed the issuance of the permit in December 1929. The stock-market crash interrupted many plans and in June 1930 Stanhope Estates sold the vacant property, with its approved plans, to Mr. Ornstein, who dropped his plans for a hotel across the intersection.

The Stanhope Estates architect had been James H. Galloway, but Ornstein retained Frank J. Schefcik, who either modified or completely redesigned Galloway's plan. Ornstein also built a nine-story hotel on the lot from Schefcik's designs. Both the garage and hotel were completed in late 1930.

The Franklin Hotel is unexceptional but the garage is a handsome work. Great vertical white stripes run up the facade, festooned with floral ornament in yellow and green, all of glazed terra-cotta.

Two automobile tires appear in terra-cotta at the top floor—the auto age's substitute for the projecting horse's head often used on stable buildings—and the elevator headhouse is covered in terra-cotta in a diaperwork pattern.

Even more striking are the words "UP" and "DOWN" and "THE ALAN GARAGE" in 2-foot-high red letters in terra-cotta relief at the ground floor. The up and down signs, relating to internal ramps, are logical but of such size that they appear slightly surreal. The Alan name—which was considered an architectural detail, not a sign, thus doubling the building's permitted number of signs—also seems unusual. It does not appear in any real-estate transactions, and last, not first names are typical for commercial structures.

According to J. Alan Ornstein, born in 1928, the garage was named for him—he was his grandfather's first grandson. The hotel was named for his brother, born in 1930; a marquee with that name was added in 1931.

The story of the Alan and Franklin is made even better by the old-time quality of the garage. The waiting room is behind a plate-glass window on the street, with the name in silver leaf. Ancient gauges mark the levels of long-gone gasoline tanks. There is a gentility about a garage purposely built, not a subbasement afterthought to a much larger building—something like the difference between the old Penn Station and the new.

The Ornstein family owned the Alan and Franklin until 1979, when they were sold to Meyers Parking System Inc. Last year a group of investors, including Mr. Gordon, took the publicly held Meyers company private. Mr. Gordon says that real-estate development is not the prime concern of the new owners of Meyers Parking, which owns 10 Manhattan properties, but the *Notice of the Annual Meeting* in 1988 forecasts "long term investments in well-selected real estate."

It is generally accepted that a garage in a prime site cannot provide a reasonable return on the value of the land. With a floor-area ratio of 12, (12 square feet of building for one square foot of land), the garage site alone could probably accommodate a 15- to 18-story building.

The Alan and the Franklin are a great New York story; but are great stories eligible for landmark protection? Lillian Ayala, a spokesperson for the Landmarks Preservation Commission, says that it has not reviewed either the Alan or the Franklin so far.

A rental-car company scraped off the beautiful silver-leaf lettering and substituted tawdry plastic. The owner cleaned the facade of the building—nice job—and followed it by stuccoing the entire ground floor—aargh!

WANAQUE APARTMENTS
An Elegant Tenement Revisited

The 1887 Wanaque Apartments, center, circa 1939.

THE FIVE-STORY, 1887 Wanaque Apartments at 359 West 47th Street, now under renovation by the nonprofit Fountain House as a residence for psychiatric patients, holds many surprises.

On a street full of speculatively built, overdecorated tenements, it is elegant and reserved—an unusual minor commission by McKim, Mead & White. Most surprisingly, Fountain House's architect, Farrell, Bell & Lennard is a direct lineal descendant of the famed 19th-century design team.

The Wanaque was put up in 1886–1887 by James C. Miller, a contractor. Miller had occupied a small house on the site and it is not clear why he built a middle-class apartment house on a street of older multiple dwellings for the working class. But what was truly unusual about the Wanaque was Miller's choice of architect—the partnership of Charles McKim, William Mead and Stanford White. They had formed their firm in 1879 and within a few years had begun landing big commissions, among them the Villard Houses in 1882, now the entrance to the Helmsley Palace Hotel on Madison Avenue between 50th and 51st Streets.

They continued to take small jobs—occasional row houses and small apartments—through the mid-1880's. But in 1886 they were at work on the $250,000 Goelet Building at 20th Street and Broadway and were about to receive the commission for the $1.3 million Madison Square Garden on Madison Square. The Wanaque, built for only $20,000, was one of the firm's last minor works.

Miller had been a carpenter and builder prior to 1885, when he first emerged as an actual developer, building and occupying a chaste row house at 47 West 119th Street. His architect there was also McKim, Mead & White. Miller was never a major figure in New York real estate and neither he nor his family appear to have had other connections with the firm. Completed in 1887, the Wanaque was simpler and more refined that the typical tenement or middle-class apartment house—both of which often had garish ornamentation.

At the Wanaque, a simple ground-floor facade of Belleville brownstone with carved rope moldings around the door and windows surrounds an elegant projecting carved stone hood in Italian Renaissance style. Except for small terra-cotta elements the upper walls are all in brick with a subtle pattern of quoining on the second through fourth floors, an elegant patterned window surround on the fifth floor and a simple corbeled cornice.

The finished work was not unlike upper-class residences such as the Gibson Fahnestock House at 30 West 51st Street, also designed in 1886 by McKim, Mead & White.

There were two railroad flats to a floor—each running front to back, with the living room at the front, then three bedrooms, then a dining room and the kitchen and the only bathroom in the back. To get from the living room to the dining room the tenant had to walk out into the public hall or march through the three bedrooms.

Miller and McKim, Mead & White apparently never worked together again. The Miller family sold the Wanaque in 1934 and by 1940 it was described as a single-room occupancy dwelling.

The more obscure commissions of McKim, Mead & White remained largely unknown until 1978 when Leland Roth, a professor at the University of Oregon, produced a list of the firm's work from its financial archives at the New-York Historical Society.

In the meantime, what started as McKim, Mead & White continued to operate, becoming most recently Cain, Farrell & Bell in 1978 and Farrell, Bell & Lennard in 1986. The firm has done eight projects for Fountain House since 1975. The partners did not know that the Wanaque had been designed by their own firm until this April.

Now John Farrell, who began with the firm in 1946, said the facade will be cleaned and the windows will be restored. But other elements of the building will disappear.

The original iron fence with unusual spiral designs needs only sanding and painting but is being ripped out and replaced with a standard modern one. The carved rope moldings on the ground-floor windows are being removed because of missing sections. "You can't get anyone to do that kind of work any more," said Mr. Farrell. And no trace of the interior is being saved.

The interior still has some of its original elements like heavy oak shutters, parquet flooring and an emerald-green, glass-tile fireplace. But they were covered in dingy yellow paint, and Mr. Farrell said he had given no thought to retaining them. The $2.5 million project will be completed in 1990.

It's a beautiful coincidence, an architectural firm renovating its own building a century after construction. But preservationists may be disappointed that much of an interesting work by a distinguished firm is being discarded.

130 EAST 64th STREET

The Mystery of Stone's Grille

Left: 130 East 64th Street in 1937. In 1958, Edward Durell Stone bought it and installed grille, center. Right: The house without grillwork today.

THE DISTINCTIVE CONCRETE-BLOCK screen, gone since 1987 from the 1956 Edward Durell Stone house at 130 East 64th Street, is beginning to fade from memory. The picture windows, originally hidden by the grillwork, now have an expansive view of the street and admit much more light to the house.

It looks like any other recent row-house alteration. It is not quite clear when the grillwork will go back up, if ever, and there are conflicting stories from all parties.

The late Mr. Stone started out as a doctrinaire modernist in the 30's, producing buildings like the original Museum of Modern Art, which he co-designed with Philip Goodwin. But a *Vogue* article in 1958 quoted Mr. Stone as saying that he had become "discontented with the uncompromising purity and aridness" of the sleek glass-and-steel structures of the International style early in the 50's.

His first major commission after his disenchantment was the United States Embassy in New Delhi, designed in 1954 in a temple-like form, decorated with gold leaf, fountains and concrete grillwork to allow cross-ventilation.

In 1956, Mr. Stone acquired an 1878 brownstone designed by James E. Ware and rebuilt it into what the *Vogue* article called "neo-Baroque"—heavy draperies, Roman-style furniture, mosaic tile coffee tables, polka-dot ashtrays and everywhere the use of concrete grillwork.

The entire brownstone facade was stripped away and replaced with large plate-glass windows, which were then covered with a projecting screen of the concrete blocks.

Critics regarded his architecture as frivolous, but he ignored them. "There isn't a taxi driver in New York who won't say that the General Motors Building is the most beautiful thing in the city," he told the *New York Times* in 1972, referring to his design at 59th Street and Fifth Avenue, which was completed in 1968.

Mr. Stone also designed the New York City Department of Cultural Affairs building at Columbus Circle, all white with a pierced facade, and the immense Kennedy Center in Washington, completed in 1971. But his house on East 64th Street has continued to be a personal touchstone for his career. The building was included in the Upper East Side Historic District in 1981.

In 1987, the second of his three wives, Maria Stone, applied to the Landmarks Preservation Commission to remove the front grillwork, saying it was unsafe. The commission agreed on condition that it be replaced with new work to match; by the fall of 1987 the grillwork was down.

But work has since stopped and the explanation depends on who is doing the telling. Mrs. Stone's son, Hicks, who occupies the ground-floor apartment in the building, says that he has served as the design architect for the restoration.

At first, he stated that the restoration stopped because he was "unaware" that the new blocks would have to be custom-cast. The additional cost, he said at the time, daunted his mother, the owner.

In a later interview, he said that the main reason the work had stopped was that the house had been rented beginning in the fall of 1987 and that the reinstallation of the facade would disturb the tenant, whom he declined to identify.

He also said that no work has been done to line up new blocks, which require an advance order for custom production, because his mother has not yet authorized any additional work.

However, he said, when the tenant vacates the premises, the grillwork will go back up. He added that he did not know when the lease will expire.

But Lillian Ayala, a spokeswoman for the Landmarks Preservation Commission, said that Mr. Stone has told them that he is actively at work on the project. Mr. Stone denies this.

Miss Ayala said that if the commission suspected that the owner did not intend to restore the grille, it would lodge a violation against the property.

Neil Berzak, an architect who assisted with the building application but who has since had a dispute over fees with Mrs. Stone, said that the additional cost of the custom grillwork was probably no more than $1,000 and added:

"I have a hunch they didn't like the screen and wanted it off."

Recently Edward Lee Cave, a real-estate broker, has begun advertising the premises for sale at $3.1 million. He said that there is no tenant in the house, that it is empty except for Mr. Stone.

Asked about the grille, he said, "It will definitely not be put back; it's a fact." Then he said he had Mrs. Stone on another telephone line and would call back. He has since declined comment on the matter.

Mrs. Stone initially did not respond to letters addressed to her house. But after these conversations, she said in a hand-delivered letter that neither her son nor Mr. Cave was authorized to speak on her behalf and that the grille would be reinstalled, although she did not say when.

Still, no grille!

THE KNICKERBOCKER LAUNDRY

A Cloudy Future for an Art Moderne Clean Machine

The Knickerbocker Laundry building near the Sunnyside rail yards in 1932.

THE ART MODERNE Knickerbocker Laundry near the Sunnyside rail yards in Queens has been vacant for three years, its 1932 streamline design competing with huge banners advertising that it is available for occupancy. Its future will probably be decided this summer, and thousands of Long Island Rail Road commuters who pass it daily will see either its facade reused in a new shopping center or its demolition.

In the early 30's, the *New York Times* estimated that laundries in the New York City area did $75 million annually in business and that the industry was dominated by small concerns. But the advent of trucking, good roads and new laundry machinery created opportunities for large, centralized operations. Many included dry-cleaning services, which became widely available around 1925, with the advent of nonflammable cleaning solvents.

In 1931, the Knickerbocker Ice Company was seeking to diversify as mechanical refrigeration cut into the demand for delivery of ice. Knickerbocker began an air-conditioning and cooling division and also established the Knickerbocker Laundry adjacent to its ice plant.

Designed by Irving Fenichel, the laundry occupied a midblock site on 37th Avenue between 43d and 48th Streets facing the Long Island Rail Road. With access to Manhattan via Northern Boulevard and the Queensboro Bridge, the two-story laundry needed an acre of space to serve its large market. Inside were huge washing, pressing, ironing, steam, dry-cleaning and other machines, and a separate boiler room. Huge windows and tiled surfaces made the interior appear as clean as a hospital.

Everything from fragile linens to great rugs were cleaned in a carefully air-conditioned, dust-free atmosphere, but the most striking quality of the Knickerbocker Laundry building was its near-public character.

Employees used a side entrance, but visitors went in through nickeled steel doors with Art Deco styling and a great solid bronze vestibule. They entered a large tiled waiting room with a vaulted ceiling and modernistic trim of black-and-gold marble. There was a stream-lined conference hall, a kitchen with surfaces covered in polished black glass and even an elevated observation window.

The whole ensemble was in line with the idea, increasingly popular at the time, that factories should be more humane workplaces, and the laundry's design aimed to reduce the historic schism between life inside and outside the factory.

The exterior made a comparable statement. Vertically streamlined end piers flanked two long bays of horizontal factory windows. Those in turn curved in to the monumental central entrance, cascading pairs of piers with a great clock and the company name carved in relief at the top. The entire facade is glass and bright white cast stone and looks more like a university library than a factory. Even the sidewalks were designed, in an alternating pattern of dark and light concrete.

The immodesty of this otherwise humble enterprise is both entertaining and unsettling. In 1932 Lewis Mumford called it "misplaced monumentality" in his "Skyline" column in the *New Yorker*.

The "series of stony billows" on the front represented "an overcompensation for the crude factory building of the past," Mr. Mumford wrote. But he was glad that "architecture is cropping up today in the least expected places."

The Knickerbocker Laundry occupied its unusual building through the 60's. Around 1970 the building was acquired by the Naarden Perfume manufacturer, which changed the name on the front and the vestibule.

Naarden moved to New Jersey in the mid-80's, and since 1987 the building has been vacant. Its owner, Richard Zirinsky Associates, has been trying to rent the space.

No one has taken it—the building still has a heavy perfume smell—and Richard Zirinsky Jr. said that he might demolish it, but that he would prefer to save at least the facade as part of a six-acre shopping center. "We're very fond of this building," he said, but it is not clear if preserving the front will work. The architects of the shopping center, Levien Deliso Songer of Queens, have prepared several designs and Zirinsky Associates has not chosen one.

Jeffrey Kroessler and Nina Rappoport, local preservationists, asked the Landmarks Preservation Commission to designate the building in 1987, but they said the commission felt there were too many other unprotected buildings of greater quality. Thus, the fate of the Knickerbocker Laundry now rests entirely in private hands.

THE OLD YALE CLUB

Make Way for the Red and Blue

The 11-story Yale Club at 30 West 44th Street, circa 1902.

THE CLUB DISTRICT in the West 40's has seen a gradual decline from its high point around 1910 as the Elks, Lambs and other social clubs have given up their buildings. But now it looks like the old Yale Club at 30 West 44th Street—the first high-rise club building and a school since 1971—will return to club use. The likely new owner is another Ivy League institution, the University of Pennsylvania's New York Club.

The notion of clubs associated with particular colleges began with the Harvard Club, which was organized in 1865. At first, the clubs were in older row houses, but in 1893 the Harvard Club built its own house, at 27 West 44th Street. Yale did not establish a club until 1897, when alumni acquired an old brownstone, freshly vacated by the Lambs, at 17 East 26th Street. By 1898, the new Yale Club had 1,000 members and a surplus of $20,000.

Perhaps with the spirit of noblesse oblige the Harvard Club gave a party in 1899 at which "members of both clubs were choked with food, drink and songs and gave each other countless long cheers," according to the club's membership book in 1981. "Invigorated by that experience, the Yale guests immediately decided they must have a bigger, better clubhouse to return the compliment."

Two years later Yale followed Harvard to an emerging club district—the West 40's near Grand Central Terminal—with its building on West 44th Street. In 1887, the Berkeley Athletic Club had opened at 23 West 44th Street. The Century Club occupied 7 West 43d Street in 1899, the same year the New York Academy of Medicine moved to 19 West 43d Street.

The Yale Club members were so uncertain of their new venture they stipulated that their building "be so constructed that if it failed it could be turned into bachelor apartments," the club history says. Evarts Tracy and Egerton Swartwout, Yale architectural graduates who had just left McKim, Mead & White to set up their own concern, designed the 11-story building, and their plans called for six floors of bachelor apartments.

The first floor had a rear grill room given by the class of 1867 and decorated with tankards and oak paneling. The second floor held a double-height library and lounge with giant columns and chestnut pilasters. Floors three through eight held 60 bachelor apartments and the ninth floor was taken up by minor dining rooms. The 10th floor was the main dining room, another double-height space, that had seating for 400. The kitchen was on the top floor. The interior is now a warren of dropped ceilings and office partitions, but it appears that parts of the first and second floors are largely intact.

Tracy & Swartwout rendered the exterior in a mixture of Beaux-Arts and neoclassical styling—with a giant arch at the 10th floor on a fairly ordinary tripartite composition in limestone and brick. Above the arch was the inscription "Qui transtulit sustinet," the state motto of Connecticut. The office of Gov. William A. O'Neill of Connecticut provided the English translation as, "He who transplanted still sustains."

The unusual thing about the Yale Club building was its obvious height. The University Club, completed in 1899 at 1 West 54th Street, had camouflaged 11 floors behind a facade that appeared to be only three, but Yale's was the first uncompromisingly high-rise clubhouse, towering over the neighboring stables and club buildings.

The *New York Tribune* quoted a member in 1901 saying, "It will be an easy matter to look down upon the Harvard and throw bouquets to them when there is occasion for doing so."

The Yale Club soon outgrew its first house. It built its present 21-story clubhouse at 50 Vanderbilt Avenue in 1915. Between then and 1933, 30 West 44th Street housed the national fraternity of Delta Kappa Epsilon and then the Army and Navy Club.

The Federal Government bought the building in 1943. In 1971, the Government valued the property at $1.15 million, declared it surplus and transferred it to the new, private Touro College.

Dr. Bernard Lander, president of Touro, says the college is "very close" to selling the property to the University of Pennsylvania Club of New York, which currently shares quarters at 15 West 43d Street with the Princeton Club.

The Department of Education approved the sale late last month but stipulated that Touro College pay the Government $450,000 out of the $15 million sale price and use most of the balance to acquire and improve a new site. The closing will take place as soon as Touro can find another location, but David P. Helpern, architect for the University of Pennsylvania Club, says he expects alteration work to start in the fall.

The headline as it ran in the paper—"Make Way for the Blue and Gold"—was written by a graduate of the University of Iowa. Penn took title in 1989, and work is still not under way.

SEAVIEW HOSPITAL

A TB Patients' Haven Now Afflicted with Neglect

Seaview Hospital on Staten Island, circa 1914.

IT'S LIKE A lost colonial outpost in the tropics—a grand complex of two dozen rotting buildings, the jungle closing in. But in this case it's a designated landmark, the 365-acre Seaview Hospital complex on Staten Island, which has been operated by New York City since its opening in 1913.

There are murmurs that some of the buildings may be restored. But decades of official neglect make it far from clear that they can survive.

At the turn of the century, tuberculosis, known as the "white plague," afflicted 30,000 people in New York City in 1903 and there was no direct cure. The only treatment known at the time was fresh air, good food and rest.

A movement grew to create a single specialized facility for such treatment and in 1905 the city's Department of Public Charities chose an elevated site in the Todt Hill section of Staten Island.

When Seaview Hospital was opened in 1913, the scheme of its architect, Raymond Almirall, satisfied several objectives. First, the elevated site with sea views and breezes was the kind of environment where tuberculosis sufferers were best treated. Second, the dispersion of the wards into a fan-shaped arrangement of separate buildings with balconies and sun rooms provided maximum light and air for the patients.

And finally, the "architecture is modern and of no historical or geographic style," as Almirall wrote in the *Modern Hospital* of February 1914, an approach considered appropriate for an entirely new kind of building. Only two municipal tuberculosis hospitals had been built when Seaview was designed, according to research by Shirley Zavin of the Landmarks Preservation Commission.

The eight free-standing open-air pavilions formed a semicircle centered on an administration building with separate residences for staff, a dining hall, a power plant and related structures—all linked by enclosed walkways and underground tunnels but surrounded by landscaped gardens. The administration building—gray stucco with a tile roof—has aspects of the Mission style, as do related buildings like the nurses' residences.

But the rectangular, stuccoed, open-air pavilions are the striking elements in the complex. They combined elements of the Arts and Crafts and Art Nouveau styles—blocky forms, unusual inset tiling, spidery open-air balconies and giant glazed rooftop sunrooms. The

tiling is restrained at the lower floors—small glazed cartouches and bands of poppies and other flowers—but explodes in color just under the cornice, with full-sized figures of doctors and nurses, seashells, and red crosses and other medical insignia, all in a six-foot-high polychrome band running around each building. It is some of the most unusual ornament in New York City.

The original complex was increased in size from 1,100 to 2,000 beds in 1917, with the addition of groups of outbuildings in more reserved styles. But the days of the open-air pavilions, the focus of the complex, were numbered.

The balconies were enclosed in the 30's, and the rooftop solariums were crudely rebuilt in the 50's, at which time modern brick fire stairs were added at the ends of the buildings.

In 1952, doctors at Seaview refined the use of Isoniazid drugs, the first successful direct treatment of tuberculosis, and in a decade tuberculosis cases at Seaview had dwindled to but a few.

In 1961, Seaview began to shift toward geriatric care and in 1973, a new 304-bed nursing care facility replaced four of the open-air pavilions, destroying the radial symmetry of the complex.

Gradually, Seaview vacated the older structures—most of the original buildings that survive are now unoccupied—and no serious attempts to seal or preserve them have been made. The empty buildings now are open to the elements and many are hidden by brush and high weed trees.

Large sections of stucco have fallen off, windows are broken, and heaps of medical equipment molder in puddles of water. The Landmarks Preservation Commission designated the buildings as part of a larger historic district in 1985. But the city's Health and Hospitals Corporation received permission from the agency last year to demolish the tall, polychrome-tiled smokestack of the power plant and it will knock it down by this fall.

Fred Winters, a spokesman for the hospitals agency, said that it would conduct a study to see if the buildings can be reused to expand the hospital's geriatric programs. But continued neglect makes the ultimate preservation of the Seaview Hospital buildings less and less likely as time goes on.

Stack is down, feasibility study under way, don't hold your breath.

THE McALPIN MARINE GRILL

The Fate of a Polychrome Grotto Hangs in Balance

The Marine Grill at the McAlpin Hotel in 1913.

IT'S ONE OF the most unusual interiors in New York City—an expansive grotto of flowing, polychrome terra-cotta. The 1912 Marine Grill in the old Hotel McAlpin at the southeast corner of 34th Street and Avenue of the Americas was developing a cult following among architectural historians and preservationists. But now the building's owner has closed the restaurant, is working on the space and won't say anything about its future.

Early 20th-century hotel construction was an exercise in quick obsolescence—with a new generation of buildings completely eclipsing the old one every three or four years. Telephone, telegraph, plumbing, elevator and other mechanical services rapidly advanced, but each new hotel also sought singular decorative schemes. The Astor Hotel had an American Indian Grill and a Pompeiian billiard room, the Plaza had the Germanic-style Oak Room and the airy Palm Court, and the Vanderbilt Hotel had an unusual Grill Room with tiled, vaulted ceilings.

The 1,500-room McAlpin Hotel, opened in late 1912, was considered the largest hotel in the world and it also attempted to outdo its predecessors. There were floors restricted to women, men and even night workers—where silence was enforced during the day. There was a tapestry gallery, a banquet room with a vaulted ceiling, a giant marble lobby, a Louis XVI-style dining room and Russian and Turkish baths.

In 1913, the *Real Estate Record and Guide* noted another unusual feature of the McAlpin. Unlike other giant hotels, the McAlpin rented out its valuable store space all along the street frontages, moving its main rooms up or, in one case, down a floor. The basement room, at first called the Rathskeller and within a few months the Marine Grill, remains one of the most unusual in New York City.

The Marine Grill is a forest of tile-clad piers that curve up and form great curved vaults, all in a glazed riot of ornament and color—brown, green, cream, silver and scarlet. Giant semicircles along the walls carry faience panels depicting the maritime history of New York.

Designed by Fred Dana Marsh, these show such noteworthy ships as the *Half Moon*, the steamer *Clermont* and the *Mauretania* against contemporary backgrounds, also in high color.

The magazine *Architectural Review* in 1913 wrote, "if there is any limit to the possibilities of colored clay for decorative purposes, this is it," and credits the overall tile work to the Atlantic Terra Cotta Company and the hotel's architect, Frank M. Andrews.

But the Marine Grill is not just a surface ornament. The upward curve of each great pier expands out to its neighbor in a series of sinuous shapes, curving in three dimensions. It is a polychrome forest of massive, stunted trees, but expressive of the room's underground location and the giant hotel bearing down on top of it.

The magazine *Brickbuilder* called it "an architectural and decorative triumph." It is far more dramatic than the corresponding, much more reserved room at the old Vanderbilt Hotel, at 4 Park Avenue, now a restaurant.

In 1951, *Hotel World-Review* reported that the Marine Grill "had been closed for several years," but would soon be reopened with "name bands."

After 1960, it was quietly operated by a succession of middle-grade restaurants all of which struggled against the invisibility of their basement location. It was generally unknown to architectural aficionados and not listed in encyclopedic works like the *W.P.A. Guide to New York City* or the *AIA Guide to New York City*.

About 15 years ago, Kent Barwick, former chairman of the Landmarks Preservation Commission and now president of the Municipal Art Society, chanced on the old Marine Grill. "The food was unspeakable, but the restaurant was exhilarating," he said.

Mr. Barwick said that he had called Elliot Willensky, coauthor of the *AIA Guide*, and told him, "Drop everything and get over to see this place."

"My jaw dropped and then I took other people just to see their jaws drop, too," said Mr. Willensky the other day, "and they did. It's one of the most memorable spaces in New York and the great thing about it was that it was completely intact, preserved quite unofficially, almost accidentally."

He gradually introduced those active in New York City preservation and history to the room—John Tauranac, William Alex, Lorna Nowvé and others. No one ever proposed the room as an interior landmark.

The restaurant closed this spring and Devorah Rankin, a spokesman for the owner, McAlpin Associates, refused without explanation a recent request to inspect the Marine Grill, saying, "There's nothing there you would want to see anyway."

She said there was work going on in the restaurant, but would add only that the space is not for rent at the moment. Whether its accidental preservation will continue is now anyone's guess.

No trace of this exquisite room survives today. Shame!

THE FOUR SEASONS

Serving Up a Restaurant for Landmark Designation

The Pool Room at the Four Seasons.

Is IT AN ENDURING landmark of the modern movement, architecturally significant and worthy of landmark protection? Or is it just a high-culture eatery in an anonymous space with a great collection of furnishings and a high-powered ambience? The Landmarks Preservation Commission now has this issue on its plate in the question of the landmark designation of the interior space occupied by the Four Seasons Restaurant.

The 1958 Seagram Building at 375 Park Avenue is a familiar success story of the modern movement. It was going to be a conventional office building designed by Charles Luckman. But in 1954, Phyllis Lambert convinced her father, the late Samuel Bronfman, the founder of Joseph E. Seagram & Sons, the liquor-distilling empire, to make the building a significant work of architecture. Mies van der Rohe and Philip Johnson were retained and designed what was at the time a stunning work—a sheer tower with a bronze-colored facade, set back on an open plaza in the middle of the prosaic apartment houses lining Park Avenue.

It appears that a ground-floor restaurant was not an integral part of the original scheme, and some accounts have it that the present Four Seasons space was at first considered for an automobile showroom.

But by 1958, Mr. Johnson was working on designs for a restaurant and the Four Seasons opened in 1959 as part of the Restaurant Associates group.

There are two large square rooms, a bar on the 52d Street side and a main dining room on the 53d Street side, connected by a travertine-lined corridor. The bar is dominated by French walnut paneling on two walls, smooth and unrelieved but cut so that the grain uncannily recalls Art Nouveau design. The restaurant is dominated by a central white marble pool of bubbling water.

Both rooms are generally open and almost cubes and each has two walls of windows, with the now-famous rippling chain draperies that exercise a hypnotic effect. Artwork and large plantings that change with the seasons abound. There is a giant Picasso tapestry in the connecting corridor and a delicate Richard Lippold sculpture of gold-colored rods over the bar, which changes from light to dark if you move only an inch.

Garth and Ada Louise Huxtable—he was the industrial designer who died earlier this month, she is the architectural critic—designed the table settings, and some of the furniture was based on designs of the 1920's by Mr. van der Rohe. The completed Four Seasons was cool, elegant and modern, an unspoken rebuke to the overstuffed French restaurants that dominated first-class cuisine at the time. It has come to be one of the most important restaurants in New York.

In 1976, Joseph E. Seagram's & Sons startled New York by applying for a landmark designation for its building, but it had not yet reached the required 30-year age limit. Ever since there have been murmurs that the building and its lobby should be designated as soon as they were eligible. But no one ever mentioned the Four Seasons.

On April 3, 1988, the Landmarks Commission voted to consider the designation of the building and its lobby at the public hearing of May 17.

Tom Margittai and Paul Kovi, now the owners of the Four Seasons, heard of this, and on April 22 wrote the commission requesting designation of the restaurant. On May 3, just before the notification deadline for the May hearing, the commission also voted to consider the Four Seasons. A decision by the commission is still pending.

Seagram's sold the building to the Teachers' Insurance and Annuity Association in 1980 with the requirement that it eventually apply for landmark designation. Both support designation of the building and lobby, but not the restaurant. Its artwork, mentioned prominently in the commission's preliminary analysis, still belongs to Seagram's, and the company doesn't want to see it locked into place.

Philip DiGennaro, vice president of the Teachers' Insurance and Annuity Association, told the commission that designation of the Four Seasons would prove "a singular benefit" to the operator of the restaurant, whose lease is up in 1999, "locking us in to restaurant use of this space." Ms. Lambert, writing in support of designation, said, "One just has to imagine the loss of presence were the restaurant not there, or it being a bank or private offices."

Teachers' architect, Paul Byard, wrote that the space alone is undistinguished and that, without the furnishings, it would be "a void, without any particular architectural character." The commission is considering the designation and has not yet clarified its point of view on the inclusion of furnishings or artwork in the designation, or whether without them, the Four Seasons could be a landmark at all.

Designated a landmark, although still contested. Before the designation, architect J. Arvid Klein noted that the "automobile showroom" story is unlikely, since auto access to what is now the restaurant would be very difficult.

THE LOTH SILK FACTORY

A Ghost Coming to Life in Washington Heights

Joseph Loth's silk factory, 150th Street and Amsterdam Avenue, circa 1890.

IT SHOULD BE the centerpiece of a 19th-century New England mill town, a long, low, brick mill building surrounded by tenements. But Joseph Loth's silk factory, completed in 1886, is not in Massachusetts or New Hampshire. It is on the west side of Amsterdam Avenue between 150th and 151st Streets.

Anthony Morfesis, the owner of the nearly vacant building, says he will clean and restore it beginning this fall and may even create a copy of the central clock tower that was destroyed in a fire in 1916.

Loth came to New York City from Hartford in 1862 and in 1875 founded a silk mill specializing in manufacturing ribbon. Taking the trade name "Fair & Square Ribbons," the Loth operation was considered the first in this country to make high-priced ribbon that competed directly with its European rivals.

In 1886, the year that the company moved its factory operations from its cast-iron building at 65 Greene Street to its new, three-story, block-long building in Washington Heights, the *New York Times* called Loth ribbons "the standard for quality" in the United States.

Early photographs show the new factory generally surrounded by vacant land, and no explanation survives as to why Loth made such a move.

But he had his new mill, which was designed by Hugo Kafka, given an "appearance more like a public building than a factory," according to *King's Handbook of New York City* of 1892.

At the center of the blockfront rose the entrance section, surmounted by a pyramidal roof carrying a clock tower. From this section radiated five wings—two north and south along Amsterdam and three at angles toward the back of the lot.

Although there is some delicate terra-cotta inset decoration, the bulk of the loft building is in simple red Philadelphia brick, skillfully manipulated in quoining, corbelling and even raised letters "Joseph Loth & Co." and "Silk Ribbons" on large panels at roof level.

Loth maintained main offices and his own home downtown, but kept 600 workers busy in his new factory making 14 widths of ribbons in 165 shades in 90 styles, selling to every major store in the United States.

He died around 1900, and although the business kept operating through the century's teen years, this factory shut down. A 1904 alteration application filed by Bernard Loth, a son, described the building as vacant. In that year the building was converted to general loft use,

A handsome polished granite entry portico, designed by Buchman & Fox, was added bearing the words "Loth Building" and storefronts were installed. In 1906, a skating rink was added and in 1907 a "moving picture show" was installed, apparently replacing the rink in a double-height space in the rear. At that time the basement was used for billiards and bowling; an inset mosaic tile panel reading "Washington Heights Idle Hour" in the basement may date from this period.

In 1916, a fire destroyed the central tower and the Loth heirs were sued by the Fire Department for the cost of extinguishing the blaze because they had disobeyed previous instructions to divide the largest areas with fire walls. In 1928, the Loths sold the building, and it gradually came to house a dozen garment and furniture operations, of which only a few now remain.

A recent tour through the building with Alexander Brooks, its longtime superintendent, presented a vanishing species for Manhattan. Huge timber joists support wide plank floors with long spans, and the radial plan of the wings give an angular feeling unusual in this rectilinear town. Brightly colored patches of fabric—ad hoc window shades—mark the touch of the garment firms. And the theater that once housed the "moving picture show" resembles a musty, dank set for a long-forgotten silent film.

On the exterior, some long-gone renovator gave the rich red brick a dulling whitewash that is now flaking away; the raised brick lettering was covered at the time and escaped the paint brush. Now exposed, it sings out in a rich red.

Mr. Morfesis says he will start his $780,000 project in September, adding that store space will go for about $20 per square foot, with loft space at about $12. Having recently discovered an old photograph of the building, he hopes to install an approximation of the old center tower, and perhaps next year the factory will once again stand out on Washington Heights.

Correspondent Michael Adams later reported that Mr. Morfesis' definition of "restoration" had been enlarged to include a garish coat of lime-green and white paint on the 200-foot-long facade.

THE CZECH GYMNASTIC ASSOCIATION CLUBHOUSE

A Two-Story Survivor Amid Upper East Side High-Rises

The New York Sokol Hall at 420 East 71st Street, circa 1935.

IT'S ONE OF a vanishing species, an element of the ethnic Upper East Side that used to be the stronghold of Central and Eastern European nationalities. The New York Sokol's 1896 building at 420 East 71st Street is one of the survivors, a two-story intermission amid a growing forest of high-rises.

At the moment it looks as if it is going to stay where it is, despite regular offers from developers and zoning that makes the site unusually attractive for new construction.

Immigration to the United States from what is now Czechoslovakia increased in the 19th century, in part because of its domination by Austria. A sokol, a club devoted to gymnastic and other athletic pursuits, had been established in Czechoslovakia in 1863 despite Austrian objections—the physical regimen of gymnastics was a mild form of resistance, as if training an army-in-waiting.

The Sokol New York was formed in 1867, and at first was on East Fifth Street, in the heart of the Czech community. But more immigration, and the establishment of the largely Czech cigar industry in the East 70's in the 1880's, led many Czechs uptown.

The sokol joined with other Czech groups in seeking to build a large hall, which was ultimately opened in 1896 at 325 East 73d Street as the Bohemian National Hall. But as plans were being drawn, Sokol New York members, feeling shortchanged over the amount of space they would have in the new building, split off to build their own structure. It, too, opened in 1896, at 420 East 71st Street.

Membership was by then about 500, but plans for a four-story hall were too ambitious, and the architect, Julius Franke, compromised at a two-story structure built for $30,000 in just a few months. Franke was to become better known as the architect of the infamous Triangle Shirt-waist building built in 1901 at Washington Place and Greene Street, where 146 workers died in a fire in 1911, partly because of skimpy exits.

The new 71st Street building, Sokol Hall, was elegant but not showy, a simple Renaissance-style facade of beige brick and terra-cotta five bays wide with a projecting granite portico. Two large tablets on the facade read "Erected in MDCCCXCVI" and "Czech Gymnastic Association." On the day the cornerstone was laid, the *New York Times* reported, "all the houses along First and Second Avenues, from 67th up to 75th Street, were decked with flags and streamers, the red-and-white banner of Bohemia mingling everywhere with the Stars and Stripes."

Inside, the new building offered a cafe, a ladies' room and a restaurant and wine cellar, but the central feature was the Great Hall,

50 feet wide and 115 feet deep. The Czechs had been able to acquire an unusual 145-foot-deep lot; most lots go only to the center line of the block, 100 feet in.

Old photographs show a space full of gymnastic equipment, ringed by a great oak gallery and painted like a European concert hall—marbleized columns and elaborate stencil and decorative work on the walls.

The hall was a centerpiece for the Czech community in New York, offering dinners, theatrical events, concerts, bazaars and a comfortable social club.

But histories of the sokol note that in the 1920's many families moved out of the area, in part because of demolition of housing and businesses by New York Hospital and other nearby institutions. By the 1930's the sokol was sharing its clubhouse with other organizations.

Gradually, the building fell into disrepair—tin ceilings bulged and were crudely patched, oak trim was painted over and cheap paneling covered areas of decorative painting. Although the original elements may survive under these later alterations, only the form of the building, the great, deep hall with its surrounding gallery, is left to awe the modern visitor.

In the 1960's the cornice and portico were crudely removed, probably destroying the building's chances for landmark designation.

The sokol, with about 180 active members, still runs gymnastic and other programs—mats and equipment cover the main hall—but it also rents rooms out for other classes.

As many of the older buildings in the area were disappearing, Halina Rosenthal, president of the friends of the Upper East Side Historic Districts, led a successful campaign in 1985 to downzone the 200-plus sidestreet blocks throughout the Upper East Side, from an R8 to an R8B classification. This reduced the allowable building height on a typical sidestreet site from 12 to 6 stories. But the City Planning Commission exempted a half-dozen midblocks between 66th and 71st Streets.

"They thought those blocks were generally owned by the institutions," Mrs. Rosenthal recalled, "and should be permitted denser development."

The sokol is in one of the exempted blocks.

Norma Zabka, president of the New York Sokol, says the organization gets regular calls from developers seeking to acquire the building and its site. But the sokol has just cleaned the facade of its building and Mrs. Zabka says it is staying put, at least for the foreseeable future.

THE PENN STATION SERVICE BUILDING

A 1908 Structure Survives a "Monumental Act of Vandalism"

The Penn Station Service Building, West 31st Street, in 1910.

THEY MISSED SOMETHING and it is a rather big something. When the Pennsylvania Railroad demolished Penn Station in 1964, it was described by the *New York Times* "a monumental act of vandalism." Many New Yorkers and architectural historians still regret the loss of the station, and aficionados search the lower depths of the present station for remnants of the old one—handrails, elevator doors, lighting fixtures and the like.

But there is one little-noted element of the old station left, a monumental building in its own right, which is itself vulnerable to demolition. It is the grimy 1908 Penn Station Service Building at 242 West 31st Street, across the street from the present station.

As the 19th century gave way to the 20th, the Pennsylvania Railroad was chafing under a peculiar burden—it had no station in New York City. Passengers had to disembark in Jersey City, crossing the Hudson to Manhattan on ferries. It was an embarrassingly awkward entrance to the nation's greatest city for one of the nation's greatest railroads, and it lost passengers bound for destinations like Chicago, who could go by a competing line, the New York Central, from Grand Central Terminal.

Tunneling under the Hudson was less expensive than a bridge, but steam locomotives could not regularly negotiate the length of the tunnel. By the turn of the century electric engines, like those on the new IRT subway designed in 1900, were being developed, even for the heavier intercity trains.

In 1902, the Pennsylvania decided to proceed with a huge new station between 31st and 33d Streets from Seventh to Eighth Avenues, a block away from the emerging Herald Square shopping district.

The station was completed in 1910, a giant pink granite Roman-style structure surrounded by old brownstones and tenements. But construction photographs of the station site in 1908—when it was just a giant hole in the ground—also show a gleaming new building on the south side of 31st Street—the station's service plant.

The service plant held the key to the railroad's new operation, for it provided the electric power for the engines in and out of New York. Research by the industrial archeologist Thomas Flagg indicates that it was also used to supply heat, light, elevator hydraulics and refrigeration

for the station as well as compressed air for braking and signaling. It even incinerated the station's garbage.

The mid-block building, 160 feet long and 86 feet high, is divided by a north–south fire wall with boilers for power generation on the west side and power distribution, offices and other elements on the east.

The station and the service plant were designed by McKim, Mead & White, specifically Charles McKim and partner William Symmes Richardson. Writing in *Transactions of the American Society of Civil Engineers* for October 1910, Richardson said that, on the station itself, "all unnecessary detail of ornamentation was omitted."

For the service building the architects assembled some of the simplest elements from the station in the Stony Creek pink granite.

The Roman Doric exterior, a row of severe pilasters bracketing ventilation windows covered with iron grilles, is about as plain as a building can get and still have an identifiable style. Cleaned, it could be a postmodern historical society or a crematorium.

When the old Penn Station was demolished the service plant was not jeopardized, for it was just another nearby building. But it gradually lost its critical function.

Now it only provides compressed air to move switches. It controls but does not generate power for the station. One of the station's engineers, Mark Wurple, said that "what goes out from here is basically just telephone lines" that could be simply relocated. The western half is sealed off because of asbestos contamination and the eastern half is only partly used.

In 1986, there were proposals to replace the present Madison Square Garden with a new office tower and talk of new buildings on the surrounding areas—including the service-plant site, which is adjacent to a large parking garage and a one-story church.

"The whole Penn Station complex is in a sort of constant flux," said Clifford Black, a spokesman for Amtrak, which owns the service-plant building. "The whole Penn Station area may be ripe for redevelopment." The current weak market in office space has dampened interest in any real development, but it may be just a matter of time until there is the opportunity for a second battle over Penn Station.

VARIETY PHOTO PLAYS THEATER

Marquee's Lights Are Dark on 1914 "Nickelodeon"

The Variety Photo Plays Theater, 110 Third Avenue, near 14th Street, in 1950.

IT'S HARD TO put your finger on what was special about it. Perhaps it was the aura of the early days of the movies, but the 1914 Variety Photo Plays Theater at 110 Third Avenue was unforgettable when it was in operation.

Now the theater's distinctive lightbulb marquee is dark, the property is vacant and being shown to potential buyers and, according to Michael Lerner, the leasing agent, a final decision—to sell, net lease or demolish the building—will come on September 12.

The earliest movie theaters were just ad hoc alterations of spaces of opportunity, like a saloon or a storefront. According to the theater historian Michael R. Miller, these turn-of-the-century nickelodeons, where admission was usually a nickel, were not superseded by specifically built movie theaters until 1908, when the Nicholand and Prospect Pleasure Palace went up in the Bronx.

By the early 1910's, perhaps 100 theaters built for movies had gone up in New York City. They were good businesses and clustered near high-traffic sites. In 1914, one promoter, Jacob Valensi, secured a 15-year lease on a plot on the west side of Third Avenue, just south of the 14th Street stop of the elevated. There he built a two-story theater, according to Mr. Miller's research, on a site previously occupied by a theater operation. Although filed as a new building, the theater actually used some of the perimeter walls of an older structure; the theater could in some ways be considered to predate 1914.

In its name—Valensi's Variety Photo Plays—it sought an association with legitimate theater endeavors, of which 14th Street had been a center since the 1850's.

Designed by Louis Sheinart, the exterior of Variety Photo Plays was in plain brick, generally unornamented except for arcaded piers projecting above a sloping tiled false roof. Mr. Miller called Sheinart "a minor, minor architect of many, many theaters" in this period.

Inside, the auditorium was fairly plain, but did have a slightly pitched floor and fixed seats, still novel touches in an industry that had started only recently with plain benches and sheets hung on a wall.

It is not clear if the walls have lost some architectural effect—they are now mostly patched plaster—but the ceiling is covered with modestly patterned pressed tin. Four large Tiffany-type half-globe lighting fixtures have somehow survived, and the simple fixed seats bear a "V" on the end panels.

There are rooftop louvered vents, still remote-controlled with chains that hang down in the middle of the theater, and a great square panel in the center, perhaps 30 feet across, is what remains of a sliding roof used in the days before air-conditioning.

Variety Photo Plays originally seated 450 and, according to Mr. Miller, probably first presented groups of two-reelers, collections of individual features, each 15 or 20 minutes long. This was at a period when the feature-length film was still uncommon and films in general were generally considered low-culture—"photo plays" or not.

By the early 1920's, nickelodeons like the Variety Photo Plays were being supplanted by larger houses seating one or two thousand, and if the Variety was ever a first-rank theater, it surely must have begun a downward slide at that time.

In 1923, a marquee was added, designed by Julius Eckman. In 1930, a balcony seating 150 and a new lobby were installed by the architects Boak & Paris, who also made over the 1923 marquee. The lobby is nondescript neo-Renaissance and it is the marquee that has made the theater special, at least to modern eyes. Boak & Paris did not change the Eckman marquee's underside, a coffered field with regularly spaced bulbs, but did add a zigzag Art Deco fascia in enameled metal and neon lighting. The fascia gives the theater's, rather than the show's, name and recalls the period when movies were more of a generic product. The lights buzzing on the underside of the marquee, when they were on, enveloped the passerby in a warm, glowing field. People going past the theater, even in the daytime, got a whiff of vintage celluloid, and at night it was intoxicating.

The film fare over the last 30 years gradually shifted from B-grade to raunchy to naughty to pornographic, and added a slightly forbidden, Coney Island spice to the building. A 10-year-old schoolboy who somehow found himself on lower Third Avenue would walk straight by but keep his eyes glued to the pictures on the billboards outside the ticket booth.

Earlier this year the Department of Health closed the Variety Photo Plays, which was operating as a gay movie theater. Now it is still and musty inside, its 1940's candy machine empty, its projection booth a small museum of antique apparatus—carbon-arc projection lighting was discontinued only a few years ago. The owner, the 110–112 Third Avenue Realty Corporation, includes members of the same families who owned it since the 1920's. In their hands lies the fate of an institution that will live on at least in the memories of many New Yorkers.

Now leased to an Off-Broadway theater. The 10-year-old schoolboy was, in fact, the author.

UKRAINIAN ACADEMY OF ARTS AND SCIENCES

Landmarking an 1898 Library

New York Free Circulating Library, 206 West 100th Street, in 1899.

WHILE THERE IS ferment in the Ukraine as nationalists seek to free it from Russian domination, there is pragmatic capitulation at 206 West 100th Street, where the Ukrainian Academy of Arts and Sciences has decided not to appeal its designation as a landmark last month.

Now the academy is making the best of the situation, applying for preservation grants and loans for its handsome little 1898 library building.

The New York Free Circulating Library was established in 1880 to serve the poor and working classes and gradually opened branches citywide. In 1896, quarters were rented at the southwest corner of 100th Street and Amsterdam Avenue. The 6,200 volumes there were in such demand that "people would sit and wait until books were returned."

In 1898, the library built a new branch at 206 West 100th Street, between Broadway and Amsterdam Avenue, a three-story Renaissance-style building designed by James Brown Lord.

Lord designed an elegant building of limestone, light-colored brick and terra-cotta, with a projecting portico supporting a giant Ionic colonnade. The lower section is simple and restrained, "modern" for its time, but the upper two floors have a decorated, Victorian sensibility—the bull's-eye windows have foliate surrounds and there is a precisely detailed anthemion band at the top.

E. Idell Zeisloft's 1899 *The New Metropolis* described the branch libraries' possibilities for poor urban children, who "depend almost entirely upon what they receive from books for moral and mental stimulus."

"Wildflowers—they rarely see them," the book stated. "They never see the stars—the street lamps blind their eyes."

Lord also designed a similar branch at 222 East 79th Street, and *New York 1900* by Robert A. M. Stern, Gregory Gilmartin and John Montague Massengale describes the Lord solution as "an elegant town house . . . an icon of humanistic reason and a refuge from the turmoil of the city."

In 1961, the Bloomingdale branch at 206 West 100th Street moved to a new building one block east and the old structure was sold to the Ukrainian Academy of Arts and Sciences, a research organization.

The Ukrainian Academy was incorporated in 1950 by emigrés fleeing Stalinist oppression and it has kept the original library interior intact, if only because of its shoestring budget, now barely $50,000 a year.

The large, light reading rooms still have their oak furniture and varnished pine bookcases, but the building is now chock-a-block with Ukrainian artifacts, especially books and magazines like *Dzvinok* (little Bell) and *Dzvinochok* (Tiny Bell), children's magazines published in Lvov in the 1930's, and the expatriate liberation journal *Tryzub* (Trident), published in Paris until 1941.

In 1986, the Landmarks Preservation Commission proposed the building for designation; as a work of architecture and as an early library structure it is of real interest. But at the hearing in November 1986, the academy's attorney, Stephen J. Jarema, resisted designation.

"Our people who were fortunate to escape from a police state are fully aware that once the government imposes a police power, no matter how innocent, it will not disappear, but grow in quest of more power," he said. "Forced obedience will replace freedom."

But the commission remained disposed toward designation and kept the matter open, even as the three-year deadline for designation neared. Meanwhile, Lionel Marks succeeded Mr. Jarema as attorney last year and reexamined the academy's position. Last month, he said that designation appeared to be "a foregone conclusion."

"It's pretty arbitrary, the way they designate," he said at the time. "The average organization just cannot sustain a challenge."

One small carrot offered by the commission is a grant program for nonprofit organizations that makes outright gifts of up to $10,000 for restoration, but only for designated landmarks.

The yearly deadline for grant applications is October 17—coincidentally, just before the three-year deadline of November 1989—and there was pressure on the academy to make the application deadline by ending its opposition. Last month, after several conciliatory meetings with the commission, Mr. Marks and Prof. Yaroslav Bilinsky, the academy's president, faced the inevitable and began to investigate applications for preservation grants and loans. The designation was made on August 29.

"Now," said Professor Bilinsky, "we'd like to do our share and maintain the building in good shape," indicating that the academy would apply for a grant. "But at the same time our main concerns are to do scholarly work."

The academy has not yet received any grant money but is hoping for $15,000 toward the cost of an estimated $75,000 in facade repairs.

17th STREET OFF UNION SQUARE

10 Houses with Collective Charm

Buildings between 120, left, and 104 on south side of East 17th Street.

EDMUND V. GILLON, JR.

IT IS HARD to pinpoint exactly what is special about the old houses on the south side of East 17th Street between Union Square and Irving Place. The individual buildings are not outstanding and most are a bit neglected, even shabby.

Despite this—and in some ways because of it—the 10 buildings combine to form a minor urban masterpiece. Whether or not the Landmarks Preservation Commission designates them, as repeatedly requested by local residents, the matter puts conventional sensibilities about preservation to a test.

Part of their distinctive character is that all the buildings didn't go up at once, in one or two rows, but by ones and twos over a half century, and they compress a wide range of styles onto one short block.

No. 104 is a crisp little red-brick Greek Revival of the mid-1840's. No. 106 is a few years later, but larger and Italianate in style. The houses at 108 and 110 were built in 1854 as two brownstone row houses in the Anglo-Italianate style, with segmentally arched window lintels. Still surviving on 110 are an elegant brownstone balcony and a remarkable overdoor decoration that looks like a superscale cabbage leaf.

The Fanwood Apartments went up in 1889 at 112 in the Romanesque style with luxurious brownstone carving and a projecting portico so commodious it looks like a carriage entrance. No. 116, a brownstone built in the 1850's, has elaborate carving in the Renaissance style.

The Irving, a narrow 1901 apartment, is the latest building on the block, an Edwardian counterpoint to its earlier neighbors. No. 120, of the 1840's, is a return to the simpler Greek Revival at the beginning of the row, which continues around the corner to 47 and 49 Irving Place; the latter is a picturesque corner assemblage of oriels, porches and a single dormer set in an unusual gambrel roof.

The 19th-century occupants were well-to-do families of business and professional men like Henry Scudder, a lawyer and Congressman who lived at 116, and James Black, a lithographer who lived in a house replaced by 118. William R. Grace, merchant and founder of the eponymous company, lived at 108 for a decade until elected Mayor in the 1880's. John Suerken, whose "saloon" later emerged as a famous eatery on Park Place, lived in the Fanwood in the 1910's.

By the turn of the century the area began to slip and most of the houses were gradually converted into apartments and came into single owner-ship—since 1954 a corporation comprising members of the Mayer family, who have neither abused nor lavished care on the properties.

The street looks like a Hollywood set of New York in the 1950's, say, for *My Sister Eileen*. The brownstone is slowly peeling in an exquisite display of age, the stoops are worn, the stone blocks are settling, and most of the little things—the rope moldings, the carving, the door frames, the ironwork—are intact. It makes a refreshing counterpoint to the north side of the street, a cool, contemporary 1961 building owned by the Guardian Life Insurance Company.

Peering into the brownstone hallways you can see old wooden stairs, statuary niches, marble and tile floors, elaborate ceiling decorations, beveled glass and Queen Anne woodwork.

The windows, some quite dirty, give intimate glimpses of bird cages, sheets hung as curtains, fancy fireplaces, a rainbow of perfectly average human habitation. Perhaps it is the last fully unbeautified block of brownstones in New York.

In 1984, the block association applied for landmark designation, a request repeated in 1985 by Jack Taylor, writing for the Union Square Park Community Coalition. This year the Gramercy Neighborhood Associates repeated the request with historical research on the build-ings, but the question of district vs. individual designation has not yet been addressed.

Samuel H. Lindenbaum, a lawyer familiar with land-use regulation, says individual designations, unlike district designations, would permit the air rights to be transferred off the block—for instance, across the street to the 27,000-square-foot site of the three-story Guardian Life Building.

Either way the beautifully worn character of the buildings will be difficult to preserve. It is hard to speak against restoration, but a pristine exterior restoration of this block—the kind that wins civic awards—is just what would dramatically reduce its character. On the other hand, given landmark quality buildings, how do you rein in the impulse to do just that?

For the moment the buildings are not going anywhere, despite the boom in new construction and renovation in the area. Anita Goldberg, speaking for the owners, said they like to "hold onto properties for years," so whatever is or is not worth preserving on 17th Street may go unresolved for some time.

Restoration was the last thing there was to worry about. In 1990 the owner methodically made mediocre "repairs" to the brownstone trim on most of the buildings.

THE KINGSBRIDGE ARMORY

A Dropped Ceiling in a Moated Bastion?

The Eighth Coastal Artillery Armory in the Bronx during construction in 1915.

IT COULD HAVE been in the *Guinness Book of World Records*, a 300 by 600 feet dropped ceiling, perhaps the world's largest. The only trouble was it was planned for the vast drill shed of the Eighth Coastal Artillery Armory, in the Bronx, completed in 1917 and now a city landmark.

But preservationists can relax: The dropped-ceiling plan for what is now known as the Kingsbridge Armory turned out to be just a bureaucratic snafu, and now it will not be built.

Armory construction in New York began in earnest in the late 19th century as military equipment increased in quantity and size and as civil disturbances like strikes and riots threatened urban areas. The medieval fortress was adopted as the appropriate style and gigantic, castle-like structures gradually appeared all over the city.

The New York Landmarks Conservancy, a nonprofit group, issued a study of armories last year prepared by Ann Beha Associates of Boston and their research indicates that the Eighth Coastal Artillery Regiment left its 1889 structure on 94th and Park Avenue for a new site in the Bronx with more room and better recruiting possibilities.

Designed by Pilcher & Tachau, the present armory covers the entire block between Kingsbridge Road and 195th Street and Reservoir and Jerome Avenues. Its drill hall was, and may still be, the largest in the world. The armory is Disneyland-huge, with two great, three-quarter-round towers centered on the vast spread of its medieval-style facade.

As Montgomery Schuyler wrote of armories in general in *Architectural Record* in 1905: "The parapets are crenellated, though nobody is expected to shoot between the crenelles. The cornices are machicolated, though nobody expects to pour hot lead from the machicoulis." Nevertheless, the design still had "an undeniable attractiveness."

As for the Kingsbridge Armory, a moat runs across the front, but any water would empty into the basement windows. Two lookouts built on lesser towers on each end are actually ventilation intakes.

The main lobby is a forest of brick columns rising to groined vaulting; the officers' quarters above are furnished simply, without elaborate paneling or finishes. High in the towers are plain circular rooms without windows, originally used for officers' dinner parties.

The vast drill shed behind the tower is roofed over with double-truss framing rising to a pointed arch 121 feet high. According to Laura Tosi of the Bronx County Historical Society, it originally contained a replica of a portion of a coast fort with a signal station, searchlights, related installations and 12-inch guns and mortars.

The drill-hall floor was originally earthen, to permit pitching tents, campfires and trenching. Ringed by a gallery of 4,000 box seats, the room is still awe-inspiring.

In peacetime, the drill hall—paved since the 20's—has been home to a variety of events, from boat shows to bicycle races to stockholder meetings, especially in the early 50's before the completion of the Coliseum at Columbus Circle.

In recent years, huge armories have suffered neglect, and Laurie Beckelman, executive director of the Landmarks Conservancy, says, "If we don't develop a strategy to extend their lives, some of these armories will definitely be lost."

The old Eighth Regiment Armory at Park Avenue and 94th Street was replaced by a school in the 60's and the spectacular but deteriorating Second Battalion Armory in Sunset Park, Brooklyn, was demolished a few years ago.

The Kingsbridge Armory is also not without its problems and the State Office of General Services evaluated it in 1985. It recommended, among other things, a dropped ceiling for the drill hall to conserve energy in the heating season, a proposal noted with alarm in the Conservancy study.

In July, the state's Department of Military and Naval Affairs stated that the dropped ceiling was still planned and only awaiting funds. But it turns out to have been a false alarm; the Office of General Services did not determine whether the drill hall was actually heated, and Malcolm Joseph, superintendent of the armory—now home to artillery units of the 42d Rainbow Division—says the heat is put on no more than two or three times a year. Both the Office of General Services and the Department of Military and Naval Affairs then agreed that the dropped ceiling will not be installed.

Financing is pending for other items like better ventilation of the vehicle fumes in the drill hall and leaks in the roof—there are pond-sized puddles on the drill floor.

But the tall west tower presents the most troublesome problem: It and the armory itself are slowly moving in different directions and a large crack between the two widens to several inches as it rises. Mr. Joseph measures the crack weekly and he will probably be the first to know when it becomes really hazardous—his office is on the ground floor.

THE BAKER MANSION

Under the Servants' Quarters, a Railroad Siding?

The George F. Baker mansion on Park Avenue at 93d Street in 1930.

IT IS CERTAINLY a drop in the giant bucket of Manhattan office space—5,600 square feet at $45 a square foot. But the space is unusual, for it is in one of the grandest houses to survive in Manhattan, the old George F. Baker Jr. residence at the northwest corner of 93d Street and Park Avenue.

The current owner, the Russian Orthodox Church Outside of Russia, now has the old servants' quarters on the rental market and will use the income to support church activities.

The core of what became the residence went up in 1917, an almost cubic house built by Francis F. Palmer, a financier, at the 93d Street corner. According to Charles Bailey, Palmer's grandson, his grandfather built the house with money he made financing British war loans in World War I.

Designed by Delano & Aldrich, it is an elegant amalgam of Federal and Georgian styling, mostly red brick with marble trim and a huge mansard roof and chimneys. Palmer also built a walled garden court on 93d Street with a fountain in the center. The mansion became the northernmost of all the grand houses built on Park Avenue, where the electrification of the railroad tracks underneath the avenue in 1903 had spurred development for the elite.

By 1927, when the house passed to George F. Baker Jr., the advent of the apartment building jeopardized the position of the grand private dwellings in Manhattan and the mansion builders retired to the side streets.

When Baker bought Palmer's house, he planned its expansion, and soon he was followed to 93d Street by the family of his sister, Florence Loew, who built at No. 56. Baker asked Delano & Aldrich to enlarge his house at the corner, adding a ballroom on the lot just north on Park and also a separate garage and a guest house just west on 93d Street.

The garden court was retained but it was now bounded by the ballroom wing on the north and the garage on the west, which has grand double-height windows for effect.

Florence Loew hired A. Stewart Walker to design her Regency-style house, now the Smithers Alcoholism Center. Walker was married to Mrs. Baker's sister, the former Sybil Kane, and some wonder why the Bakers did not also retain Walker's firm, Walker & Gillette.

According to research by Michel Scherbinine, of the Russian Orthodox Church, Mrs. Baker said, "My brother-in-law is a fine man, but I would not let him design even a doghouse for me."

For the Bakers, Delano & Aldrich expanded and refined their original work, using the same formula of high ceilings, marble and wood floors, simple styling and their signature mix of traditional and Art Deco lighting fixtures.

Baker succeeded his father as president of the First National Bank and accumulated and inherited tens of millions of dollars. He was also a director of the New York Central Railroad, and there is a persistent but unconfirmed story that there is a private railroad siding underneath the house. Members of the Palmer family deny that there was such a siding in their time.

George F. Baker 3d, who lived in his grandfather's garage in the 70's, said he never heard of the siding until a telephone repairman told him that cables ran into such an area.

Dan Brucker, a spokesman for Metro-North Commuter Railroad, says that no trace of the siding exists from the track side underneath Park Avenue. In the main house there is no evidence of such a feature—except for an unmarked elevator button for a level someplace below the cellar.

George F. Baker Jr. died in 1937 and his widow closed the main house at the beginning of World War II. She kept it empty until 1958, when she sold it to the Russian Orthodox Church Outside of Russia, established in 1920 after the Revolution. The church cut a vehicular entrance into the garden courtyard and added an exterior stairway to the second-floor ballroom, which was then converted into the sanctuary.

Church officials have changed very little in the rest of the house and it remains much as it was when the Bakers occupied it, broad, cool floors and big, quiet rooms. For many years the church leased the area under the ballroom—originally the servants' quarters—to the Russian Orthodox St. Sergius High School, but the school left last year.

Now the church has taken the unusual step of offering the space for rent, not to a church-related tenant, but as professional space.

According to Paul Wexler, the vice president at Douglas-Elliman in charge of the property, "It's unusual to find such a large block of professional space on the Upper East Side," where typical offices are much smaller.

The space has its own entrance on Park Avenue—the Bakers' former service entry—and windows onto the garden court but no access to it. Even if the railroad siding does exist, Mr. Wexler doubts its value in attracting tenants. "The location and the space are special enough," he said.

Part of the space has been rented out to Carnegie Hill Neighbors.

THE GRAND CENTRAL VIADUCT

An $8 Million Revival for a Midtown Masterpiece

The Park Avenue viaduct south of Grand Central Station in 1919.

IT'S ONE OF those things one doesn't really notice, fading as it does into the familiar background of midtown. But the 1919 Park Avenue viaduct, running between 40th and 42d Streets, will begin to stand out again next year as an $8 million restoration by the Grand Central Partnership reestablishes the structure—including the roadway hugging the terminal—as a central focus for the Grand Central area.

The original Grand Central Terminal was built in 1871 and, with its wide marshaling yards to the north, formed a great barrier to north–south traffic that became serious by the turn of the century. A design competition for a new terminal in 1903 brought forward the idea of covering the yards with streets and buildings and unifying the southern and northern sections of Park Avenue.

Reed & Stem, later working with Warren & Wetmore, produced a planning masterpiece for the terminal, an intricate mix of rail traffic—suburban, intercity, elevated and subway—with pedestrian and vehicular access. The terminal itself became a sort of grand pedestrian thoroughfare from one building to another. Around the outside the two firms developed a circumferential roadway that took traffic between 46th and 40th Streets, bridging busy 42d Street.

The terminal was completed in 1913, but the viaduct was not finished until 1919 and the elevated structure was then credited in the architectural press solely to Warren & Wetmore. In the same year an appeals court ruled that Warren & Wetmore had improperly excluded Reed & Stem from subsequent work around the terminal, awarding the latter firm $219,000 in fees.

The viaduct is three arches in length and all were originally open. An ornamental iron railing with shell medallions runs along most of the roadway and elaborate bronze street lights originally stood atop granite piers.

According to *Architecture* magazine in 1919, "esthetic considerations called for arches" in spanning the three openings but the spaces were too cramped to allow footings for true arch construction. So the architects and Olaf Hoff, the engineer, designed great steel girders, curved as if built as arches but actually cantilevered out from the opposing piers. The steel members were up to 136 feet long and were pulled by a 52-horse team from 19th Street and the East River to the site.

The completion of the viaduct suddenly changed Park Avenue from an inconvenient local street to the most modern highway in New York.

Indeed, the viaduct, which was built without sidewalks, may be the earliest thoroughfare in New York designed solely for vehicles, without any accommodation for pedestrians.

But gradually Park Avenue became one road among many and the viaduct's prominence diminished. A gritty sameness settled over midtown, especially as International-style architecture seemed to force all older structures into one undifferentiated lump.

In 1939, in association with the World's Fair, the open space between 41st and 42d Streets was filled in with a tourist information center, an Art Moderne amalgam of glass block and streamlined bronze, perhaps designed by the city's Department of Public Works.

But as Grand Central Terminal's fortunes began to rise again, so, too, did the viaduct's. The Landmarks Preservation Commission designated it a landmark in 1980 and the designation report by Rachel Carley calls it "the finest example of Beaux-Arts civic planning in New York."

The Grand Central Partnership, a neighborhood civic organization, was founded in 1985 partly to address the problems of a midtown of older structures. With what the Partnership says was the approval of all of its commercial property owners, a business improvement district roughly from 38th to 48th Street and from Second to Fifth Avenue was approved by the Board of Estimate in 1988 and 10-cent-per-square foot commercial-property surtax was assessed.

Using funds from the surcharge, the group plans a comprehensive program of plantings, sidewalk renovations and sign guidelines from 38th to 48th Street and from Second to Fifth Avenue. Central to its efforts will be cleaning and repairing the viaduct and roadways around Grand Central and repairing and reinstalling the original lamps, most of which have been in storage since the early 80's.

According to Arthur Rosenblatt, architect for the project, the Art Moderne–style work of the 30's under the central arch will be demolished and replaced with a glass-walled cafe. All traffic except airport buses will be banned from the two arms of Park Avenue leading to 42d Street. The Landmarks Preservation Commission will review the proposed changes on November 28 and, if approval is granted, work should begin next year on this unusual restoration project.

I have since discovered that the Moderne-style infill under the central arch was designed by Eggers & Higgins.

CENTRAL PARK TRANSVERSES

Neglected and Abused Crosstown Roads

The transverse at 85th Street, looking east through tunnel, in the winter of 1892.

THEY ARE BY far the most visited sites in Central Park and generally are conceded to be among its most significant features. But as millions of dollars are spent restoring Central Park, its four transverse roads receive little attention, sometimes even abuse.

The twisting, serpentine rock canyons are thrilling experiences of movement, but a system of split governance seems designed to keep them as neglected masterpieces.

According to William Alex, president of the Frederick Law Olmsted Association, the requirements for the original 1858 Central Park design competition were generally silent on providing for crosstown traffic. But the winning Olmsted–Calvert Vaux design included sunken transverse roads at 65th, 79th, 85th and 97th Streets.

In their submissions, the designers wrote, "inevitably they will be crowded thoroughfares, having nothing in common with the park proper," serving "coal carts and butcher's carts, dust carts and dung carts."

The transverses, all with sidewalks, were designed to twist and turn under bridges and behind embankments to keep them hidden from the park, but the barrier worked both ways. "The public cannot be secured safe transit through large open spaces of ground after nightfall," Olmsted and Vaux wrote, and the park was closed at night. But the transverses had to remain open.

The first transverse road was opened in 1859, part of a larger circulation plan as complicated as that of Grand Central Terminal. Olmsted and Vaux had to incorporate often parallel paths for carriages, equestrians and pedestrians in their overall Romantic design, but they also wanted to provide east–west crossings without interfering with the park's sense of remove.

Each transverse wall is a masterpiece of stonework. Local Manhattan schist was cut on the site and laid in delightful irregularity, some finely dressed, some so roughly faced they bulge out in near-comic fashion. And the 79th Street rock tunnel is a gigantic, cave-like room, certainly one of the great interior landmarks in New York, blasted through in 1859.

Nineteenth-century views show elaborate lighting fixtures—now long gone—at each tunnel entrance. Most transverse entrances were enlarged for additional traffic in the 1930's, but away from Fifth Avenue and Central Park West, they are almost entirely unchanged.

The transverses have always been considered key elements in the park's design; Elizabeth Barlow Rogers, now Central Park Administrator, described them as "brilliant" in her 1972 book, *Frederick Law Olmsted's New York*.

Central Park's fortunes have revived in recent years as Bow Bridge, Bethesda Terrace and other elements have been burnished and restored. But the transverses seem to have been neglected. Dirt sometimes a foot thick clogs the sidewalks, which have not been cleaned in years. Coarse modern light fixtures run down the center of a majestic rock tunnel, which is itself filthy from half a century of exhaust fumes. Conduits, piping, wires and other impedimenta have been draped carelessly along the walls.

The greatest disaster is the Department of Environmental Protection's replacement of a 100-foot section of the 79th Street transverse wall in 1983. The department demolished the original curving wall, discarding the original schist—now very hard to find—and rebuilt it to crude design in granite, which sticks out like a very sore thumb. The department did not submit the project for review to either the Art Commission or the Landmarks Preservation Commission, as required.

But that is fairly typical for the transverses. Everyone acknowledges that responsibility for the four roadways is a confusing overlap, split among the Departments of Parks, Transportation and Environmental Protection. The transverses are simultaneously roads, walls, bridges, monuments, landscape elements and more.

Ironically, the transverses are the most used elements in the park. The new Central Park Zoo had 1.3 million visitors in the last 12 months, but the 79th Street transverse alone had 7.3 million vehicle crossings in the same period. But few who would walk a mile to see the exquisitely restored Belvedere Castle have walked down the specially designed staircase—the only one in the transverses—to the equally majestic rock tunnel below it. And the Central Park Conservancy's 1985 master restoration plan, called *Rebuilding Central Park*, describes them as simple roads of only utilitarian significance.

Someday the transverses may receive their due, but for the near term they seem destined to remain just roads, not part of Central Park's grand design, but simply a way through it.

WILLIAMSBURGH SAVINGS BANK

Resolving the Case of Missing Muntins

The Williamsburgh Savings Bank on Ashland and Hanson Places in Brooklyn in 1929. The bank is altering 906 windows installed without approval of the Landmarks Preservation Commission.

THE BIGGEST VIOLATION ever of New York City's landmarks law has been settled by a compromise, and the Williamsburgh Savings Bank in downtown Brooklyn has begun to alter the 906 windows it installed without the approval of the Landmarks Preservation Commission.

The bank could have been required to remove all the illegal windows and replace them with replicas of the originals, or even fined, but now need only add decorative muntins (bars that divide the panes); it is either justice or simply an accommodation, depending upon one's perspective.

In 1929, the bank, which was established in 1851, built the tallest structure in Brooklyn, a 512-foot-high, neo-Romanesque office building at the northeast corner of Ashland and Hanson Places. Designed by Halsey, McCormick & Helmer, it contains a great banking hall and two floors of banking offices. The rest was built as rental offices.

The main lobby and banking area are elegant, affecting the grand style designed to make every depositor feel like a millionaire. The banking room is a vast, cathedral-like space of limestone, marble and mosaics, and the soft afternoon sun, filtered through tinted-glass windows, gives the room a feeling of great antiquity.

But the building is even better known for its exterior. The buff-colored brick walls rise in successive setbacks to a tower capped by a gold dome. Near the top is a four-faced clock 27 feet in diameter, with colored hands designed to be visible 30 to 40 miles away. In 1928, the *Real Estate Record & Guide* predicted that the building would "long be the borough's dominant landmark."

In 1977, the Landmarks Preservation Commission, with the bank's endorsement, designated the exterior a landmark, and earlier this year the bank, owned since 1987 by the Republic National Bank, celebrated its 60th anniversary with a restoration project for its great banking hall. According to Dan Burgess, a spokesman for the bank, representatives of the landmarks agency attended one of the ceremonies and complimented the bank on its work.

At about the same time, however, a commission staff member noticed news accounts of the restoration work. Lillian Ayala, spokeswoman for the commission, said the staff member called the bank to make sure the work described did not affect the exterior. Bank representatives confirmed that all the work was on the interior, except for "the new windows"—906 new windows.

The commission then issued a violation and at a public hearing on July 25 more of the story came out. Tom Fitzgerald, a retired vice president, testified that in 1983 the bank found that the steel, 2-over-2 industrial-style windows were in bad condition and decided to replace them without notifying the commission because it didn't want to delay installation. The commission's vice chairman, Elliot Willensky, noted skeptically that time did not seem to be an issue because it had taken the bank six years to replace 906 of the 935 windows.

At the same hearing, eight out of 22 applications had to do with illegal work, already performed. Ms. Ayala, the commission's spokeswoman, said that at most hearings about a third of the items on the agenda concern illegal work. As for fines for noncompliance, she said they are rarely assessed.

No one can say how much more illegal work goes on that the commission does not catch. The window work at the bank went on for six years before anyone noticed.

Speaking at the hearing for the Historic Districts Council, a New York City watchdog group, Eric Allison urged a vote against legalizing the windows, calling it a "willful disregard of the law by a corporation that was clearly aware of its responsibilities."

The commission then denied the request to legalize the installation, noting that the new 1-over-1 aluminum windows "do not replicate the configuration, profiles, finish and detail" of the originals, and this "significantly affects . . . the significant role the windows play" in the building's appearance.

But last month the commission approved an unusual compromise. The bank was permitted to install false muntin strips on the 1-over-1 panes to make them look like 2-over-2. Some specialized windows will have to be removed, but most can now become legal with minor work.

Windows make up about half the building's facade. Ms. Ayala was unable to explain how a single muntin could cure problems with the "configuration, profiles, finish and detail" and did not respond to a request for comment from either the chairman, David Todd, or Mr. Willensky.

Mr. Allison commented later: "How are you going to tell the owner of some brownstone that they should have correct windows but that it doesn't apply to that big building over there? The commission is violating its own standards."

139 GREENE STREET

The Longest-Running Restoration in New York City

The 1825 Federal house at 139 Greene Street, in 1940.

THINGS JUST SEEM to take more time in New York City—like renewing a driver's license, Christmas shopping and, most of all, restoration projects.

The restoration of the Woolworth Building in the 70's, the New York Landmarks Conservancy's Archives Building project in the 80's, and the current exterior work on the San Remo on Central Park—all these approached or surpassed a decade.

Now the longest-running restoration project seems to be 139 Greene Street, a trim little 1825 Federal house south of Houston Street that has been undergoing alterations by fits and starts since 1974.

Early in the 19th century, migration of the elite residential areas tended to follow a northward pattern along Broadway, which variously served as the city's main shopping, entertainment and residential street. After the 1810's, development pushed up past Canal Street, and surrounding side streets were filled up with private residences. In 1824, Anthony Arnoux, a merchant tailor living at 144 Fulton Street, bought the lot at 139 Greene Street and built the present house.

The completed building represented the height of late Federal styling. Subtly varying deep red and orange brick is set off against details in marble: paneled window lintels, a rusticated basement and a molded elliptical stone arch around the doorway. A photograph at the New-York Historical Society taken in August 1937 shows an elegant eight-paneled door flanked by fluted Ionic columns.

According to Regina Kellerman, executive director of the Greenwich Village Historical Society, the use of marble was common in New York building in this period, in part because the warden at Sing Sing, using convict labor to cut Tuckahoe marble, was undercutting normal prices by two-thirds.

Arnoux did not move in until 1834, and it is not clear who initially occupied the house. The 1850 Census suggests that, by mid-century, he was a widower, living there with children Gertrude, age 48, Emily, 32, Alfred, 30, William, 25, and Edwarde, 20, along with Dana Weisenden, a servant.

By the 1850's, a wave of large hotels and restaurants had invaded Broadway in this section. Parts of the present SoHo district, particularly Greene Street, were rife with prostitutes. The Arnoux family moved out in 1860 to a house at 20 East 32d Street.

Timothy Guilfoyle, author of a forthcoming history of prostitution in

New York City, called *City of Eros*, said in an interview that a woman named Mary Ann Temple was arrested for running a brothel at 139 Greene Street in 1862, and that the 1870 edition of *Gentleman's Companion* lists a "Miss Whalen" as running a similar establishment there. At the time, he said, there were 13 other brothels on the block.

In 1890, the *Real Estate Record & Guide* described Greene Street as a center for the hatter's trade and noted the end of its former status as a center of prostitution, saying: "A man can walk through now without being himself too frequently accosted through closed window shutters."

The house at 139 Greene remained more or less intact and telephone directories after the 1920's give a succession of typical SoHo businesses: trucking, rags, paper stock and wastepaper.

One tenant built a loading dock right on top of the marble steps. Another punched a new, wider doorway through one of the first-floor windows. After 1968 it was owned by the art dealer Richard L. Feigen. In August 1973—the same month that SoHo was designated a historic district by the Landmarks Preservation Commission—Peter W. Ballantine bought the house for his residence.

Mr. Ballantine received permission from the landmarks agency in 1974 to reopen the first floor windows, reopen the main entrance, put in new six-over-six sashes and perform other work, and his plans were approved. In 1975, he filed plans with the Department of Buildings for interior changes, but according to Vahe Tiryakian, a spokesman for the agency, the application was not pursued and expired.

But Mr. Ballantine did make progress on the exterior and installed a temporary plywood door. Over time, he has begun to fill in the enlarged first-floor window and is now about half done—the opening is covered with plywood. But the six-over-six windows have yet to be installed.

Mr. Ballantine, who is doing some of the restoration work himself, declined a request for an interview, saying "it isn't the right time." Permits from the Landmarks Preservation Commission have no expiration date and the house, obviously unfinished, yet occupied, has become well known in SoHo.

A neighbor at 143 Greene Street said he has known Mr. Ballantine for 20 years and that he is indeed restoring the building, but has had trouble with the size of the brick. But, he added, "I think its's going to be a lifelong thing."

U.S. RUBBER COMPANY BUILDING

Restoring Luster to a 1912 Lady

THE 20-STORY HEADQUARTERS Carrère & Hastings created in 1912 for the U.S. Rubber Company at 1790 Broadway, at 58th Street, is a building of discreet qualities. It cannot claim any superlatives, and most of the guidebooks omit it, but it has what many better known buildings lack: good manners.

Now, after some rough handling over the years, it is being cosseted and given a civilized shine. And the changes planned for the lower floors constitute what may be the most radical restoration since the marketing of older office buildings for their historic architecture began several years ago.

Longacre—later Times Square—developed as a center of the carriage industry in the mid-19th century. Later, the automobile transformed Broadway north of 42d Street and by 1910 there were at least 75 automobile businesses up to 59th Street. But the evolution of Times Square into a theater center beginning in the first decade of the century also forced up values on Broadway frontages. Automobile companies moved as far north as 70th Street.

In 1911, the U.S. Rubber Company, a major tire company needing a presence in this automobile center, bought a plot at the southeast corner of 58th Street and Broadway and commissioned as architects Carrère & Hastings, then just finishing their monumental building for the New York Public Library on Fifth Avenue at 42d Street.

As at the library, the architects used Vermont marble over the entire structure, unusual for New York commercial buildings, which were typically faced with brick, limestone and terra-cotta. According to Channing Blake, a landscape gardener and expert on Carrère & Hastings, the company's use of the Modern French style was also unusual in a city that favored the Italian Renaissance and Gothic styles for its tall buildings.

A grand arcade covered the first two floors. Above that, the building rose with a dramatic verticality, emphasized by the tall marble tiers alternating with metal and glass window bays. Most of the delicate, carved-marble ornament was kept toward the lower floors. Up close the building is all debonair urbanism—it could be a Paris bank or London hotel—but from afar the marble ornament is harder to see and it becomes a sleek skyscraper.

U.S. Rubber rented out the second to 13th floors but kept the ground floor as a tire showroom and the upper floors for its own offices. These have oval rooms, marble fireplaces, wood paneling and unusual interlocking rubber-tile floors with marble trim.

In 1940 U.S. Rubber moved to a new headquarters at 1230 Avenue of the Americas (then Sixth Avenue). Its previous building passed through various hands and was acquired in 1951 by the West Side Federal Savings and Loan Association.

At first the bank made small alterations, installing a neon sign on the Broadway side designed by Herbert Tannenbaum, who apprenticed with Emery Roth in the 30's. But in 1959, according to Mr. Tannenbaum, "they wanted more punch" and asked him to prepare more extensive schemes.

"I gave them several alternatives but urged them not to destroy the beauty of the building," he says. "But landmark buildings were not in vogue then" and the bank demanded a completely new facade for the lower two floors. Mr. Tannenbaum produced a sleek International-style scheme of polished gray marble with stainless-steel trim. The original marble base was jackhammered off.

"It's a good design, but on the wrong building," he said. "I was always unhappy with it."

Mr. Tannenbaum may soon be able to limit his regrets. The bank, taken over by the First Nationwide Savings Bank in the 70's, sold the building in 1985 to 1790 Broadway Associates, a partnership headed by John Phufas.

Mr. Phufas has just completed a convincing restoration of the marble and gilt lobby, designed by Richard Rice, which had also been largely destroyed by the bank. He is set on keeping and restoring the original

U.S. Rubber Company building at 1790 Broadway, at 58th Street, circa 1940.

metal windows on the office floors and he monitors tenant changes with restoration in mind. He is also planning a proper cleaning of the marble facade and copper cornices, which were indifferently cleaned by the bank in 1984 in preparation for its sale.

But the most dramatic change will take place on the lower floors. Although the bank's lease there extends to 1995, others have already expired and the owner and Mr. Rice plan a full-scale restoration of the ground-floor facade, using original elevation drawings and in consultation with Mr. Tannenbaum.

"I've spent millions," said Mr. Phufas, "but there is a payback." The building is now a center for communications companies, including the Public Broadcasting System, Virgin Atlantic Records and *Connoisseur* magazine.

THE B. & O. FREIGHT WAREHOUSE

Wrapping a West Side Landmark in a Truck Shop

The B. & O. Freight Terminal at 26th Street and 11th Avenue in 1914.

MAYBE IT WAS more interesting as a view than as a building—a plain white neoclassical rectangle silhouetted against its much larger sibling to the north, the streamlined Starrett-Lehigh Building.

If that's the case, then the 1914 B. & O. Freight Warehouse at the southwest corner of 26th Street and 11th Avenue will soon be lost as New York City wraps a tall Department of Sanitation repair shop around the older building, erasing the last vestiges of the railroad's great two-square-block rail yard.

Beginning in the 1840's, the West Side waterfront developed into a center of the city's rail operations when the Hudson River Railroad established service upstate. Its trains crossed the Harlem River at Spuyten Duyvil. At the time, rail operations were centered around what is now TriBeCa. By the late 19th century some rail-freight structures began appearing north of 14th Street.

For shipping between New York and points west, most railroads had to ferry freight cars on special barges across the Hudson. By the 1890's, the West Side waterfront was a welter of different rail lines for different carriers. In 1897, the Baltimore & Ohio—then running freight service into Staten Island—acquired the block bounded by 25th and 26th Streets and 11th and 12th Avenues for a marshalling yard and small terminal facilities. In 1912, it began building a new freight terminal/warehouse.

According to Thomas Flagg, an industrial archeologist, the railroad needed to keep most of its yard open to permit the shifting of cars to sidings. So it built its nine-story terminal/warehouse on a 67- by 352-foot plot in the northeast corner of its block, which measured 200 by 593 feet. It was designed by Maurice A. Long, a staff engineer.

According to an article in *Railway Review* in 1914, the all-concrete building was the largest such structure in New York City. It was also an early example of the flat-slab method of construction that rests concrete floors directly on the vertical columns of the floor below. This eliminates the need for intermediate girders, which reduce light and headroom.

The exterior is typical of factory construction of the time, handsome in a utilitarian way, decorated principally with wide bays of rustication and large painted letters of identification. Mr. Flagg said the building, which typically served the garment industry, was designed to handle the shipping of smaller parcels at a time when there was no United Parcel

Service. Goods could be picked up at the warehouse rather than at a pier, as other railroads required.

While the rail yard was used for unloading direct to trucks, rail cars could also come alongside and even inside the building in cases where goods were to be held on the upper floors.

A plot plan published in *Railroad Review* indicates that a twin to the 1914 building was planned for the southeast corner of the plot, at 25th Street and 11th Avenue, but this was never completed. In 1931, the Starrett-Lehigh Building was built just to the north, and in the mid-1930's the B. & O. acquired the next block to its south, between 24th and 25th Streets, and doubled the size of its rail yard.

Little has changed since that time, and the B. & O. warehouse became a prominent, if unintended, landmark to those traveling past its more conspicuous neighbor, especially visible from the West Side Highway.

Overlooking its two open blocks of rail sidings, it is a chastely elegant appetizer to the flashy main course of the Starrett-Lehigh structure.

Freight rail service generally declined after World War II, but Mr. Flagg said the B. & O. yards did not close until the early 70's. Around that time a private developer, the Mishkin Construction Corporation, proposed the construction of a 30-story housing project over the yards but nothing came of it. At some point in the 70's, the building changed to light industrial use, its role at the present.

In 1981, the yards and freight building, by that time owned by the CSX Corporation, were sold to Bulgroup Properties, a partnership including Coleman Burke. According to Mr. Burke, the partnership sold the southerly portion of the site to the Postal Service in 1986, which built a modernistic new garage-repair shop there in 1987.

In the same year, New York City condemned the remaining portion of the northerly block, an L-shaped parcel that wraps around the old B. & O. building. According to Michael Friedlander, a design project manager for the Department of Sanitation, plans for a new repair shop on the site for department vehicles are going out to bid, and construction should begin this summer.

The new building will be 82 feet high, butting up against the south side of the 100-foot-high B. & O. building. Soon a familiar vista of a memorable structure will be consigned to memory.

THE VIEW DOWN FIFTH AVENUE

Tower Now Blocks the Prospect

Spire of the Empire State Building peeks over new tower at 56th Street.

I T WAS THE most evanescent of unofficial landmarks, a haphazard alignment of buildings spanning half a century along a mile-long stretch of Fifth Avenue. The view south toward the Empire State Building—actually a gradually rising succession of buildings—was long familiar to tourists and New Yorkers walking down the avenue along Central Park from as far north as the Cooper-Hewitt Museum at 91st Street.

Now the new 56-story tower above the Rizzoli and Coty Buildings at 56th Street has squarely blocked this view, and the loss serves as an admonition that the most familiar and delightful things in New York can also be the most fragile.

Early in the 19th century, the appreciation of scenic vistas was oriented toward mere distance, and only views from tall structures—like the high embankment of the Croton Reservoir at 42d Street and Fifth Avenue—were generally considered of interest.

Although Olmsted & Vaux's Central Park design of 1858 emphasized picturesque juxtapositions of natural features, it was not until skyscrapers began going up at the tip of Manhattan at the turn of the century that haphazard views of otherwise unrelated buildings began to be appreciated.

There were early attempts to control buildings along certain streets, like the advice of a Fifth Avenue Commission in 1911, which, fearing that "the continued erection of high buildings on both sides of the street will clearly be disastrous," proposed a 150-foot height limit. John M. Carrère, a commission member, urged more sensitivity by owners and architects to the relation of their buildings to neighboring ones, saying: "No matter how beautiful a building may be, it does not improve the neighborhood if it jars with all the other buildings in the perspective."

Most planning theory at the turn of the century was based on the study of European cities, especially those with wide, radial boulevards centered on major public buildings or squares, and New York's mean little grid plan was always found wanting. But New York developed dramatic, if coincidental, views like that of midtown from the East River Drive, the Central Park West skyline across the park from Fifth Avenue, and vice versa, the view of the Chrysler Building down Lexington Avenue and, by 1931, of the Empire State Building from upper Fifth Avenue.

The Fifth Avenue prospect was really a view of a succession of buildings, beginning with the mansard roof of Bergdorf-Goodman at 58th (1926) rising to the exuberant Heckscher (now Crown) Building tower at 57th (1921) past the lush green cornice of the Gotham Hotel at 55th (1905) to the streamlined mass of 500 Fifth Avenue at 42d (1931) to the Empire State itself at 34th (1931).

It was a sort of accidental architectural waterfall, nicely balanced, and the 666 Fifth Avenue building at 53d (1957) fit right in. The prospect was most apparent between 91st and 64th Streets. At 64th, the buildings melted into the midtown view.

But last year the new tower, at 712 Fifth, began rising. Topped out but not yet opened to the public, it already has come to overpower what was a nicely balanced grouping. Now, from 79th Street, its giant rectangular mass blocks everything but the disembodied TV tower of the Empire State Building.

A landmarks controversy erupted around the little Coty and Rizzoli buildings in 1985. Originally, the tower's developers proposed razing them. Eventually, the commission not only refused that, but also required that Solomon Equities and the Taubman Company set their tower 25 feet back from the buildings' facades.

William Pedersen, whose firm, Kohn Pedersen Fox, designed it, says, "If you had to consider every view when every building was built, it would stop everything."

At the time of the landmark controversy, no one brought up the question of the view, and in any event the landmarks agency has no authority to regulate such a vista. Only in the last year has the new building become obvious from a distance.

But other cities have been evaluating whether views are just as important to preserve as buildings. According to Constance Beaumont, senior policy analyst at the National Trust for Historic Preservation, many American cities now protect certain views, among them Austin, Texas, which since 1984 has regulated sight lines to the State Capitol.

And according to Warren Huff, senior center-city planner in Philadelphia, a law passed this November preserves views of its City Hall over private property from such disparate locations as the steps of the Philadelphia Museum of Art and Interstate 95.

New York does not yet protect views, but the new 712 Fifth Avenue building may serve as a constructive reminder of that to anyone who still remembers the architectural waterfall that has now dried up.

When I first conceived this story, I had some doubt: Was I inflating a minor, barely noticeable change into a major issue? This fear vanished with the architect's first response in our interview. I said I was calling about the new building, but that I was focusing on an aspect different than the landmark buildings at the base. "Oh," he said, with a nervous laugh, "You mean the view down Fifth Avenue." I had the distinct impression that he was just waiting, during the Coty–Rizzoli controversy, for the view question to come up, and was relieved when no one thought of it.

THE CIVIC CENTER SYNAGOGUE

Contrasting Styles Are Startling on White Street

Far right: The building at 47 White Street, center, in 1945. Right: The Civic Center Synagogue replaced the loft building at 47 White Street in 1965.

OFFICE FOR METROPOLITAN HISTORY

ROBERT GALBRAITH/WILLIAM N. BREGER

THE CIVIC CENTER Synagogue at 47 White Street is just the kind of building planners warn against. Built in 1965, it replaced an unusual 1866 neo-Grec loft building, startlingly interrupting an otherwise intact 19th-century streetscape, one of the finest in the four proposed TriBeCa historic districts, or even in the city.

It is unabashedly different from its neighbors in materials, form, detailing and fenestration. Still, it cannot be said that the all-white, curving synagogue is anything but a welcome addition to the street, and it presents a conundrum for preservationists: If it really does all those bad things, why is the result so good? And if it is just the type of building that is not allowed in historic districts, will the Landmarks Preservation Commission regulate it as a nuisance or as an attraction, if and when pending historic districts are approved?

The Civic Center Synagogue was founded in 1938 for weekday worship by civil servants working in the area and by the early 1960's occupied a loft building at 80 Duane Street. But the construction of the Federal building on the site displaced the congregation, which bought an old building at 47 White Street in 1965, the year the Landmarks Preservation Commission was founded.

This was a time when only the most important landmarks—like the Customs House at Bowling Green—were being advanced for landmark designation, and the congregation demolished the existing building without protest. Designed in 1866 by Charles Alexander, the early 47 White Street had unusual neo-Grec detailing carved in brownstone, an interesting counterpoint to the more conventional Renaissance-style iron and marble buildings on the rest of the street.

Completed in 1967, the synagogue was intentionally startling. Faced with white marble bricks, its broad, bowed shape seems to float above a plaza, connected to the ground only by three small rectangular pods, the middle one serving as the main entrance. The front has no windows and curves back at the top, blank and expressionless—pure form.

Inside are two ordinary basement levels, but the sanctuary above is remarkable, a gigantic dove-shaped space dominated by a narrow skylight and the curved inside of the bowed facade faced in strips of wood—more like an airport building than a center-city temple. William N. Breger, the architect, and Paul Gugliotta, the structural engineer, received an award from the American Institute of Architects for the project.

To a walker down White Street the synagogue first appears as a round white nose. It gradually expands and rises until, viewed from a point directly opposite its huge double curve, it seems to be gently suspended between the adjacent buildings.

The rise of historic preservation has led to definite ideas about new buildings in historic areas. In most cases, the ideal choice is obviously contemporary, without phony historicism, but deferring to its environment.

The Civic Center Synagogue—without a cornice or windows anywhere on its big bulging form—can hardly be said to follow anything except its own very interesting lead. It is radically different from, but not hostile to, its neighbors.

In 1988, the congregation's president, Mark Brecker, supported a proposal to raze the synagogue and build a tower above, with a conventional infill facade below, pushed to the street wall. According to Rabbi Jonathan W. Glass, membership among office workers has declined drastically and space is needed for school, social and other activities to serve the area's growing resident population. But amidst controversy over the height of the new building, the plan never advanced.

This year the landmarks agency calendared a proposal for four historic districts covering most of the TriBeCa area, including the synagogue. A preliminary commission survey in 1985 rated the synagogue a "2," a category typically including bland buildings of marginal value.

"Buildings like this break all the rules, but what preservation needs is a new language," said William J. Higgins, a preservation consultant. "We have terms for style and for history, but we have trouble describing how buildings fit together—whether well or poorly. Instead of taking away from the street, this building sets it in motion."

Rabbi Glass said that the redevelopment project is now dead and that "we're here to stay." But he noted that the synagogue, built to seat 290, has an active congregation of a little more than 60 and that new membership from Battery Park City and other areas has not yet met expectations. He said the synagogue has not taken a position on landmark designation, but adds that the modernity of the building provides flexibility.

The synagogue never took a position on designation, and the Commission has not yet voted on the matter.

INDEX

In this index, city agencies are alphabetized without "New York" preceding.